Printed Circuit Board Design Using AutoCAD

Chris Schroeder

Newnes

Boston   Oxford   Johannesburg   Melbourne   New Delhi   Singapore

Newnes is an imprint of Butterworth–Heinemann

Copyright © 1998 by Butterworth–Heinemann

 A member of the Reed Elsevier group

 Butterworth–Heinemann supports the efforts of American Forests and the Global ReLeaf program in its campaign for the betterment of trees, forests, and our environment.

Library of Congress Cataloging-in-Publication Data

Schroeder, Chris, 1954–
    Printed circuit board design using AutoCAD / Chris Schroeder.
       p.   cm.   -- (The EDN series for design engineers)
    Includes bibliographical references and index.
    ISBN 0-7506-9834-9 (alk. paper)
    1. Printed circuits--Design and construction--Data processing.
2. AutoCAD (Computer file)   3. Computer-aided design.   I. Title.
II. Series.
    TK7868.P7S344   1997
    621.3815'31--dc21   97-22001
                                             CIP

British Library Cataloguing-in-Publication Data

A catalogue record for this book is available from the British Library.

The publisher offers special discounts on bulk orders of this book.
For information, please write:

Manager of Special Sales
Butterworth–Heinemann
313 Washington Street
Newton, MA 02158-1626
Tel: 617-928-2500
Fax: 617-928-2620

For information on all Newnes electronics publications available,
contact our World Wide Web home page at: http://www.bh.com/newnes

10 9 8 7 6 5 4 3 2 1

Printed in the United States of America

To Dr. Heinz Schroeder,
who encouraged his son's dreams

The EDN Series for Design Engineers

C. Schroeder   *Printed Circuit Board Design Using AutoCAD*

J. Lenk   *Simplified Design of Data Converters*

F. Imdad-Haque   *Inside PC Card: CardBus and PCMCIA Design*

C. Schroeder   *Inside OrCAD*

J. Lenk   *Simplified Design of IC Amplifiers*

J. Lenk   *Simplified Design of Micropower and Battery Circuits*

J. Williams   *The Art and Science of Analog Circuit Design*

J. Lenk   *Simplified Design of Switching Power Supplies*

V. Lakshminarayanan   *Electronic Circuit Design Ideas*

J. Lenk   *Simplified Design of Linear Power Supplies*

M. Brown   *Power Supply Cookbook*

B. Travis and I. Hickman   *EDN Designer's Companion*

J.Dostal   *Operational Amplifiers, Second Edition*

T. Williams   *Circuit Designer's Companion*

R. Marston   *Electronics Circuits Pocketbook: Passive and Discrete Circuits (Vol. 2)*

N. Dye and H. Granberg   *Radio Frequency Transistors: Principles and Practical Applications*

Gates Energy Products   *Rechargeable Batteries: Applications Handbook*

T. Williams   *EMC for Product Designers*

J. Williams   *Analog Circuit Design: Art, Science, and Personalities*

R. Pease   *Troubleshooting Analog Circuits*

I. Hickman   *Electronic Circuits, Systems and Standards*

R. Marston   *Electronic Circuits Pocket Book: Linear ICs (Vol. 1)*

R. Marston   *Integrated Circuit and Waveform Generator Handbook*

I. Sinclair   *Passive Components: A User's Guide*

Contents

Chapter 3. Single Sided PCB Design   79

Chapter 7. Importing HPGL Files for Manufacturing Documentation   211

Chapter 8. Importing Gerber Artwork Files for Viewing   235

Chapter 9. Importing Excellon Format NC Drill Data

Appendix A. Gerber Format   **283**

Appendix B. Excellon Format   **289**

Appendix C. HPGL Format   **291**

Preface

This book is about printed circuit board (PCB) design using AutoCAD. Unlike the hundreds of books written about mechanical and architectural applications of AutoCAD, this is the first one that covers PCB applications. *Printed Circuit Board Design Using AutoCAD* was written in recognition of the fact that many companies use AutoCAD for this purpose because their requirements do not justify the acquisition cost and learning curve associated with specialized PCB design software. *Printed Circuit Board Design Using AutoCAD* also covers the subject of schematic drafting with AutoCAD and surface mount technology. The book is organized into a series of tutorial exercises, preceded by an introductory chapter that gives an overview of PCB manufacturing technology and design techniques. The tutorial exercises focus on specific projects: schematic drafting, designing single sided, double sided, and surface mount PCBs, and importing PCB design related data into AutoCAD from other systems. Each tutorial contains a mix of theory and practice.

The disk that accompanies *Printed Circuit Board Design Using AutoCAD* contains the AutoPADS conversion utilities and sample files for the tutorial exercises. The AutoPADS utilities allow bidirectional transfer of Gerber format photoplotter data and Excellon format numerical control (NC) drill data from AutoCAD. The AutoPADS utilities also allow input of HPGL (Hewlett-Packard Graphics Language) data from other computer aided design systems into AutoCAD. Gerber and Excellon formats are industry standards for the data that board manufacturers expect to receive. *Printed Circuit Board Design Using AutoCAD* places particular emphasis on creating data and documentation that meet current industry standards.

Certain prerequisites exist for the use and understanding of the material presented in this book. The reader is assumed to be familiar with AutoCAD and have some knowledge of electronics and schematic drafting. *Printed Circuit Board Design Using AutoCAD* is not intended to be an introductory text for someone who has never used AutoCAD. Some degree of PC and DOS literacy is also required. In order to complete the tutorial exercises, the reader will require a minimum 486 class PC with AutoCAD Release 12 or 13 or AutoCAD LT for Windows 95 and an attached inkjet or laser printer compatible with AutoCAD. A color inkjet printer such as the Hewlett-Packard DeskJet 850 series is highly recommended.

Acknowledgments

First, the author would like to thank Michael Levy. Many years ago, Michael and I were involved in a business venture appropriately named Printed Circuit Design & Development in Ann Arbor, Michigan. Michael taught me much about printed circuits and the realities of running a small business.

The author was fortunate enough to have worked for both Gerber Scientific and Excellon. Both companies pioneered technical advances and set standards during the early days of the PCB industry.

Gerber Scientific is an outstanding company that represents the best aspects of the American entrepreneurial spirit. The company was started in the late 1940s by H. Joseph Gerber, an Austrian immigrant. Mr. Gerber started out making precision measuring devices and other small scientific instruments in his garage, hence the name of the company. Government contracts during the space race years of the early 1960s brought the company into the computer graphics arena. Mr. Gerber made a point of knowing all of his salespeople on a first name basis. All new employees had dinner with Mr. Gerber during which he personally explained the company's tradition of high quality and strict business ethics. The author went to work for Gerber as a sales engineer not long after graduating from the University of Michigan. This was my first introduction to computer graphics and capital equipment sales. In 1980, Gerber had just introduced a new low-cost digitizing system that included a small photoplotter for just under $100,000. I went to work for them shortly before Thanksgiving and by Christmas had already taken orders for several systems. My first commission check was almost as much as what some of my friends made in a year.

In 1982 IBM introduced the PC, and soon after came the first release of AutoCAD. Advances in laser systems and electro-optics made possible fast laser photoplotter systems that were not encumbered by Gerber's patents. Low-cost workstations and shrink-wrapped software followed. Those of us who had become accustomed to the big commission checks moved on. For years afterwards, some of us would still gather at the NEPCON West show (the big event in the PCB industry) in Anaheim, California, and reminisce about the good old days at Gerber. Barely 30 years old, we were already veterans of an electronics industry less stable than the shifting sands of the California desert.

There were many mirages that appeared in that desert, and an opportunity as product manager for imaging systems at Excellon Automation in Torrance, California, proved to be one of them. Excellon was one of the early pioneers of numerically controlled drilling equipment for the PCB industry. Excellon had just introduced one of the first commercially available laser photoplotting systems and was working on advanced laser imaging systems for directly exposing photoresist materials and optical inspection. Excellon had become a division of Esterline Technologies, a large conglomerate. The professional managers brought in by Esterline did not understand the complexities inherent in laser imaging. After one down quarter in early 1985, they dumped the imaging program, many of the talented people involved with it, and the company's future.

Today, after a prolonged downturn, Excellon sells only drilling equipment. Gerber Scientific had some tough years too, but they now sell an advanced line of laser photoplotters and optical inspection systems. Mr. Gerber is still president and chairman of the board.

The author learned a basic lesson from this. The best places to work are where a gray-haired founder's name appears on the building and where he still has a steady hand on the tiller. Watch out when the MBA types arrive bringing endless paper work, procedures, and policies. With no respect for the company's traditions and lacking any clear vision for the future, they quickly drive out the creative talent. All too often, they mortgage the company's future in order to collect a bonus for the current quarter's results, and a once proud company is run into the ground.

I would like to thank the staff at Crane Cams for encouraging me in this project. Special credit goes to my boss, Bill Gaterman, the vice president of engineering, for giving me the freedom to pursue creative activities that do not always show an immediate return on investment. I am also grateful to Rob Chamblin and Troy Weippert for their suggestions after trying some of the techniques presented in the book.

On a final note, I would also like to thank the staff at Butterworth-Heinemann, including Jo Gilmore and Liz McCarthy.

Dedication

This book is dedicated to the memory of my father, who passed away several years ago. He was a physician who had always wanted to be an engineer. He had planned to write and pass on some of his experience after he retired. But the demands of a busy practice and the needs of his patients always came first and his time ran out.

About the Author

Chris Schroeder received his B.S. in Engineering from the University of Michigan in 1976. He is currently chief engineer for the automotive electronics business unit of Crane Cams in Daytona Beach, Florida, and has previously been involved with sales and marketing of computer graphics equipment, laser imaging systems, and design of industrial electronics. He enjoys flying small airplanes, playing with electronics, and writing. Chris lives with his wife, Tina, and young son, Garrett, in Ormond Beach, Florida.

1

Introduction to PCB Design

Printed circuit board (PCB) technology evolved from early efforts to miniaturize electronics during World War II. The first PCBs were actually conductive inks screened on ceramic materials — a technology now known as hybrid circuits. PCBs based on plastic laminates with copper conductors did not see general use until the 1950s. Improvements in the manufacturing process reduced PCB costs and played a leading role in the consumer electronics product revolution that started with Japanese transistor radios in the early 1960s and that continues today with laptop computers and cellular telephones. In the late 1970s, traditional manual design and drafting techniques gave way to computer aided design (CAD). Today's trends include surface mount technology and multi-layer boards.

PCB Classifications

PCBs are classified according to the number of layers and types of holes. Figure 1-1 shows a cross section of the most basic PCB. This is a single sided PCB with conventional through hole components. Through hole technology is sometimes referred to as part-in-hole (PIH). The base material for single sided boards is generally phenolic or a fiberglass and epoxy laminate. Phenolic material is inexpensive but has a limited temperature range and is quite brittle. Glass epoxy laminates can withstand more severe environmental stress. The PCB shown in Figure 1-1 is referred to as a single sided board because the conductive copper pattern is confined to only one side of the board. The conductive copper pattern occurs on the solder side of the PCB, and components are mounted on the opposite side, referred to as the component side. Once parts are inserted into the PCB, the leads are soldered to the conductive copper pattern.

The first commercial PCBs were single sided. Single sided PCBs are still used for many low-cost consumer products. The fact that circuit traces occupy a single layer and cannot cross over one another poses a significant design problem. Jumpers are used where signals must cross. As the board size and complexity increase, the number of jumpers required tends to increase geometrically. This places severe limits on single sided boards.

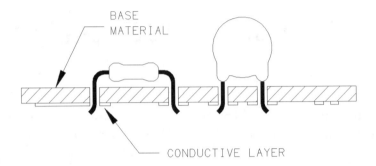

Figure 1-1   Cross Section of Single Sided PCB

A double sided board is shown in Figure 1-2. Conductive copper patterns occur on both sides of the board. The holes drilled in the board are not plated through. Double sided boards of this type are not widely used today. Automated wave soldering equipment can solder only the bottom layer. Component leads must be hand soldered to copper traces on the top side of the board. This type of double sided board was used in the early days of the industry to increase circuit density by allowing signal paths to cross over one another. Signal traces were predominantly routed in one direction on the component side and at a 90 degree angle on the solder side. Connections between sides were made by inserting bare wires through the holes and soldering the wires on both sides.

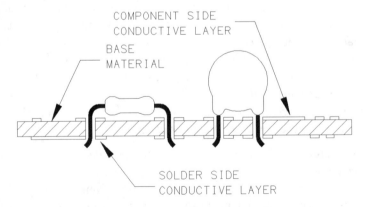

Figure 1-2   Cross Section of Double Sided PCB

These wires were called *Z wires*. The name came from the shape that the wire formed when the ends were clinched over to keep the wire from falling out of the hole. Rivets also were used for the same function as the Z wires.

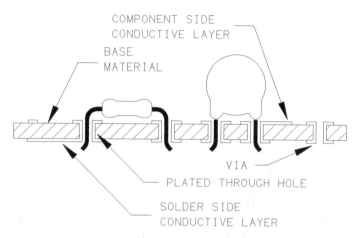

Figure 1-3   Cross Section of Double Sided PTH PCB

By the 1960s, the technology was developed to plate a copper layer on the inside of holes. A board with plated through holes appears in Figure 1-3. The abbreviation PTH is used for plated through holes. PTH allow much denser packing of circuitry. Holes used to connect traces between layers are referred to as *via holes* or simply *vias*. Until the mid 1970s, PTH technology was sometimes unreliable. Stress from repeated thermal cycling (temperature changes) would cause some plated through holes to fail. The plating that formed the copper barrel through the hole would separate from the copper pattern on the surface causing a loss of electrical connection. Processing techniques have greatly improved, and failures of plated through holes are now a rare occurrence. Costs also have come down to the point that PTH PCBs are frequently more cost effective than an equivalent single sided PCB.

PTH boards are now considered more reliable than single sided boards in demanding applications. Thermal stress and vibration can cause components to break loose on single sided boards. The component leads are soldered to the copper pattern on the bottom of the board. The adhesive between the copper and the base material is the only thing holding the components in place on single sided boards. Plated through holes provide much better support for component leads. During the soldering process, solder wicks up through the holes. The effect is the same as a solid rivet. After soldering, plated through holes can survive substantial forces and deformation before dislocating from the base material.

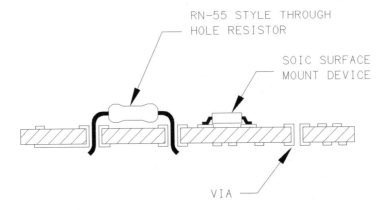

Figure 1-4   **Cross Section of Surface Mount PCB**

Figure 1-4 shows a PTH PCB with mixed through hole and SMT (surface mount technology) parts. SMD is the abbreviation used for surface mount devices. Note the proper terminology. When referring to individual parts, use the term SMD. When referring to the general technology or a board, use the term SMT. Figure 1-4 shows a conventional through hole part, an RN-55 style resistor and an SMD part, a small outline integrated circuit (SOIC). SMD parts have small bent leads or metallized surfaces that make contact with pad patterns on the PCB. Solder paste is screened onto these pads, and the SMDs are then placed onto the board. The solder paste helps to hold the SMDs in place. The board assembly is then sent through an oven that causes the solder paste to melt and form electrical connections between the pads and the parts. This process is called *reflow soldering*.

Today, most new designs use SMD parts wherever possible. SMT reduces product size and cost. SMD devices are much smaller than equivalent through hole parts. SMD parts can also be mounted on both sides of the board. Some automated part placement machines can install upwards of 30,000 parts per hour with minimal operator intervention. SMT is one of the enabling technologies for new products such as cellular phones and laptop computers. The low labor content inherent in SMT has allowed U.S. companies to regain a competitive edge and is a primary factor in the resurgence of our consumer products industry.

PCB Manufacturing Considerations

As discussed earlier, most new designs use SMD parts and double sided boards or even multi-layer boards with PTH holes. Different processes exist for manufacturing these boards. SMT boards require a well defined solder mask.

Serious soldering defects can occur if the solder mask is not precisely registered or deforms during the reflow soldering process.

Until about 10 years ago, most boards were solder plated over the entire conductive surface. The solder mask was then applied over the solder plated surface, with the exception of pad areas. This conventional solder mask over solder process requires special design considerations and can cause certain manufacturing problems. Solder mask materials do not adhere well to solder plating. When the board is heated during the soldering process, the solder plating under the solder mask can melt. After the board cools, the solder mask coating may wrinkle, the edges around pads can become deformed, and the coating may even flake off entirely in some areas. Ground plane areas must be crosshatched to avoid large solid areas, which are particularly prone to wrinkling and flaking. Unfortunately, crosshatched ground plane areas are less effective at shielding electromagnetic interference (EMI).

Within the last few years, most companies have switched to the SMOBC/HASL board process. SMOBC/HASL stands for solder mask over bare copper/hot air solder leveling. The term SMOBC is commonly used by itself and is understood to include HASL. SMOBC boards have solder mask applied directly over the copper conductive layer. A shiny solder coating is applied to pad areas by dipping the board in molten solder and then using a hot air process to level the solder. Large solid ground planes do not pose any problem with SMOBC. Reflow soldering conditions during SMT assembly operations have less effect on SMOBC boards. The solder mask material also adheres better to the copper conductive surface.

During the early development of the SMOBC process, the steps that involved stripping of solder plated resist, solder dipping, and HASL sometimes caused extreme stress on PTH resulting in subsequent reliability problems. These process steps have been refined. When consideration is given to the overall board manufacturing and assembly process, SMOBC is now considered the most cost effective and reliable approach.

In the following section, the SMOBC manufacturing process steps are examined in detail. Variants exist for some of the processing steps. A good working knowledge of this subject material is essential, from the standpoint of both design decisions and evaluation of potential vendors. Environmental regulations have driven many process changes in the last 15 years. The Environmental Protection Agency (EPA) has recently mandated restrictions on the use of formaldehyde, which is a major component of some plating baths. On-shore vendors still using formaldehyde and other restricted chemicals are likely to encounter process difficulties when they are finally forced to switch to more environmentally acceptable materials.

Solder Mask over Bare Copper Process

SMOBC boards are generally constructed from organic substrates. The most common substrate consists of layers of woven glass cloth impregnated with epoxy resin. This is referred to as a laminated substrate. In the United States, .062 inch thick FR-4 (the FR stands for flame retardant) is the most widely used laminate. As shown in Figure 1-5, the SMOBC process starts with a laminate that is copper clad on both sides. The thickness of copper and other metal plating is often given in ounce (oz.) units. This unit of measurement refers to the weight of copper (on a single layer) for a one square foot area. One ounce copper is equivalent to a thickness of .0014 inch or 35 microns. The manufacturing process generally starts with ½ or one oz. copper clad FR-4 laminate. Board manufacturers set their equipment up for a given panel size, such as 18 × 22 inches. The first step is to cut the material to this panel size.

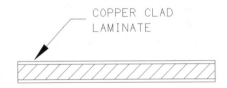

COPPER CLAD
LAMINATE

Figure 1-5   Starting with Copper Clad Laminate

Step 2, shown in Figure 1-6, is to drill the panel. High speed computer numerical control (CNC) drilling equipment is used for this purpose. The small drill sizes require spindle speeds up to 80,000 rpm for reasonable throughput. Panels are normally stacked three high between sheets of entry and backup material. Aluminum clad plastic materials are widely used as entry and backup materials. The entry and backup materials prevent burrs on the exposed copper cladding of the laminate and help cool the drill bit. A pin registration system locates and retains the stacked panels.

Drilling very small holes poses a major challenge. One of the limiting factors is that the depth drilled should not exceed ten times the drill diameter. When drilling through three .062 inch thick panels and the associated entry and backup materials, the smallest drill size is approximately .020 inch. This places a limit on the smallest via hole that can be used. PTH holes are generally drilled about .003 inch larger than the finished size to take into account plating thickness. Based on drilling limitations, the minimum via size for conventional boards is approximately .030 inch pad diameter with a .018 inch hole diameter.

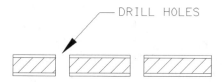

Figure 1-6   Drilling Holes in the Copper Clad Laminate

Step 3, shown in Figure 1-7, involves the initial formation of the PTH. This area has always been the focus of intense research and development and many different process technologies have been tried. Regardless of the process used, the goal is to generate a conductive surface inside the holes for subsequent plating operations.

The most commonly used process involves a two step catalyzing bath consisting of a $SnCl_2$ sensitizer solution followed by a $PdCl_2$ activator solution. After the inside of the holes is catalyzed, an electroless copper deposition bath based on a Cu-EDTA complexing agent is used to build up an initial metal layer with a thickness of .00001 to .0001 inch. Note that an electroless plating bath does not require the flow of electricity as the basis for the plating action. The use of a $SnCl_2$-$PdCl_2$ catalyzing bath was first described in a paper by Fred Pearlstein of Kollmorgen Corporation in 1953. A team led by P.B. Atkinson of General Electric applied for a patent on a Cu-EDTA based electroless plating solution in 1956. With the combination of a $SnCl_2$-$PdCl_2$ catalyzing bath and Cu-EDTA electroless plating solution, PTH technology became a practical reality in the early 1960s. Recent restrictions on formaldehyde, which is used as a reducing agent in electroless copper plating baths, are now driving new PTH process technologies.

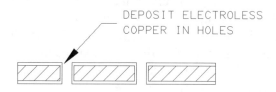

Figure 1-7   Initial Formation of Plated Through Holes

Direct metallization technology (DMT) offers environmentally acceptable alternatives to the conventional PTH process by eliminating the requirement for electroless copper deposition. About a dozen DMT processes have been commercialized. Most are based on palladium or carbon/graphite systems. The palladium-based systems deposit a thin conductive layer of palladium or palladium sulfate inside the holes, which can then be directly electroplated. The carbon and graphite systems use suspensions of these conductive materials to coat the inside of holes prior to electroplating. In addition to the favorable environmental aspects, DMT also facilitates processing of Teflon and polyimide board substrates, which are difficult to plate with electroless copper.

Step 4, shown in Figure 1-8, involves the application of a plating resist pattern to the board. In the depicted SMOBC process, the plating resist covers the entire board surface except those areas where conductive material is required. The plating resist pattern is a negative of the board artwork. Many plating resist materials and process variations exist. Two broad categories are screen printed resists and photoimaged resists. Screen printed resist materials are inexpensive but generally limited in terms of feature resolution to trace widths above .012 inch.

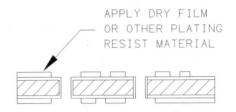

APPLY DRY FILM
OR OTHER PLATING
RESIST MATERIAL

Figure 1-8   Application of Plating Resist

Photoimaged resist materials are preferred for fineline boards. Photoimaging technology can image line widths well below the limits of the remaining manufacturing processes. Photoimaged resists fall into two categories: dry film and liquid. DuPont Riston dry film materials are widely used and are based on a photopolymer chemistry. Riston dry film consists of photopolymer resist sandwiched between an outer Mylar protective and an inner polyolefin separator layer. Riston dry film is supplied on rolls and simultaneously laminated onto both sides of the PCB substrate panel with automated equipment using hot rollers and pressure. The separator layer is removed during the lamination process. The outer Mylar layer protects the resist during the exposure process. An optical exposure unit simultaneously exposes both sides of the PCB panel. Phototools are drawn into direct contact with the dry film by means of a vacuum system. Registration pins ensure proper alignment between the PCB panel and the phototool. Ultraviolet (UV) light exposure initiates polymerization in the dry film material. After the contact exposure, the Mylar protective layer is removed and the photopolymer resist is developed. Areas polymerized by UV exposure remain intact while the developer dissolves the unexposed material. The original DuPont Riston materials required a solvent-based developer. Today the majority of companies employ dry film materials compatible with an aqueous process. A weak alkaline solution is used as the developer. Later, after copper and solder plating, the remaining resist is stripped off with a strong alkaline solution.

The image resolution is approximately equal to the thickness of the resist material. A thin photoresist layer is capable of finer image resolution. This is due to light diffusion effects during exposure and undercut effects on edges during subsequent development. Dry film gives acceptable results down to about .008 inch feature size. Liquid photoresists can be applied as a very thin coating and are capable of higher resolution than dry film. Disadvantages include the requirement for more expensive equipment and complex process controls.

Phototools are either diazo or silver halide materials on a Mylar base. The life of a phototool used in contact printing may be as low as 20 to 50 panels. Many phototools are directly plotted on high speed laser systems and disposed after the completion of a production run. The laser photoplotting process is explained in greater detail in the next section. Direct laser imaging of resist materials was first tried in the early 1980s. So far this technology has not made significant inroads into the marketplace because of extremely high cost and low throughput.

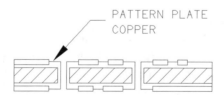

PATTERN PLATE
COPPER

Figure 1-9   Copper Pattern Plating

Step 5 in the SMOBC process is shown in Figure 1-9. This is a conventional electroplating operation. At this point the entire panel surface including the inside of the holes is conductive. Plating resist covers the areas where copper plating is not desired. In most cases, 1 oz. copper (.0014 inch thick) is deposited on the panel. Features such as circuit traces will grow in width by approximately the same amount. For fineline boards with .008 inch or smaller features, feature sizes on the phototool must be adjusted to compensate for this growth effect. This is one of the reasons why board manufacturers prefer to generate phototools in-house and have the customer supply artwork in the form of electronic data.

Electroplating of copper is an electrochemical process that requires current flow through an electrochemical cell consisting of cathode, anode, and electrolyte solution. Metal plating racks holding the board panels form the cathode. The racks are immersed in an electrolyte solution of copper sulfate acidified with sulfuric and hydrochloric acids. This plating solution also contains proprietary organic additives that improve characteristics such as the "throwing power" (the ability to plate deep inside small holes) and surface finish. Solid copper bars form the anode. A power supply causes electric current to flow from the cathode racks to the copper anodes. Two half-reactions occur in this electrochemical cell. One half-reaction termed *reduction* occurs at the cathode and involves absorption of electrons. Copper cations in solution plate out at the cathode surface. The other half-reaction is termed *oxidation* and involves giving up electrons at the anode. Copper atoms at the anode surface become oxidized and go into solution.

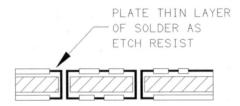

PLATE THIN LAYER
OF SOLDER AS
ETCH RESIST

Figure 1-10   Solder Plating

Step 6 is shown in Figure 1-10. A thin .0002 inch layer of solder (60% tin and 40% lead) is electroplated on top of the copper from the previous step. This solder plating forms a resist for the subsequent etching process in step 8. Step 7, as shown in Figure 1-11, involves stripping the plating resist from step 4. At this point the desired board features are covered with solder plating and the remaining area is the original copper cladding.

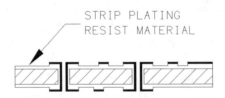

STRIP PLATING
RESIST MATERIAL

Figure 1-11   Stripping the Original Plating Resist

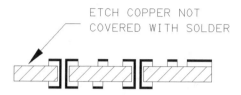

Figure 1-12   Etching the Circuit Pattern

In step 8, shown above in Figure 1-12, the remaining copper cladding is etched from the panel, leaving only the desired circuit pattern. The most common etchant solution is based on ammonium hydroxide (also referred to as alkaline ammonia). Closed loop continuous process systems are now widely used. These systems regenerate the etchant solution and allow recovery of the copper. The closed loop system recovers copper as copper sulfate, which can be returned to the copper plating bath. Etching always results in a certain amount of undercut at feature edges. The degree of undercut is referred to as the *etch factor*. Etch factor is defined as the ratio of depth to side attack. A high etch factor results in less feature distortion from undercut. Undercut during etching partially compensates for feature growth during the copper pattern plating in step 5.

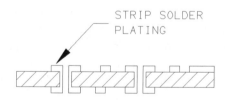

Figure 1-13   Stripping the Solder Plating

In step 9, shown above in Figure 1-13, the thin solder plating used as an etch resist is stripped from the panel. SMOBC requires this step in order to create a bare copper surface. Solder stripping aroused controversy during the early development of the SMOBC process. Solder stripping requires harsh acids that can attack the exposed substrate material. Excessive time in the solder stripping bath can result in measling (small white spots) and crazing (surface defects appearing as small cracks). Investigations conducted by the Institute for Interconnecting and Packaging Electronic Circuits (IPC) revealed that these minor surface defects did not affect the long-term reliability of the finished board.

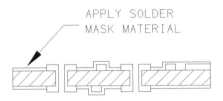

APPLY SOLDER
MASK MATERIAL

Figure 1-14   Applying the Solder Mask

Step 10, shown in Figure 1-14, involves applying the solder mask (also referred to as *solder resist*) material to the panel. The circuit pattern on the panel now consists entirely of bare copper. With the exception of pad areas to which solder connections will be made during board assembly, the entire board area is covered with solder mask.

Solder mask application techniques and process choices are similar to those available for plating resists. Solder mask can be screen printed or photoimaged. Photoimaged solder mask materials come as a dry film or in liquid form. Screen printed, heat cured epoxy inks have been successfully used for many years and are still the industry mainstay. Dry film solder mask materials were popular some years back. More accurate registration and thicker coatings are possible with dry film than conventional screen printed solder mask. Dry film materials with a typical thickness of .002 to .003 inch have proven to be a disadvantage on fine line/fine pitch SMT boards. Dry film solder mask has difficulty covering small areas between tightly spaced pads. In recent years dry film usage has declined, and the trend is to use liquid photoimagable solder resist (LPISR) materials such as Ciba-Geigy's Probimer 52. LPISR is recommended for all SMT boards.

The use of solder mask was by no means universally accepted during the early days of the PCB industry. Spaces between traces and pads were often so large that unmasked boards could be successfully wave soldered. Boards were sometimes afflicted with conductive chemical residues trapped under the solder mask. These residues resulted from improper processing during PCB manufacturing or flux wicking through cracks during wave soldering. As the board geometry shrank, excessive solder shorts during assembly forced companies to start using solder mask. With better process controls and the improved solder mask adhesion inherent in SMOBC, problems with conductive residues under the solder mask are now a very rare occurrence.

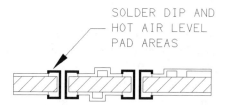

SOLDER DIP AND
HOT AIR LEVEL
PAD AREAS

Figure 1-15   Applying a Selective Solder Coating

Step 11, the last step in the SMOBC process is shown in Figure 1-15. A solder coating is selectively applied to the pads. The panel is first dipped in molten solder and the resulting rough solder coat is then leveled by a hot air process. The term *HASL* is used to refer to this process step. As with the solder stripping process in step 9, HASL aroused controversy during the early development of SMOBC technology. Critics argued that HASL exerted extreme thermal stress on the board, which caused some PTH to fail. They ignored the fact that the board is subjected to even more severe thermal stress from the wave or reflow soldering during normal assembly operations. Plated through holes that fail during HASL would most likely fail anyway in later processing steps. Today most production boards are subjected to bare board electrical test as a final step in the PCB manufacturing process. HASL weeds out marginal boards in the same manner as the thermal cycling conducted during MIL-SPEC tests.

The SMOBC process is now complete, but several steps remain before the board is finished. These steps include gold plating edge connectors, screen printing the component legends, depanelizing the individual boards, inspection, and a bare board electrical test. Industry trends have affected many of these operations.

Gold plated edge connectors were once commonly used. While edge connectors are inexpensive and reliable, they are not suitable for applications that require repeated mating cycles or high signal densities. Personal computer buses such as the AT bus and PCI bus are among the few remaining widespread applications for gold plated edge connectors. High performance buses such as the VME bus use pin and socket connectors directly soldered onto the PCB.

Screen printing of component legends on the board helps identify components during assembly, test, and field repair operations. Additional information screened on the board may include the product name, part number, and switch and jumper positions to aid customer setup. The terms *component silkscreen* and *legend silkscreen* are commonly used to refer to this printed information. A heat cured, epoxy-based ink gives the best results. The white ink traditionally used over green solder mask gives excellent visibility.

Depanelization involves separating the individual boards from the panel. If automated component placement equipment will be used during assembly operations, the boards are usually left on the panel. The outside of the panel is trimmed, and slots or V grooves are cut around the periphery of the individual boards to allow easy removal after assembly. CNC routing equipment is widely used for depanelization and profiling of board outlines. The board manufacturer generates the numerical control (NC) routing program in-house based on the customer's board outline drawing or data from artwork files. For very high volume production or odd shapes, the board outline may be blanked (punched). CNC routing is typically done with a .125 inch diameter cutter. Outside corners of the board can be routed square, but internal corners will have a .0625 inch radius. Square internal corners require a separate notching operation.

Bare Board Electrical Test

While bare board testing may not be cost effective for initial prototype runs or some low-cost consumer products, SMT and fineline technology generally dictate such testing for all production boards. Advances in bare board test equipment have greatly reduced the cost. Testing a moderate-size board with several hundred pads costs less than $.25 per board in production quantities. This is much less than the cost of rework. The Rule of 10s is often cited as justification for bare board testing. The Rule of 10s states that the cost of an undetected fault increases by a factor of ten throughout each stage of the production process. Figures cited for industrial products are: $10 at the assembled board stage, $100 at the system integration stage, and $1000 in the field.

A bare board electrical test checks for continuity between interconnected pads and isolation between separate circuit patterns. The maximum resistance threshold for continuity tests is in the range of 10 to 50 ohms. Test currents are generally under 100 milliamps. Continuity tests will not detect a "neckdown" fault. The minimum resistance threshold for isolation tests is 2 megohms with an applied potential of 40 to 100 volts. Isolation tests detect gross faults such as conductive "whiskers" between traces, but may not detect more subtle faults such as surface contamination that cause small leakage currents and wreak havoc with sensitive analog circuitry.

The equipment for bare board electrical tests falls into two broad categories: moving probe and "bed-of-nails." Moving probe testers use two or more probes that rapidly move from pad to pad on the board surface. Moving probe testers do not require a dedicated fixture for every board.

Setup time and cost are low, but so is the throughput. These systems are generally used for prototype and short run production. Bed-of-nails testers use a dedicated test fixture for each board. The board is held against spring loaded probes that contact the pads. Typical test time is only a few seconds per board. The cost per board is low, but the dedicated bed-of-nails fixture will cost upwards of $500 for a small board. The board manufacturer can extract pad location and connectivity data for building the test fixture and programming the tester from the customer's artwork and NC drill data files.

PCB manufacturing is a highly specialized business that requires a substantial investment in capital equipment. Few electronics companies still maintain in-house board manufacturing capability. Most companies use multiple outside vendors. It is not unusual to find that a company uses one vendor for fast turn prototypes, another for fineline SMT boards, and an offshore source for high volume production.

Historical Overview of PCB Design Techniques

The original techniques used for PCB design were borrowed from the graphic arts industry. In larger companies, the process involved several distinct disciplines, each of which was the realm of a different specialist. After a product had been breadboarded, the engineer usually drew up a rough schematic and board outline and then submitted this information to the drafting department. The first task involved drafting the schematic. After the draftsman completed the schematic, the PCB designer did a board layout drawing. This drawing showed the board outline, arrangement of parts, and signal interconnections. Different colors were used to identify the various layers. For double sided boards, blue was used for the component side and red for the solder side. The mnemonic "red is hot" made this color scheme easy to remember, since the solder side was the "hot side." The layout drawing, also known as a linestudy, was done at 2:1 or 4:1 scale on a .1 inch grid. PCB design was a specialty considered more demanding than traditional drafting, and skilled PCB designers were well paid. Many successful PCB designers came from graphic arts backgrounds.

After the color-coded layout was completed, another drafting specialist prepared the artwork and board documentation. The layout was placed on a light table. Successive overlay sheets representing artwork and documentation were created on the basis of the underlying layout. A pin registration system ensured that all sheets remained precisely aligned. The first sheet was the pad master. The pad master consisted of black pad patterns for all the components on the PCB.

Several companies specialized in supplying self-adhesive component patterns and colored tapes used to speed the process — one of the best known was the now defunct Bishop Graphics. For double sided boards, circuit traces were often formed on the same sheet as the pad master with various widths of red and blue tape. For multi-layer boards, a separate sheet was generally used for each circuit layer. Artwork for a legend silkscreen and documentation for manufacturing drawings was also prepared on separate overlay sheets. This drafting specialty was referred to as *taping* and required long hours working on a light table with an X-Acto knife. The person doing the work was known as a "taper."

The next step in the process was to photographically separate the layers and at the same time reduce the artwork to the final 1:1 scale. In the case of a double sided board with a red/blue artwork master, this was done through the use of colored filters. For example, using a red filter caused the red traces to drop out, leaving the blue component side traces and black pads. The process was then repeated with a blue filter for the solder side artwork. The solder mask artwork was created by slightly overexposing the image without any filters so that both red and blue dropped out, leaving just the black pads. Various photomechanical means where then used to create the slightly oversized pad image required for the solder mask artwork. One method involved a deliberate overexposure, which caused the pads to bloom out. Another method used a device called the Byers Micromodifier. This device moved the pad artwork in an oscillatory circular pattern while making a contact print. By controlling the amplitude of the movement, the Byers device could generate oversize pads accurate to within a few thousands of an inch.

The photographic work for PCB artwork required a specialized engineering camera and film processing equipment. Photoreducing a 4:1 size artwork master for a large PCB required a giant engineering camera that would occupy an entire room. This work was sent out to a service bureau, since it was difficult to justify the expense of the equipment for in-house use. At first these service bureaus were the same companies that did color separations and halftones for the graphics arts industry. In time, service bureaus evolved that specialized in artwork for PCBs.

Introduction of Computer Aided Design and Manufacturing

The first attempts at CAD for PCBs started in the early 1960s. These first systems were often based on IBM mainframe computers. By the early 1970s, the mainframes had started to give way to powerful minicomputers such as the Digital Equipment Corp. VAX series. Initially the emphasis was not on automating the design phase, but on reducing the tremendous amount of labor required for taping the artwork and drafting documentation.

The PCB designer still did the board layout 2:1 or 4:1 size at a drafting table. Once the layout was completed, it was digitized. Some of the early digitizers were electromechanical attachments to drafting machines mounted on large light tables. A cross hair on a transparent reticule replaced the standard ruler mechanism on the drafting machine. The reticule was linked through a series of cables and pulleys to optical encoders that read position information into the computer. The operator moved the reticule and aligned the crosshair with various features on the layout. Usually pad locations were digitized first, followed by the end points and corner points of the traces. Digitizing all the layers of a large board could take several days, but this was still a great time savings compared with manual taping.

Photoplotting of PCB Artwork

Once the information had been digitized and was available in the computer, the artwork could be plotted out. Most systems also featured some interactive graphics for adding text annotations or minor engineering changes. The less expensive systems utilized pen plotters for plotting the artwork. In this case the artwork was still plotted 2:1 or 4:1 scale and then photoreduced. One of the early innovations that had a significant impact on the PCB design process was the photoplotter. This technology was pioneered by Gerber Scientific of Hartford, Connecticut, during the early 1960s. The first generation of photoplotters were modified flat bed pen plotters. The pen plotter head was replaced with an optical projection mechanism that moved over the film. The photoplotter head worked much like a slide projector. Instead of a slide carousel, the head had a wheel containing 24 optical patterns, called *apertures*. Each aperture was a unique pattern that could be projected onto the film. A shutter mechanism controlled the light source. Pad shapes were "flashed" on the film with a momentary opening of the shutter while the head remained stationary at the required location. Traces were drawn with round aperture patterns by means of leaving the shutter open and moving the head over the film, similar to drawing with a pen. The system was controlled by a minicomputer that read data from magnetic tape. The photoplotter shared many similarities with CNC machines and used a variant of RS-274 NC control language that came to be known as *Gerber format*.

Having been the first company to bring a photoplotter to market, Gerber established their data format as an industry standard. It remains so today and is supported by most CAD systems. During the 1980s, the mechanical photoplotters were replaced with laser photoplotters. These devices scan a laser beam across the film in one axis while the film moves in the other axis. The basic operation is similar to that of a laser printer, except that the laser beam exposes film instead of a toner drum. Pen plotters and the older Gerber photoplotters are referred to as *vector devices*. These mechanical plotters require vector data. Lines or traces are drawn from point A to point B. The vector data for each line consists of the X and Y coordinates for the end points and the width of the line. A Gerber pad flash is a special case in which the data consists of the X and Y coordinates for the pad center location and the pad shape.

Laser photoplotters and laser printers such as the Hewlett-Packard LaserJet series are raster devices. The image consists of individual picture elements (pixels). The number of pixels along a 1 inch line is referred to as the *resolution* and is expressed in dots per inch (DPI). Laser printers are either 300 or 600 DPI. The resolution of a laser photoplotter is usually 2000 or 4000 DPI. The higher resolution allows imaging of fine details. A rule of thumb for PCB artwork is that the plotter resolution should be one fourth the size of the smallest feature. A laser photoplotter with 2000 DPI resolution can produce very high quality artwork with traces as small as .002 inch. It is possible to image even smaller traces at this resolution, but a noticeable stair stepping pattern will start to emerge on traces running at 45 degree angles. While laser photoplotters require raster data for the laser imaging system, the input data is still in the old Gerber format. The Gerber vector data is converted into raster data by a powerful workstation or embedded controller. This conversion is analogous to conversion of ASCII text or Postscript to a raster image by a laser printer.

Numerically Controlled PCB Drilling

Most PCBs require a substantial number of drill holes. Even boards that contain 100% surface mount devices still have via holes between layers. High speed numerically controlled drilling machines are used to drill the holes during the board manufacturing process. The CNC drilling machines used in the PCB industry are highly specialized. The drill spindles must be capable of rotational speeds up to 80,000 rpm to achieve acceptable productivity levels. Vacuum systems are used to fixture the boards and remove the fine dust generated by the drilling operation. Since cutting fluids and lubricants common in metal working equipment would seriously contaminate the PCB materials, air bearings and closed-loop fluid cooling systems are used instead. One of the first companies to offer a high speed NC drilling machine for PCB applications was Excellon corporation. As was the case with Gerber photoplotters, Excellon used a variation of RS-274 NC data format for their drilling equipment, and this became the industry standard.

In the mid 1970s, when the author first started working in the electronics industry, PCB manufacturers typically received a 1:1 size photographic artwork and fabrication drawing from their customers. Some of the larger board manufacturers had their own camera equipment and could accept a taped up 2:1 or 4:1 artwork master, but in most cases photoreduction work was subcontracted out to a service bureau. The board manufacturer used the photographic artwork to image a resist pattern for etching and plating the PCB. Equipment limitations and economics dictated the use of a standard panel size such as 18 × 22 inches throughout the manufacturing process. Images for smaller boards were stepped and repeated to fill up this panel size. Several different boards could also be combined to obtain the most efficient panel utilization. A contact printing process was used to go from the photographic artwork supplied by the customer to the phototool used in actual etching and plating operations.

Generating NC drill data from the customer's artwork was a time-consuming task. An optical programming system was used for this purpose. The optical programmer consisted of a light table with a movable magnifying head, somewhat similar to that of an optical comparator use in metal-working industries. The operator guided the optical head with two hand wheels and pressed a foot pedal whenever the head was centered over a pad location where a drill hole was required. X and Y location data giving the position of the optical head was then written out on punched paper tape by a teletype machine. Data for different hole sizes could not be sorted. While tool changes in the NC drill were done under program control, repeated tool changes greatly slowed the machine down. The operator had to mark up the artwork and plan the path that the NC machine would follow for each required drill size. You can imagine what an ordeal it was to generate the NC drill tape for a large board with hundreds of holes. Back in those days, donut-shaped pads were often used on the board artwork. The small clear hole in the center of the pad made it easier to align the optical programmer with the pad center. A common misconception was that the donut pads made it easier to drill the board, since presumably the drill bit would not have to pass through copper. In fact, this was a fallacy since in most manufacturing operations the first step was to drill the board, which still had solid copper surfaces.

Evolution of PCB Design Tools

Digitizing systems were the first PCB CAD tools. Digitizing systems eliminated manual preparation of artwork and documentation but did not directly affect the design process. As very large scale integrated circuits (VLSI) drove up pin counts and electronic systems became more complex, the need arose for PCB design automation. Recal-Redac introduced one of the first commercially available design automation tools in the late 1970s. The Recal-Redac system included interactive graphics and an autorouter. This system sold for almost $200,000. The starting point of the design automation process was the creation of a netlist (list of components and signal interconnections). The first Recal-Redac systems did not include schematic drafting capability (also referred to as *schematic capture*). The designer worked from the schematic, redlining each signal connection as the netlist was slowly entered at a terminal. Using the interactive graphics display, the designer then created the board outline and placed the components. Some tools were available to aid the component placement process. A rats nest display mode showed pin to pin signal connections. By examining the density of traces in the rats nest display, the designer could optimize the component placement to minimize path lengths and crossovers.

Additional tools were available for automatically swapping pins and gates to further reduce path lengths and crossovers. Rules entered into the component library determined which device pins and gates were electrically equivalent for swapping purposes. For example, the two pins of a discrete resistor could be swapped, but not the pins of a diode or polarized electrolytic capacitor.

After the component placement had been optimized, the autorouter automatically routed the board traces. Percentage of completion depended on the design rules (minimum trace size, pad sizes, and grid spacing) and the designer's skill in placing the components. On boards of moderate complexity, completion rates approached 95%. After autorouting, the designer interactively routed the remaining traces. Interactive routing was a slow and cumbersome process. A Tektronix storage tube display was used for the interactive graphics. This was a monochrome display that made distinguishing between layers somewhat difficult.

The system had limited capability to allow checking of the final design for spacing violations. This feature is now referred to as *design rules checking*. The last step was to pen plot the various drawings and to create data files for computer aided manufacturing (CAM). Gerber data for the various artwork layers was output on magnetic tape. Excellon NC drill data was output on punched paper tape. Note that these media were used until well into the 1980s. CAM data is now transferred by means of floppy disk or on-line, but the term *drill tape* is still widely used for NC drill data.

Racal-Redac claimed productivity improvements ranging up to 5:1 over digitizing systems such as those sold by Gerber. The high cost, and the fact that a Gerber photoplotter was still required for plotting artwork, limited initial acceptance of the Racal-Redac system. Even with a 5:1 productivity improvement, potential labor cost savings hardly offset the amortization of the equipment. Only a few large companies and PCB design service bureaus could afford design automation. However, Racal-Redac had set the stage. All present electronic design automation (EDA) tools for PCB design follow the same basic concept pioneered by Racal-Redac.

Today a number of vendors offer Windows-based PCB EDA software priced as low as $1500. These software packages generally include schematic capture, autorouting, interactive editing, design rules checking, and CAM output (Gerber and Excellon format data).

Impact of Manufacturing Requirements on PCB Design

Manufacturing requirements drove the development of the early CAD tools. This trend continues today as advances in packaging technology such as fine pitch SMD and dense ball grid array devices drive up board complexity and force design rule changes to accommodate smaller feature sizes.

Early CAD systems used for digitizing board layouts generated both high quality photoplotted artwork and NC drill tapes. Whereas optical programming of NC drill information was usually accurate to within ±.003 inches, CAD generated drill tapes had absolute accuracy. Even the older mechanical photoplotters were quite accurate. During the 1960s Gerber already offered mechanical photoplotters capable of ±.0001 inch accuracy when plotting on glass plates. Most photoplotting is now done on 7 mil Mylar film. Temperature changes during processing are the major factor influencing the accuracy. Careful environmental controls allow 16 × 20 inch artwork accurate to within about ±.002 inches.

Most new designs use SMT and board manufacturers now routinely handle the required .008 inch trace widths and .018 inch via holes without any significant cost penalty. Companies whose products that do not take full advantage of the available manufacturing technology quickly lose market share in today's competitive environment.

Precise photoplotted artwork and accurate NC drill data have become absolute requirements. Photoreduction of pen plotted artwork is no longer a viable option. Modern board manufacturers do not like to accept film artwork from customers. Film artwork is easily scratched by careless handling. Exposure to humidity and temperature extremes can cause dimensional changes that are not easily corrected. For the same reasons, most manufacturers do not keep phototools. Each time a job is run, they plot out a new phototool. Many manufacturers now have in-house laser photoplotters. They also have CAM tools that can generate a step and repeat pattern for an optimum panel layout. Few manufacturers still have optical programmers for generating NC drill data. If a customer cannot supply Excellon format NC drill data, the artwork must be sent out to a service bureau. The service bureau scans the artwork using a document scanner and electronically generates the required NC drill data. This service costs money, and one way or another the customer pays for it.

Most customers now send Gerber and Excellon files to the board manufacturer. There is no physical transfer of artwork or documentation. Often the only document received by the manufacturer is the purchase order, and even that is usually faxed or sent by means of EDI (electronic document interface). The board manufacturer has a electronic bulletin board system (BBS) that the customer dials up using a PC equipped with a modem and communication software. The files representing the board design are then transferred on-line. The files are compressed with a compression utility such PKZIP and uploaded to the manufacturer's BBS with a file transfer protocol such as ZMODEM. Only a few minutes are required to transfer the files for an average-size board. Both PKZIP and ZMODEM have error detection capability that virtually eliminates the possibility of data corruption. This process has proven to be very efficient and reliable. Board manufacturers usually leave their BBS up 24 hours a day and 365 days a year. This facilitates business conducted across time zones and continents in a global economy. The BBS also allows E-mail messages, which further enhances communication. Few other industries have reached this level of sophistication as far as electronic transfer of manufacturing data is concerned.

Application of AutoCAD for PCB Design

AutoCAD is the most widely used CAD software, with several million users worldwide. While 90% of AutoCAD users are primarily involved in traditional mechanical disciplines and the architectural field, the remaining 10% have some involvement with electronics. Many use AutoCAD to draft schematics, design PCB artwork, and prepare detailed fabrication and assembly drawings for PCBs designed on other EDA systems.

Companies that use AutoCAD to draft schematics or design PCB artwork often lack the workload to justify the acquisition cost and learning curve associated with specialized EDA software. In time, they may see their requirements grow, but in the interim AutoCAD offers a readily available, low-cost solution.

AutoCAD was not intended to be used for PCB design. Autorouting and design rules checking are not available. AutoCAD also lacks drivers for Gerber and Excellon format data output. Third-party add-on tools and utilities are available to fill the voids, but some of them cost almost as much as entry level EDA packages. In the absence of proper tools, users resort to pen plotting artwork at 2:1 or 4:1 size and photoreduction. For the reasons outlined in the previous section, this technique is incompatible with modern board manufacturing.

Tutorial exercises in the following chapters show proper techniques for using AutoCAD to draft schematics and design PCBs. The disk included with this book contains utilities for transfer of Gerber and Excellon format data into and out of AutoCAD and a library with many common through hole and SMD parts.

Overview of the PCB Design Process Using AutoCAD

The PCB design process outlined in the rest of this chapter is based on the use of AutoCAD as an interactive design tool. The first step is to determine what design rules will be required to make the parts on the schematic fit within the board outline. In most cases the board outline is determined by the envelope or nature of the product. For example PC AT bus add-on boards follow a standard outline. The predetermined board outline may include location requirements for parts such as connectors or front panel controls (switches, pots, and displays). If a board outline has not been determined, part of the PCB design process may be to calculate the minimum required board size.

Floor Planning Metrics

The process of determining the required board area for component placement is called *floor planning*. Two relatively simple floor planning metrics are used throughout the industry to aid in the process: chip equivalents (CE) and density. The CE figure is an overall measure of the amount of circuitry on the PCB. The term *integrated circuit (IC) equivalents* also is used.

$$CE = \text{Total Number of Device Pins on PCB} / 14$$

The CE figure is based on a 14 pin IC and relates the total amount of circuitry to an equivalent board with 14 pin ICs. Calculation of the CE figure is straightforward. The designer adds up the device pins for all the parts shown on the schematic. Any unused pins, such as spare pins on connectors or unused gates on ICs, are included.

The next step is to calculate the board density in terms of CE per square inch of useable board area:

$$\text{Density} = \text{Useable Board Area (sq-inch)} / CE$$

Useable board area excludes any areas where components cannot be located, including clearance areas around mounting hardware.

CE and density metrics as calculated above apply to most digital boards. Analog and power supply boards often contain large devices with relatively few pins. Common examples include transformers and large electrolytic capacitors. A rule of thumb is that any devices with less than 10 pins per square inch merit special consideration.

The area of these large devices is deducted from the useable board area in the density calculation. This gives reasonable results in most cases.

The calculated density gives a good indication of the complexity of the board and the type of design rules that will be required to successfully complete the layout. The lower the numerical density figure, the less area is available per component. When PCB designers talk about a high-density board, they mean a board with a low numerical density figure. The theoretical density limit for a digital board using ICs in dual inline packages (DIPs) is .45 sq-in/CE. This limit is based on the assumption of 14 pin DIPs separated by .25 inch margins. For surface mount boards using SOICs with .050 inch pad centers and .1 inch margins, the theoretical density limit is about .23 sq-in/CE.

These theoretical density limits are difficult to achieve and would likely require a multi-layer board. Table 1-1 gives practical density limits for PIH and surface mount boards using various design rules. The design rules are explained in detail later. The boards are assumed to contain a mix of digital and analog components. Note that the dimensions are expressed in mils (1 mil = .001 inch).

Table 1-1   Density Guidelines for PCB Design

Board Technology	Design Rule	Density Limit (Sq-In/CE)
Single sided PIH	50 mil grid/25 mil trace	1.25
Double sided PIH	50 mil grid/25 mil trace	1.0
Double sided PIH	25 mil grid/13 mil trace	.70
Double sided PIH	16.7 mil grid/8 mil trace	.50
Double sided SMT	25 mil grid/13 mil trace	.35
Double sided SMT	16.7 mil grid/8 mil trace	.25

PCB Design Rules

Design rules consist of a grid spacing and minimum trace width. PCB designs are always based on a grid. Component pads and trace corners are located on the grid. In most cases the minimum trace width is approximately one half of the grid size. This provides an optimum balance between trace width and trace-to-trace space. Additional design rule parameters include the minimum pad size, via size, and pad-to-trace space. Poor registration of the solder mask can leave traces near pads exposed and cause solder shorts. Consequently, the pad-to-trace space tends to be a critical parameter.

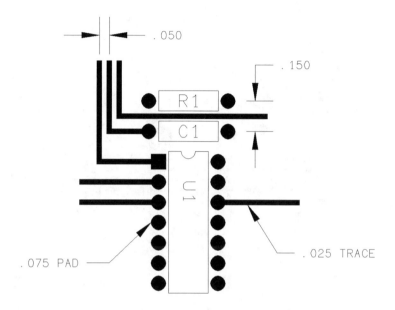

Figure 1-16   50 Mil Grid and 25 Mil Trace Design Rule

Figure 1-16 shows a section of a board designed on a 50 mil grid with 25 mil minimum trace width. This design rule was typical of single and double sided boards manufactured 20 years ago. Table 1-2 gives two common variations of the 50 mil grid design rule. Minimum pad and via sizes can be either .075 or .062 inch. The choice of pad size affects the pad-to-trace space. Traces cannot run between the pads of DIP ICs with pins on .1 inch centers. This severely limits the maximum density. Today, the 50 mil grid/25 mil trace design rule is virtually obsolete. It might still be used on single sided boards for very cost sensitive consumer gadgets or homemade boards for hobbyist applications.

Table 1-2   50 Mil Grid Design Rules

Min Pad	Via	Min Trace	Trace-Trace	Pad-Trace
.075	.075	.025	.025	.025
.062	.062	.025	.025	.031

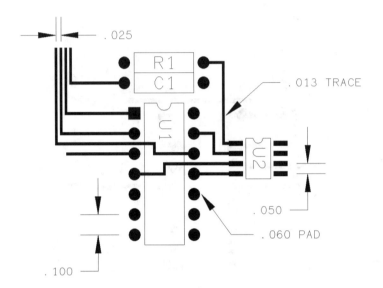

Figure 1-17   25 Mil Grid and 13 Mil Trace Design Rule

Figure 1-17 shows a section of a board designed on 25 mil grid with 13 mil minimum trace width. Table 1-3 gives two variations of the 25 mil grid design rule. The use of a 25 mil grid design rule is typical for boards in cost-sensitive products when size is not a major constraint. The use of .060 inch pads for DIPs and 13 mil traces is preferred for most applications.

Note that the 25 mil grid design rule allows running a single trace between pads of standard DIP ICs. This increases the maximum density and facilitates design of large boards with long rows of ICs. SOIC devices with pads on .05 inch centers can also be accommodated, even though traces cannot be run between these pads. By today's standards, 12 to 13 mil traces are not considered difficult to manufacture. Resist patterns can be applied by means of an inexpensive screen printing process.

Table 1-3   25 Mil Grid Design Rules

DIP Pad	Via	Min Trace	Trace-Trace	Pad-Trace
.062	.055	.013	.012	.012
.060	.055	.013	.012	.013

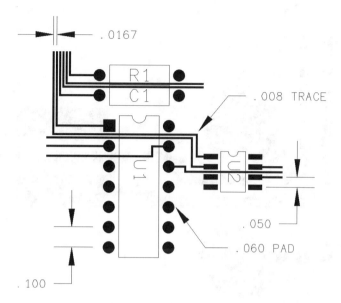

Figure 1-18   16.7 Mil Grid and 8 Mil Trace Design Rule

Figure 1-18 shows a section of a board designed on 16.7 mil grid with 8 mil minimum trace width. This design rule is typically used for SMT boards in a wide range of consumer and industrial products. Two traces can run between the pads of DIP ICs with pins on .1 inch centers. One trace can run between SOIC pads on .05 inch centers. Most PCB manufacturers can handle 8 mil traces. Dry film or liquid photoimageable resist materials are recommended; 100% bare board electrical test is also highly recommended once production volumes are reached.

Note that the 16.7 mil grid results in four grid points between SOIC pads on .05 inch centers and seven grid points between DIP IC pads on .1 inch centers. When traces are run between pads, the traces are offset 1/2 grid location for proper centering and optimum spacing. This is shown more clearly in Figure 1-19. This is easily done in AutoCAD by setting the grid to 16.7 mils and the snap to 8.35 mils.

Figure 1-19 also shows 45 degree beveled corners on traces. Various schools of though exist regarding 45 degree beveled corners. Sharp 90 degree corners represent an electrical impedance discontinuity for fast signals with rise times in the nanosecond range. Such discontinuities can cause signal ringing and excessive EMI. Logic boards using BiCMOS, ECL, Schottky TTL, or other high speed logic families will benefit from beveled corners. Most boards using analog circuits, CMOS, standard TTL, and LSTTL will see little if any benefit from beveled corners.

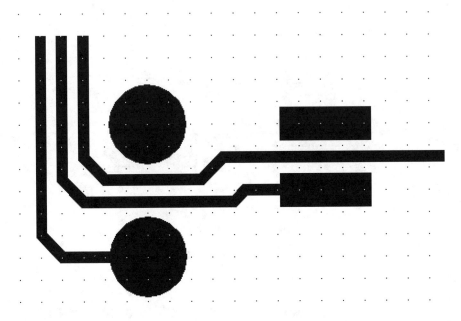

Figure 1-19   16.7 Mil Grid with Traces Offset 1/2 Grid

Trace Width and Spacing Requirements

The PCB designer must also determine the feature width and spacing required to safely handle the anticipated current and voltage levels. The trace width and via hole size determine the maximum current carrying capacity. Spacing between features (trace-to-trace, pad-to-trace, and pad-to-pad) determines the maximum voltage. Tables 1-4, 1-5, and 1-6 list IPC standards for current carrying capacity and required spacing.

Table 1-4   Current Carrying Capacity of Traces

Trace Width	Max Current (amps)	Resistance (ohm/ft)
.008	1.0	.37
.013	1.5	.22
.025	2.5	.12
.050	4.0	.06
.100	7.0	.03
.150	9.0	.02
.250	13	.012

Table 1-5   Current Carrying Capacity of Vias

Via Pad/Hole Size	Max Current (amps)
.030/.018	2.5
.055/.031	4.0

Current carrying capacity is based on a 10 degree Celsius temperature rise with standard 2 oz. copper plating for traces and 1 oz. copper in PTH vias. This provides a reasonable safety margin for most consumer, industrial, and automotive applications. Eight mil traces (the smallest used in the examples in this book) carry sufficient current for most signals on analog and logic boards. Even small vias can carry significant current. A .055 inch via can carry the same current as a .050 inch trace. Wider traces will require multiple vias to maintain the maximum current carrying capacity. Note that in most cases, the resistance of the trace is the limiting factor, not the current-carrying capacity. Using Ohm's law ($E = I \times R$), a .050 inch wide trace that is 1 foot long and carrying 4 amps current would experience a voltage drop of .24 volt. This voltage drop could affect the operation of analog circuits or appreciably reduce the noise margin in a digital circuit.

Table 1-6   High Voltage Spacing Requirements

Minimum Spacing	Max DC Voltage	Max AC Voltage
.008	30	20
.012	40	28
.025	150	100
.050	300	200
.100	500	350

The minimum spacing requirements in Table 1-6 are based on IPC standards for uncoated boards operated below 10,000 foot altitude. Solder mask and conformal coating will increase the maximum allowable voltage. Operation at high altitudes decreases the maximum allowable voltage. Note that using the 16.7 mil grid/8 mil trace design rule results in a minimum spacing of 8.67 mils and a maximum voltage level of only 30 volt. This is marginal, but is widely used for analog circuits with ±15 volt supplies. Power supplies and other high-voltage circuits connected to the AC lines are usually subject to regulatory agency requirements, such as UL or IEC/VDE. UL considers any circuits operating above 40 volt DC to be high voltage. UL requires a minimum of .1 inch spacing for 120/250V AC circuits. IEC/VDE requires up to 4 mm (.157 inch). Allowing for manufacturing tolerances and a large safety factor, a minimum spacing of at least .175 inch is suggested for all 120/250V AC circuits.

Board Outline and Component Placement

If the board outline is predetermined by product requirements, the board area is known. CE and board density metrics can be calculated and an appropriate design rule chosen on the basis of the density limits given in Table 1-1.

If the board outline is not predetermined, the minimum required board area can be calculated. First calculate the CE. Next, select an appropriate design rule. The density limit for the selected design rule can then be used to calculate the minimum board area:

$$\text{Minimum Board Area (sq-inch)} = \text{CE} \times \text{Density Limit}$$

Once a design rule has been selected and calculations have shown that the parts will fit onto the board outline, the floor planning task is complete. The next step in the PCB design process involves analysis of the required part patterns. A part pattern consists of the pads, drill holes sizes, component outline, and reference designator text that make up the part as it appears on the board.

Part patterns are organized into a parts library so that once created for a particular design, they can easily be accessed and reused in the future. Many companies have PCB design parts libraries with hundreds of different part patterns created over a number of years. The parts library is a valuable company resource. Maintenance of the parts library is a key aspect of efficient PCB design.

AutoCAD uses the term *block* to refer to stored graphics patterns. PCB part patterns are created as AutoCAD blocks. This text uses the term *part pattern* to refer to such AutoCAD blocks. Other CAD and EDA systems use terms such as *part symbol* or *part decal*. You may see this terminology in books and magazine articles. The disk included with this book includes AutoCAD drawing files that contain libraries of common PIH and SMD part patterns defined as AutoCAD blocks.

For most PCB designs, 90% of the required part patterns will already be available in the company's parts library. The remaining parts will require definition and creation of new part patterns. Information for definition of part patterns can be found in manufacturers' data sheets. Information required for conventional through hole parts includes the lead spacing, body outline dimensions, and lead diameter. Information required for SMD parts includes the pad shape, pad spacing, and the body outline. Manufacturers' data sheets usually include a drawing with the suggested part pattern and detailed dimensions.

Standard practice dictates that the view orientation for all board documentation is looking down on the component side of the board. The CAD system is also set up so that the designer views the artwork layers as seen from the component side. Some part data sheets show the pad pattern as viewed from the solder side. This can cause confusion. The author has seen many instances in which experienced PCB designers inadvertently created mirror image part patterns. Always verify the view orientation when referring to data sheets.

The bill of materials for the board is an excellent document to use for analysis and planning of the required parts patterns. Schematic capture software generates a bill of materials as part of the schematic drafting process. If you are using AutoCAD to draft the schematic, you can extract a bill of materials using the techniques shown in the next chapter. Suggested practice is to write the name of the required part pattern next to each item on the bill of materials. This is also a good time to create a file folder for all the documents related to the design. Keep the marked-up bill of materials in the file folder for future reference.

Once the part patterns have been identified and any required new patterns created, the component placement process begins. The component placement process involves placing the part patterns within the board outline. This is the most critical phase of the PCB design. Novice designers always underestimate the importance of a good component placement. They tend to rush through this phase of the design. A novice designer should plan on spending 80% of the total design time in planning the component placement. A well-planned component placement lends itself to easy routing of signal traces. A poor component placement may prove impossible to route. A sure sign of poor placement is when routing difficulties are encountered on a board that is within reasonable density limits for the selected design rules.

The component placement should minimize total signal length and crossovers. The best place to start is with a well organized schematic. Today, especially in smaller companies, the engineer often draws the schematic and does the PCB design. Dividing the schematic into functional blocks and grouping these functional blocks for a logical pattern of signal flow facilitates subsequent PCB design. Time spent organizing the schematic will pay off later on and reduce the total time to complete the project. The schematic flow will suggest the parts placement on the board.

Mechanical and packaging considerations also play a major role in the parts placement. Certain components such as connectors, switches, displays, and power devices on heat sinks often have predetermined locations. Thermal considerations may influence component location. Heat dissipation is a factor for most power supply boards and computer boards using high speed CPUs. Regulatory agency requirements, such as UL and IEC standards, may dictate spacing between high voltage components. The designer must consider all of these factors during the component placement.

The designer should have an overall plan for the board before placing individual components. Parts should be grouped in an array with rows and columns. An array organization also facilitates proper power and ground busing. Channels between rows and columns should provide sufficient space for routing the anticipated number of signal connections. All ICs should face in the same direction. Polarized discrete parts such as diodes and electrolytic capacitors should also have uniform orientations. Manufacturing process considerations, such as the use of automatic insertion equipment, may dictate the minimum spacing between parts. All of these considerations are discussed in detail in subsequent chapters.

Routing Connections

After completion of the component placement, the next step involves routing the board. Power and ground connections are routed first. These connections are typically made with .05 inch wide traces. The recommended power and ground busing scheme for digital logic is shown in Figure 1-20. Note that a bypass capacitor is used at every IC location. The main power and ground buses are on the solder side (shown as shaded traces). Cross connections between rows are on the component side (shown as solid black traces).

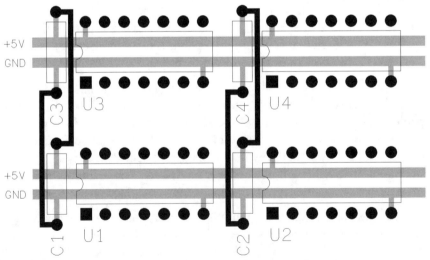

Figure 1-20   Power and Ground Busing Example

The grid pattern of power and ground connections is tied to solid copper areas that run around the outside edges of the board. By convention, the ground plane is placed on the solder side and the power plane (+5V) is placed on the component side. Typical width of these copper planes is .1 to .25 inch. General practice is to place an electrolytic or tantalum capacitor with a value of 1 to 10 uF between power and ground at the edge connector or where power enters the board.

Figure 1-20 shows power and ground buses running parallel to the IC pins on the solder side. This establishes the horizontal axis as the preferred direction for traces on the solder side and the vertical axis as the preferred direction for traces on the component side. Thus traces between IC pins run predominantly on the component side. Minor solder mask registration errors could leave copper exposed on traces between pins. Running traces between pins on the component side reduces the likelihood of solder shorts. Another benefit relates to unused pins for spare gates on ICs. If these pins are tied to ground on the solder side, they remain readily accessible. Engineering changes that require the use of a spare gate can be implemented without having to unsolder the IC.

After completion of the power and ground connections, the remaining signal connections are routed. Most designers focus their initial attention on short signal interconnections that can be routed on a single layer without the use of a via. Each layer has a preferred routing axis. Routing a trace along the wrong axis may block subsequent traces. The designer generally places a limit of 4 to 10 grid locations that a trace can be routed in the wrong direction during this initial routing. Signal traces that must run in a diagonal direction beyond this "wrong way" limit will require one or more vias.

Signal traces that must run a considerable distance are routed in channels. Vias are used to connect the traces in the channel to device pins. Figure 1-21 shows a channel routing strategy that maximizes the number of signal traces in the available channel width. Note how the signal traces are diagonally displaced around vias. N traces can be routed in a channel with a width of N+2 grid points. This channel routing strategy works with either 25 mil or 16.7 mil grid design rules.

A specialized routing strategy used with memory ICs is shown in Figure 1-22. This routing strategy is referred to as a "daisy chain." Data and address lines in memory arrays are generally bussed to the same pins on each device. The daisy chain pattern accomplishes this data and address line bussing between adjacent ICs without requiring vias. Figure 1-22 shows an example of a daisy chain for a 16 pin TTL PROM. Note that two basic trace patterns are stepped and repeated to form the entire daisy chain pattern.

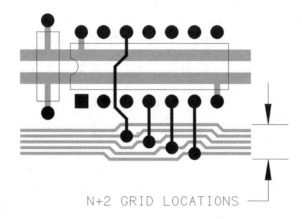

Figure 1-21   Channel Routing Example

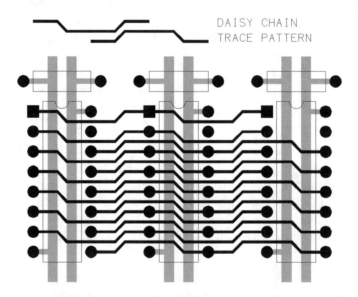

Figure 1-22   Daisy Chain Routing Example

During the initial routing, signals are predominantly routed along the preferred axis on each layer. This requires the use of a large number of vias. After all the signal connections have been routed, 10% to 25% of the vias can usually be eliminated by dropping the restriction on wrong-way routing.

Final Steps in the Design Process and Postprocessing

After cleanup of the routing, final steps in the design process include adding additional power and ground plane copper patterns and editing and positioning reference designators used to identify components. At this point the PCB design is substantially complete. The next step is to run check plots and look for design rule violations. Gross violations include shorts caused by signal traces that cross and spacing violations. More subtle violations might involve drill holes that are too close together and vias that are too close to SMD pads. Once any design rule violations have been corrected, postprocessing steps for the output of CAM files (Gerber and Excellon data) and preparation of manufacturing drawings complete the design task.

Conclusion

In the following chapters, schematic drafting and PCB design techniques will be presented in a series of hands-on tutorial exercises. Some suggested books and reference materials on PCB manufacturing and design are listed below for readers interested in additional sources of information:

Clark, R. H. *Printed Circuit Engineering*, New York: Van Nostrand Reinhold, 1989.

Coombs, C. *Printed Circuits Handbook*, 4th ed. New York: McGraw-Hill, 1995.

Gilleo, K. *Handbook of Flexible Circuits*, New York: Van Nostrand Reinhold, 1992.

Ginsberg, G. L. *Printed Circuit Design*, New York: McGraw-Hill, 1991.

Solberg, V. *Design Guidelines for Surface Mount and Fine-Pitch Technology*, New York: McGraw-Hill, 1996.

2

Schematic Drafting

Schematic diagrams are used to represent graphically the components and interconnections of electrical circuits. In the past, schematics were drafted by means of manual drawing techniques. Up until the late 1970s, the only schematic drafting aids were plastic drawing templates. Other than the use of templates and new symbols for solid state devices, little had changed for almost 50 years. Engineers usually drew up a rough schematic by hand. The circuit was then prototyped on a wire-wrap board. Once the circuit was debugged, the drafting department redrew the schematic and started the PCB layout. Today most engineers do their own schematic drafting using CAD tools. This chapter will show you how to draft schematics using AutoCAD.

The assumption is made that the reader has some knowledge of electronic schematics and the use of AutoCAD. This chapter starts with a review of schematic drafting standards and concludes with a tutorial exercise that shows how to use AutoCAD for schematic drafting.

Introduction to Electronic Schematics

Electronic schematics consist of symbols that represent the individual electronic parts used in the circuit. These symbols are interconnected with lines that represent the actual electrical connections. Figure 2-1 shows symbols for the most common of all electronic parts, the resistor. On a typical schematic, each symbol represents an individual part. The symbols are annotated with text. The basic schematic symbols are highly standardized, since the most common parts such as resistors and capacitors have been in use for almost a century.

Reference Designators

Each symbol is annotated with text that includes a reference designator, for example R1 or R2, and a description of the part. In the case of R1 on Figure 2-1, the description consists of the value (10K or 10,000 ohms). Other descriptive text might include a wattage rating (such as .25 watts), a tolerance (such as 5% or 1%), a voltage rating, or a manufacturer's part number.

It is very important to clearly understand the importance of the reference designator and the rules for assigning reference designators. An alphanumeric reference designator is used to uniquely identify each part. A given circuit might have ten 2.2K resistors used in different locations. Each of these resistors is given a unique reference designator, for example, R1, R5, and R7. In addition to the schematic, the reference designators also appear on the PCB legend silkscreen, assembly drawing, and bill of materials. Manufacturing uses the reference designators to determine where to stuff parts on the board. Field service uses them to identify and replace failed parts.

Standards have evolved for assigning reference designators. A reference designator consists of an alphabetic prefix and a numeric suffix. Each class of electronic parts has a one or two letter prefix. Most companies use the ANSI (American National Standards Institute) reference designator prefixes with minor modifications as given in Table 2-1. The numeric suffix is numbered starting from one for each class of part, for example, C1, C2, C3, R1, R2, U1, and U2. Preferred practice is to number each class starting at the upper left-hand corner of the schematic and then going from left to right in rows from top to bottom.

Some parts, such as logic ICs, consist of multiple subparts or gates. In this case, common practice is to add an additional alphabetic suffix to the reference designator, starting with the letter A. For example, the four individual gates of a CMOS 4001 quad NOR gate might be designated U5A, U5B, U5C, and U5D.

Table 2-1   Reference Designator Prefixes

A	assembly, subassembly, device, or function block that is separable and/or repairable
AT	attenuator, isolator (RF devices)
B	fan, motor
BT	battery, photocell
CB	circuit breaker
CP	coupler, junction (RF devices)
D	diode, any two terminal semiconductor device including LEDs
DC	directional coupler (RF device)
DL	delay line
DS	alarm, buzzer, visual, or audible signaling device
E	antenna, any miscellaneous electrical device
F	fuse
FL	filter
G	generator (rotating machine)

Table 2-1   Reference Designator Prefixes (Cont'd)

H   hardware
HY circulator (RF device), hybrid circuit
J   receptacle (stationary connector)
JP jumper plug (common usage on computer boards)
K   contactor, relay; **CR** is often used in industrial electronics
L   inductor, coil (single winding — may have multiple taps)
LS loudspeaker, horn, any audio/ultrasonic output transducer
M   meter, clock, strain gauge, any miscellaneous instrument
MG motor generator
MK microphone, any audio/ultrasonic input transducer
MP mechanical device without any electrical connections
P   plug (removable connector); **PL** is used in industrial electronics
PS power supply
Q   transistor, MOSFET, SCR, any three-terminal semiconductor
R   resistor, any fixed or variable; **RN** is widely used for resistor network
RT thermistor
RV varistor
S   switch, thermostat, thermal cutout
T   transformer, including autotransformer with single winding
TB terminal board (obsolete)
TC thermocouple
TP test point
U   integrated circuit (use of IC is obsolete), nonrepairable assembly
V   electron tube, vacuum/ion device including high power RF
VR obsolete usage for zener diode or voltage regulator
W   waveguide, transmission line (RF device)
X   socket for lamp or fuse
Y   crystal, ceramic resonator, tuning fork device
Z   tuned cavity or circuit, other miscellaneous RF networks

Table 2-1 is by no means all-inclusive. Some companies and industries use varying practices, and evolution is ongoing. For example, the prefixes IC and VR are obsolete, with U now being used for integrated circuits including voltage regulators. In some areas of industrial controls, CR is used to refer to relays and contactors and PL is used for plugs.

On a final note, remember that the reference designator gives information only about the class of part (resistor, diode, integrated circuit) and the location of the part on the schematic. The reference designator does not give any information about the electrical parameters of the part.

Part Descriptions

The part description must give concise information about all relevant electrical properties. An appropriate part description depends on the type of part. At first glance, it might appear that many passive components such as resistors and capacitors have been highly standardized and only the part value and tolerance would be required to specify the part. For example, one might assume that all 1000 ohm .25 watt 5% tolerance resistors are interchangeable, and therefore the part value and tolerance should be a sufficient description. In fact, most schematics are still drawn with such assumptions.

An important factor to consider is the bill of materials. When CAD is used for schematic drafting, the bill of materials can be extracted from the CAD data. In AutoCAD, reference designators and part values can be defined as attributes. These attributes can be extracted from AutoCAD and imported into database and spreadsheet programs. The bill of materials can then be completed with only a few minor edits. With this procedure in mind, it is good practice to enter as much information as possible into the part description while drafting the schematic.

SMT is another factor driving the need for more detailed parts descriptions. Today, a 1000 ohm .25 watt 5% resistor could be axial lead through hole, cylindrical metal electrode face (MELF) or Electronics Industry Association (EIA) 1210 size rectangular chip. Because of considerations of voltage standoff requirements or pulse power handling capability, a design could have a mix of both through hole and SMT devices with the same electrical parameters. To avoid errors on the bill of materials, the part description must be accurate and complete. Suggested guidelines as to what information should accompany individual classes of parts are given in the following sections.

First, let's review the units and associated symbols used to describe the values of electrical circuits and parts commonly found on schematics. There is an immediate problem that needs to be addressed. ANSI/IEEE standards call for a mix of upper case and lower case letters and some Greek letters, such as Ω for ohms, which is the unit for resistance. This is in direct conflict with the drafting convention that only upper case letters appear in drawings and with the limitations of ASCII keyboards and output devices. AutoCAD supports custom fonts that could theoretically accommodate special characters. However, problems can occur when extracting bill of materials information. The use of mixed capitalization or special non-ASCII characters is not recommended.

Table 2-2 gives multiplier prefixes for use with engineering units, and Table 2-3 gives the most common electrical units and associated symbols used by convention.

Table 2-2   Multiplier Prefixes

UNIT	ANSI SYMBOL	MULTIPLIER
femto	f	10^{-15}
pico	p	10^{-12}
nano	n	10^{-9}
micro	μ (use u)	10^{-6}
milli	m	10^{-3}
kilo	k	10^{3}
mega	M	10^{6}
giga	G	10^{9}

Micro and milli prefixes appear to be a problem if only upper case letters are used. The situation is not as bad as it appears, because there are no common devices where both these prefixes are likely to occur. Resistors are usually in the range of .01 ohm to 22 megohm. By convention, when M is used with resistance values, it always stands for megohm (for example, 10M is 10 megohm).

Inductors are usually in the .1 microhenry to 10 henry range, with millihenry values quite common. By convention, MH stands for millihenry.

Table 2-3   Engineering Units

UNIT	CONVENTIONAL SYMBOL
Capacitance	
picofarad	PF
nanofarad	NF
microfarad	UF or no symbol (MFD is archaic)
Inductance	
microhenry	UH
millihenry	MH
henry	H
Resistance	
milliohm	write out in decimal, for example .001
ohm	no unit symbol (R used in Europe)
kilohm	K
megohm	M
Electrical Units	
microampere	UA
milliampere	MA

Table 2-3   Engineering Units (Cont'd)

UNIT	CONVENTIONAL SYMBOL
Electrical Units (Cont'd)	
ampere	A
microvolt	UV
millivolt	MV
volt	V
kilovolt	KV
milliwatt	MW
watt	W
kilowatt	KW
Mechanical Units	
microsecond	US or USEC
millisecond	MS or MSEC
second	SEC
minute	MIN
hour	HR
mil (.001 inch)	MIL
inch	IN
foot	FT
centimeter (.01 meter)	CM
meter	M
ounce	OZ
pound	LB
gram	GM
kilogram	KG

While on the subject of units, let's briefly discuss numbering. Preferred schematic drafting practice is to use decimal values rather than fractions. Use .25 watts rather than 1/4 watt. Unlike practice on some mechanical drawings, leading zeros are not used in front of decimal points. Again, problems may occur when extracting the bill of materials if these considerations are not observed.

Dropping the units symbol is accepted practice with resistors. The appearance of ohms or the proper Greek symbol (Ω) is now rare. In Europe, the letter R is sometimes used both as a unit symbol and decimal point place holder. A 4R7 resistor is 4.7 ohms. Good practice is to add a text note to the schematic indicating that all resistance values are in ohms unless otherwise specified.

Common film and electrolytic capacitors are in the microfarad range. The use of the symbol UF is common. The usage of MFD has become archaic. The trend is to entirely drop the units symbol for microfarad range parts. Again, good practice would dictate a text note to this effect.

Symbols for Electronic Parts

This section provides an overview of some of the most widely used types of schematic symbols. The symbols shown in this section are in the AutoCAD schematic parts library file included on the disk supplied with the book. The name of the corresponding AutoCAD block is listed below each symbol. Block names are derived from the reference designator prefix. Most symbols have reference designator and part value attributes as part of the block definition. More detailed information on the AutoCAD schematic parts library is given in the tutorial exercise at the end of this chapter.

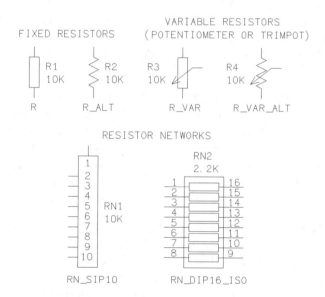

Figure 2-1   Resistor Symbols

Figure 2-1 shows symbols for the ubiquitous resistor, the most common of all electronic parts. Two styles are used for fixed resistors. R1 is the more modern style used in Europe and industrial controls in North America. R2 is the traditional style. The modern R1 style more closely represents film resistors, whereas the R2 style was derived from the wirewound construction of resistors dating back to the turn of the century. The author strongly suggests using the R1 style for all new projects.

The complete description of a discrete resistor such as R1 or R2 should include the part value in ohms, wattage, tolerance, temperature coefficient for precision resistors, material and package size. Materials include wirewound (usually high wattage power resistors), carbon composition, carbon film, and metal film. Carbon composition resistors have almost been entirely supplanted by low-cost carbon film types that can easily be manufactured in tighter 5% tolerance. In fact, they are so widely used that one can safely assume, if no other information is provided, that a fractional watt 5% resistor is carbon film. However, relying on such assumptions is not good drafting practice.

Axial lead resistor sizes are well standardized for fractional watt parts, and it is usually not necessary to specify additional package size information when the wattage rating is given. Schematics often have notes such as ".25W RN55." The RN55 is an old MIL-SPEC package size designation commonly used for 1% metal film resistors. Years ago, .25W 1% metal film resistors were the size of .5W carbon resistors (MIL-SPEC RN60 package size) and RN55 parts were rated only .125W. Better processing techniques have raised the wattage rating of RN55 size parts. The ".25W RN55" statement precludes the use of older style parts that may be too large.

Resistors with wattage ratings greater than 1W do not have well-standardized package sizes. Good practice dictates that you include a manufacturer's part number or series or type designation in the description or in a separate text note. Surface mount chip resistors have standardized package sizes, but a given wattage rating may be available in several sizes. For example, .06W resistors come in both 0603 and the new microscopic 0402 chip sizes. Again, good practice dictates that you include the size designation along with the wattage rating.

RN1 and RN2 are resistor networks. Most resistor networks with less than 14 pins are understood to be single inline package (SIP) devices and those with 14 or 16 pins to be dual inline package (DIP) devices. Construction and voltage ratings vary, so adding the manufacturer's part number to the description is usually a good idea. Variable resistors, such as R3, can be either small trimpots used to calibrate analog functions or panel mounted potentiometers (pots) for user adjustments. There are many different styles, materials, shaft configurations, and pin arrangements. Therefore, a specific part number should be included in the description or in a separate text note.

Much of the information about the resistors on a given schematic is redundant and can be summarized in a few text notes. The use of text notes eliminates unnecessary clutter and makes the schematic more readable.

For example, the notes might state:

1. All resistors are .25W 5% carbon film unless otherwise specified.

2. All 1% resistors are .25W RN55 size metal film with 50 ppm temperature coefficient unless otherwise specified.

3. All 5W resistors are Clarostat series VC5E or equivalent wirewound.

4. All variable resistors are Bourns 3386P series single turn cermet trimpots.

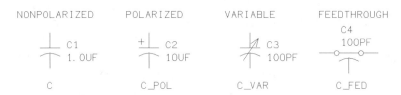

Figure 2-2   Capacitor Symbols

Figure 2-2 shows capacitors. The unit for capacitance is the farad (F), but most capacitors are in the microfarad or picofarad range, so the units UF and PF are used. Standard capacitor symbols are shown above. By convention, the capacitor symbol is always oriented toward ground or the lowest DC voltage. For circuits where the DC voltage is not fixed or known, nonpolarized capacitors are drawn with the convex side facing right or down. Additional information required to describe a capacitor includes the voltage rating, tolerance, and construction. Fixed value capacitors can be nonpolarized and polarized. Capacitors are classified according to the electrode and dielectric materials used in their construction. Other than surface mount devices, where a standard size code can easily be added to the part description, there are no real standards for capacitor sizes, and the manufacturer's part number should be included in the description.

Nonpolarized types include ceramic, silver mica, and various metal foil-film and metallized films such as polystyrene, polyester, polypropylene, and polycarbonate dielectrics. Older types using oil or wax impregnated paper dielectrics are obsolete. Polarized capacitors include tantalum and aluminum electrolytic types.

Ceramic capacitors have two or three character alphanumeric designations for the dielectric properties that determine initial tolerance and temperature characteristics. Ceramic capacitors used to bypass power at integrated circuits are usually .01UF to .1UF Z5U +80 −20% types. Oscillator, RF, and timing circuits often require more precise and stable ceramic NPO or COG 5% parts with values ranging up to about 1000 PF. Coupling and filtering applications commonly use ceramic Y5P and X7R 10% types ranging up to about .47 UF. It is not uncommon to find circuits where .1UF Z5U types are used for bypass and identical value .1UF X7R types for timing and filtering. The author can recall one incident in which an improper schematic description resulted in the inadvertent substitution of a Z5U ceramic capacitor into a critical circuit that subsequently malfunctioned.

Film capacitors with metal foil or metallized film are used for specialized applications that require tight tolerance, high voltage, or pulse power handling capacity or very low leakage. A detailed discussion of the design choices and tradeoffs for the various film capacitors is beyond the scope of this book. However, any incorrect substitutions in high voltage or pulse power applications can have disastrous and life-threatening consequences. In addition, parts that have regulatory agency (UL, CSA, VDE) approvals are required for many antenna coupling and power supply across-the-line applications. The author suggests that a specific manufacturer's part number be given for such critical parts.

Similar considerations apply to polarized capacitors, especially the aluminum electrolytics. High-frequency switching power supplies using aluminum electrolytic capacitors require that the parts be characterized for load life at high temperature, internal resistance (ESR), and ripple current handling capability. Inclusion of a specific manufacturer's part number is highly recommended. A final note of warning on capacitors has to do with polarity. Reverse polarity on a polarized capacitor can cause fire or explosion. Errors can easily occur when general rules of schematic flow (discussed later in this chapter) are not followed and polarized capacitors are drawn with varying orientations on the same sheet.

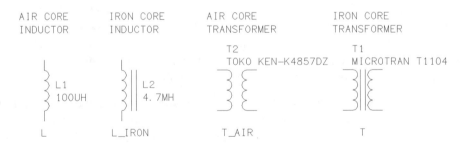

Figure 2-3   Inductor and Transformer Symbols

Inductive devices are found in RF circuits and power supplies. Inductive device symbols included in the schematic library are shown in Figure 2-3. The unit for inductance is the henry (H), but as with capacitors, practical inductors have much smaller values. Inductors for RF circuits are usually air core or ferrite core (drawn same as iron core) in the microhenry (UH) range; those for power supplies can range up to hundreds of millihenry (MH) and are usually ferrite or iron core. Two basic transformers are shown in Figure 2-3. Most power transformers have more than two windings or multiple taps on windings, requiring the user to create a custom schematic symbol for the part.

Almost all applications of inductors and transformers involve consideration of a complex set of electrical parameters (Q factor, leakage inductance, winding resistance and capacitance, and core magnetic properties). A basic description of the device in terms of inductance for inductors or turns ratio, impedance ratio, or voltage levels for transformers is helpful for testing and troubleshooting purposes. A manufacturer's part number is required to specify the device, since there are no standards or generic parts.

Drawing a transformer on the schematic also requires attention to pin numbering. Pin numbers on the schematic must match those that will be used on the PCB. Most transformers have bobbins with defined pin numbers. This information can be found on the manufacturer's data sheet.

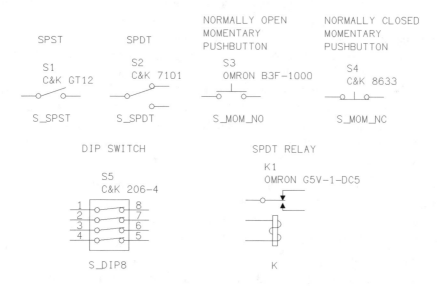

Figure 2-4   Switch and Relay Symbols

Common switches and a relay are shown in Figure 2-4. For anything other than these generic devices, the user will have to create a custom schematic symbol. As with transformers, the user must pay attention to relay pin numbers. The manufacturer's part number should be included in the description of any part for which no industry standards exist. Good practice also dictates adding text to label switch functions and positions.

Good practice is to group multi-pole switch sections together, as is done with the symbol for the 4PST DIP switch. This makes the schematic more intuitive than individual switch sections scattered throughout a sheet. It also facilitates board setup and troubleshooting

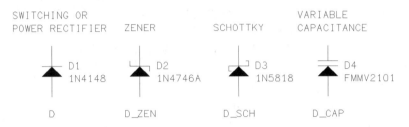

Figure 2-5   Diode Symbols

Common semiconductor diodes are shown in Figure 2-5. Optoelectronic devices (LEDs and photodiodes) are covered further on in this section. An industry standard numbering and part registration system was started in the 1950s using 1N prefixes for two-terminal diode devices and 2N prefixes for three-terminal transistor devices. In theory, all devices with the same number, for example 1N4148 diodes or 2N4401 transistors, should be fully interchangeable. In general this holds true for low voltage, low frequency, or low power parts manufactured using mature technology. For high voltage, high power, or high speed devices, there are usually significant differences in electrical parameters between vendors' parts. Good practice is to specify at least one qualified vendor.

In recent years, registered numbers have given way to proprietary vendor part numbers, for example the FMMV2101 varactor (variable capacitance diode) shown above. Purchasing agents are bedeviled when looking at bills of materials calling out such devices. The vendor name should always be included.

Figure 2-6 shows the most frequently used transistors and other three-lead semiconductor devices. Note that all of the devices in Figures 2-5 and 2-6 appear without any outer circle. Usage of an outer circle around semiconductor devices is considered archaic. Registered transistors and SCRs start with 2N for U.S. and 2S for Japanese devices; some older MOSFET devices start with 3N. Any part number starting with a letter is usually a part that originated with a particular vendor. The description guidelines suggested for diodes in the preceding section also apply to transistors and other three-lead semiconductors.

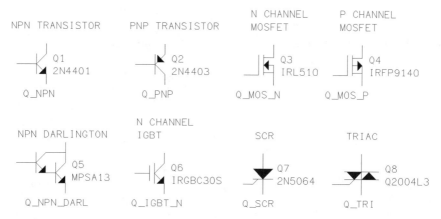

Figure 2-6   Transistor Symbols

A recent development is the introduction of so-called smart power devices. This category includes transistors, MOSFETs, and IGBTs with on-chip features such as current limiting, short circuit protection, gate or output voltage clamping, and over temperature protection. In a true sense these devices are really three-lead integrated circuits. Accepted practice has been to use the basic symbol that most closely represents that output device and simply ignore the presence of the other circuit elements. There are pro and con arguments for this approach, but the author suggests that if it is done, an explanatory text note should be included. This note should include the maximum current, clamping voltage, or other applicable parameters.

Devices in Figure 2-6 are shown in their preferred orientation with current flowing from top to bottom. The schematic should be drawn with the devices in the preferred orientation. The resulting schematic will be easier to understand.

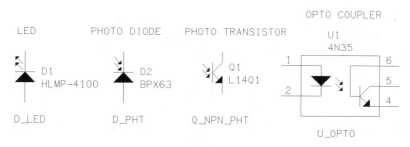

Figure 2-7   Optoelectronic Symbols

Considerations discussed for diodes and transistors apply to the optoelectronic devices shown in Figure 2-7. LEDs, photo diodes, and photo transistors have an optical function, such as a power on indicator or an IR (infrared) communications link. Good practice is to include a text label explaining the intended function.

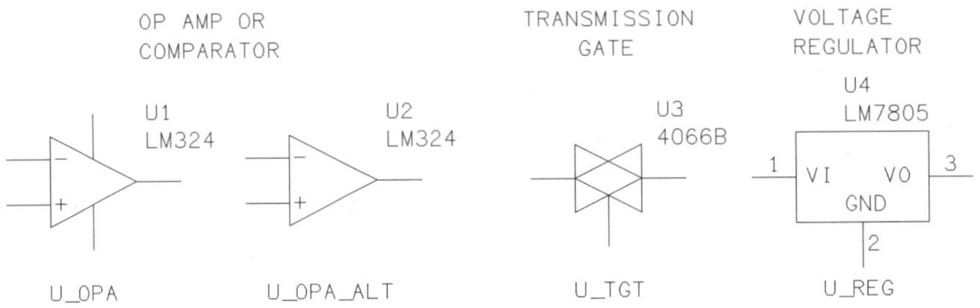

Figure 2-8   Analog Integrated Circuit Symbols

The term *analog* or *linear* refers to circuitry with signals that can vary over a range of voltages. Analog integrated circuits, such as the examples shown in Figure 2-8, require certain unique considerations when drawn on a schematic. A triangular symbol has been in use for many years to indicate operational amplifiers (op amps) and comparators. All op amps and comparators use the same symbol, but the pinouts vary. Many op amp and comparator integrated circuits contain multiple devices. The most common convention is numbering the individual devices with an alphabetic reference designator suffix starting with the letter A. For example, if a LM324 quad op amp is assigned reference designator U1, the four individual devices would be labeled U1A, U1B, U1C, and U1D. Power and ground pins should appear only on the first device, U1A.

Proper schematic "flow" dictates that certain rules be followed when drawing op amps and comparators:

- Draw op amps and comparators with the triangle symbol pointing from left to right as shown in Figure 2-8. This assures compatibility with the requirement that signals should flow from left to right.

- Draw the "–" inverting input on the top. Most electronics engineering textbooks and references show classic op amp feedback networks and comparator circuits with the inverting input terminal on top. Failure to follow this rule can lead to confusion and difficulty understanding circuit operation.

Transmission gates, once a novel part, are now widely used. Various symbols have been used for transmission gates, but the symbol shown for U3 in Figure 2-8 has now become the industry standard. This symbol, which is based on two back-to-back buffers, is highly intuitive, since an analog transmission gates functions similar to a bidirectional buffer. It also resembles a piping symbol for a valve.

No standard symbols exist for more complex analog integrated circuits. A simple rectangular block with labeled and numbered pins is used. Good practice is to include every pin on the device, even if it is not used or not internally connected. Pins should be arranged with inputs on the left, outputs on the right, power on top, and ground at the bottom. Multiple signals such as data or address should be arranged in order from top to bottom. An older practice is to arrange all pins in the same physical order as on the actual IC. This archaic practice usually results in a extremely messy arrangement of signal interconnections.

Most analog ICs have part numbers that provide an adequate description. Many part numbers have alphabetic prefixes that identify the original vendor, for example CA for RCA (now Harris), LM for National, MAX for Maxim, and TL or Texas Instruments. Often second source vendors will use the same prefix. The LM series is widely sourced. Including a vendor name with the part description would only be a requirement for relatively new or unique parts. Part numbers usually have an alphabetic suffix that identifies the package. The suffix may also identify the temperature range or other electrical parameter such as offset voltage, speed, or power consumption. An LM324N comes in a 14 pin DIP, an LM324M comes in a SOIC surface mount package, and an LM324AN is a low-power DIP version.

Schematics are sometimes drawn as part of a reverse engineering project, and an entire book could easily be written on this subject. Determining the correct part number for a device can be difficult. Date codes can be mistaken for part numbers. The electronics industry uses four-digit date codes for most ICs. The first two digits are the year and the last two digits are the week. A part manufactured the 12th week of 1997 would be stamped 9712. Products manufactured in very high volume often have in-house part numbers, even on generic devices. Identifying these devices and finding an equivalent commercial part number can be difficult.

The term *digital logic* refers to circuitry with signals that are restricted to a limited number of logic states. A detailed description of digital logic functions and theory is beyond the scope of this book. Logic families in widespread use today include TTL and CMOS. Both use standard Boolean logic with 0 and 1 states. Zero is represented by a low voltage (near ground) and 1 by a high voltage (2.5V or higher depending on the device). Some devices have an additional high impedance or "off" state. This allows the outputs of multiple devices to be connected together, such as on a computer data bus, with only one device enabled at a time and the others in the off state.

BUFFER	INVERTER	OR	NOR
U1	U2	U3	U4
74ALS34	74LS04	74LS:	74LS02
U_BUF	U_INV	U_OR	U_NOR

AND	NAND	EXCLUSIVE OR	EXCLUSIVE NOR
U1	U2	U3	U4
74LS08	74LS00	74LS&	74LS266
U_AND	U_NAND	U_XOR	U_XNOR

Figure 2-9   Digital Logic Gate Symbols

The four basic digital logic functions include the buffer, OR, AND and XOR (exclusive OR). Symbols for these logic functions are shown in Figure 2-9. The four basic functions can also have inverted outputs. In this case they are referred to as the inverter (NOT), NOR, NAND, and XNOR (exclusive NOR). The symbol is drawn with a small circle on the output. The small circle indicates an inverted signal, either input or output. Logic functions, when implemented in electronic circuitry, are referred to as *gates*. Buffer and inverter gates can only have a single input and output. XOR and XNOR gates, by nature of their logic function, can only have two inputs. All other gates can have two or more inputs.

Digital logic ICs may contain from one to six gates. Treat digital ICs with multiple gates using the same principles as discussed in the previous section on analog ICs with multiple devices. A part number description is generally sufficient for digital logic, since most parts are sourced by multiple vendors. TTL is the most widely used logic family. Some TTL part numbers are shown in Figure 2-9, such as the 74LS02 NOR gate. The 74 prefix identifies the part as commercial temperature range (0 to 70 degrees C); a 54 prefix is used for military temperature range parts (–55 to 125 degrees C). The LS designates the part as belonging to the low-power Schottky logic family. The original TTL logic had no special designator. The part number for the quad NOR gate would have been 7402.

Many different logic families have been introduced, each with its own two or three letter designator. In fact many of these new families are not even based on transistor technology. CMOS variants, such as a 74HC02, use MOSFET technology with somewhat different logic levels but retain the popular device functions and pinouts originated with TTL. This is an advantage for the user who has created a library of widely used parts. If a new design requires a 3.3V logic device such as a Phillips 74LVT373, one can use an existing part such as the 74LS373 and simply edit the name. This is much more convenient than creating a new part.

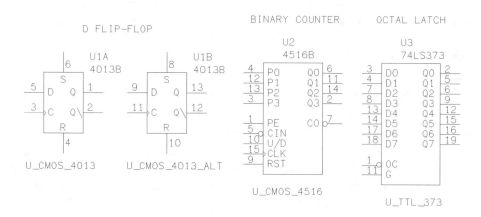

Figure 2-10   Advanced Digital Logic Symbols

Figure 2-10 shows some advanced digital ICs. As with advanced analog ICs, these devices are drawn as rectangular blocks with named and numbered signal pins. Note that U2 and U3 both have inverted signal inputs and outputs denoted by a small circle. U1A also has noninverted and inverted outputs. Here the inverted output on pin 2 is denoted by a backslash after the signal name. An additional convention used to represent inverted (active low) signals is an overbar above the signal name. This is difficult to do in AutoCAD, and the backslash after the signal name is the preferred convention. Both the small circle and backslash (or overbar) conventions are used on a rather arbitrary basis in manufacturers' data sheets. Most 4000 series CMOS part data sheets use an overbar. The small circle appears on most TTL data sheets. Another signal convention is the use of a small triangle to represent edge-triggered clock inputs, as shown on U1A pin 3 and U2 pin 15.

Special considerations apply to programmable memory and microcontroller devices. These devices, and others such as the broad class of programmable logic devices, contain firmware. Firmware is the same as software, except it is more or less permanently programmed into the device. With the advent of electrically erasable memory devices, the distinction between software and firmware has become more blurred, but convention is still to refer to any code loaded into non-volatile memory as firmware.

Whenever devices requiring or utilizing firmware appear on a schematic, it is good practice to add a note, either to the device description or as a separate text note, that gives the firmware name and the earliest compatible version. Why note the earliest compatible version? Today schematics are usually generated at the start of a design project — not as part of the documentation created after the fact. Often earlier revisions of a product will exist. Firmware used with earlier board revisions may not be compatible. Firmware seems to go through rapid changes and multiple firmware versions usually are released before the board hardware is updated. Noting the earliest compatible version can help prevent mistakes during manufacturing, final testing, and field servicing.

Memory devices usually have a read or write access time, which is a very critical parameter in high-speed computer systems. Often the part number has a dash suffix, such as -150, where the number identifies the access time in nanoseconds. If this parameter is critical and the device is available in multiple speed grades, this information must be included on the schematic. A similar consideration applies to programmable devices, where the programming voltage often varies between different vendors. If relevant, programming voltage information should also be included.

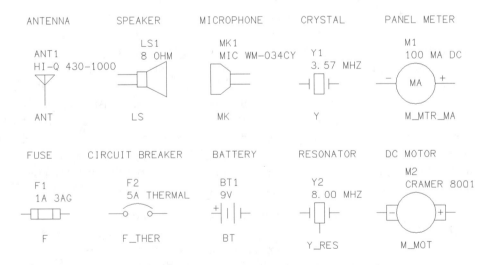

Figure 2-11   Miscellaneous Symbols

Figures 2-11 and 2-12 complete the overview of circuit symbols. Batteries are represented by the symbol shown for BT1. As drawn, BT1 shows a two-cell battery. To be technically correct, a 9V alkaline or carbon-zinc battery should be drawn showing six 1.5V cells. In today's environment of complex computer systems, such details are usually glossed over. As long as the battery is correctly described, use of the symbol shown for BT1 should not cause any confusion.

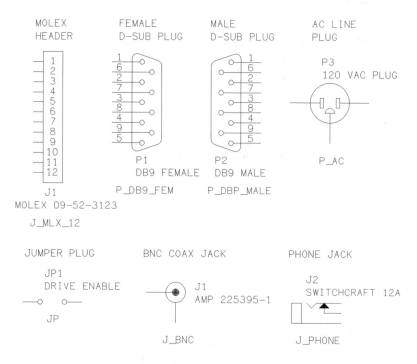

Figure 2-12   Connector Symbols

Some of the commonly used connector symbols are shown in Figure 2-12. By convention, any fixed connector attached to a panel or motherboard is referred to as a *jack* and uses reference designator J. A removable connector, including the card edge connector on a daughterboard or PC bus expansion board is referred to as a *plug* and uses reference designator P or PL. Since a circuit board is often a removable part of a larger system, some companies consider all connectors on the board as plugs.

With the advent of user-configured computer expansion boards, the jumper or jumper plug has become ubiquitous. Jumpers are typically incorporated onto a circuit board as paired pads on .1 inch centers. For user-configurable board options, a header can be installed and a removable jumper provided to make the connection. Jumpers used for manufacturing options or calibration functions are often normally closed with a small trace between the pads. The trace can be cut with an X-Acto knife to open the jumper. If required, a wire can be soldered between the pads to re-establish the jumper connection. It is very important to clearly describe the function of jumpers and whether the function is asserted with the jumper open or closed. For complex functions set with multiple jumpers, a table listing is good practice. Normally closed jumpers should be shown with a line drawn between the circles, similar to a normally closed switch.

Good practice is to describe the physical configuration of all connectors, give a vendor name and part number if applicable, and add a text note that describes the function served or the connecting device.

Special Schematic Symbols

The special symbols shown in Figures 2-13 and 2-14 represent power, ground and signal flow. Power and ground symbols are shown in Figure 2-13. The figure also shows special symbols used to represent signal flow between sheets in multi-sheet schematics.

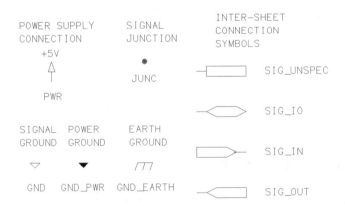

Figure 2-13   Power, Ground, and Signal Flow Symbols

Power and ground symbols are used to represent connections to power and ground. Three different styles of ground symbols are shown in Figure 2-13: signal ground, power ground, and earth ground. The signal and power ground symbols are used to represent ground planes on a circuit board. The only proper use of the earth ground is to represent a system ground that actually connects to an earth ground, such as a water pipe or ground rod. An earth ground should never appear on a PCB schematic.

The value attribute of the +5V power symbol can easily be edited to represent other voltage levels. Modern schematic drafting practice is to place an appropriate symbol wherever a power or ground connection occurs, rather than tying these circuit points together with lines. This reduces clutter and improves the readability of the schematic.

Modern practice calls for using the junction symbol to represent an electrical connection between lines that cross. Otherwise, lines that cross are not considered connected. Older drafting practices called for small breaks at crossover points where no connection existed. Do not use this archaic practice with CAD drafting.

The concepts of lines that represent signal connections and symbols that represent junctions, grounds and power connections are familiar to most persons with experience in schematic drafting. These concepts generally cause few problems in making the transition from manual drafting to CAD. The intersheet signal connection symbols shown in Figure 2-13 may be less familiar. With the advent of fast laser printers and the growing complexity of electronic products, the trend is toward multi-sheet A size (8.5 × 11 inches) schematics. Intersheet signal connection symbols are used to show the connections between sheets.

Intersheet signal symbols are not connectors. They do not represent physical parts and should never be used in place of connectors. Their only purpose is to route signals between sheets. Four common intersheet signal symbols are shown in Figure 2-13: input, output, bidirectional, and unspecified. The sense or direction of the symbol refers to the sheet on which it occurs. This is shown more clearly in Figure 2-14. Input symbols represent signals coming from another sheet. Output symbols represent signals going to another sheet. Bidirectional symbols are used for data buses where signals can flow in both directions. Unspecified symbols are used for power and reference voltage connections between sheets or other signals when the concept of a directional flow is not applicable.

Recommended practice is to place input symbols on the left and output symbols on the right side of the sheet. Placement of bidirectional and unspecified symbols should correspond to the predominant "flow" direction. For example, AC power coming into a power supply board should appear on the left and DC power generated by the board should appear on the right

Figure 2-14 introduces two additional schematic drafting concepts: bus structures and labels. The use of bus structures to represent a group of related signals, such as a data or address bus, became widespread practice after microprocessor technology was introduced in the early 1970s. Representing an eight bit data bus or 16 bit address bus with a single broad line is more convenient than drawing out each signal. Besides the obvious time savings in drafting, the signal flow becomes much clearer and easier to understand. With the advent of 32 and 64 bit bus structures, drawing out each signal is no longer an option.

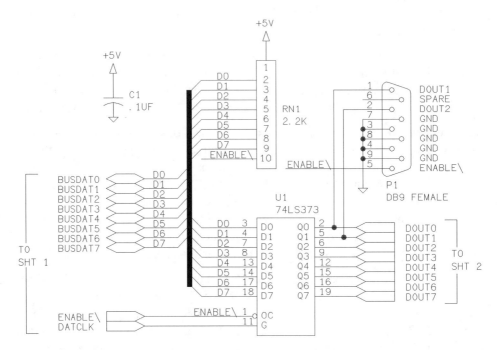

Figure 2-14   Schematic with Bus Structure and Labels

Certain conventions are followed in the drawing of bus structures. All signals enter (or exit) a bus via a short 45 degree diagonal line. This convention allows other signal lines to cross a bus at right angles without any confusion about whether or not a connection is intended. A uniform name should be used for all signals on a bus, for example D0, D1 . . . D32 or ADDR16, ADDR17 . . . ADDR24. The name should consist of an alphabetic prefix and a numerical suffix. Individual signal labels such as D2 or ADDR17 must be placed on all signal lines connecting to the bus.

Signal labels are used to identify and connect line segments representing the same signal. Figure 2-14 shows the ENABLE\ signal routed to pin 10 of RN1 and pin 5 of P1. This results in a neater appearance than if additional lines were routed to these pins. By convention, signal labels should be placed on top of horizontal lines or immediately to the right of vertical lines.

Preferred Schematic Drafting Practices

So far, the discussion of preferred practices has largely focused on the use of schematic symbols and the content of descriptive information. The subject of schematic flow requires further discussion. Proper flow is critical to assuring readability of the finished schematic. Figure 2-15 shows a schematic with poor flow. Figure 2-16 shows the same circuit redrawn with improved flow.

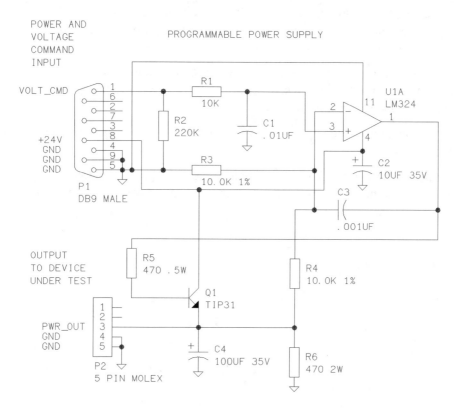

Figure 2-15   Schematic with Poor Flow

Schematic Flow

Electronic systems can be broken down into blocks of circuit elements. This concept is shown in Figure 2-17. Each circuit element contains interconnected parts that carry out a particular signal processing function. Information and electrical power flow from circuit element to circuit element. *Schematic* flow refers to a logical layout of these circuit elements. Drafting recommendations for schematic flow are given in the following list:

- Signals should flow from left to right and in rows from top to bottom, as shown in Figure 2-17. Place connectors according to the predominant signals: input connectors on the left and output connectors on the right.

- Orient devices in accordance with the signal flow principle. Normal orientation is with inputs on the left and outputs on the right, positive power on top and negative power or ground at the bottom.

- Arrange circuitry so that voltages increase from bottom to top for each row. Locate ground symbols facing down at the bottom of rows. Locate power symbols facing up at the top of rows.

- Use bus structures to relieve signal congestion for all data and address signals. Use labels to implicitly join separated segments together rather than routing the signal lines over great distances.

- Orient op amps and comparators so that their "–" inverting inputs appear at the top.

- Connect device power and ground pins to individual power and ground symbols. Do not tie many leads together at a single power or ground symbol.

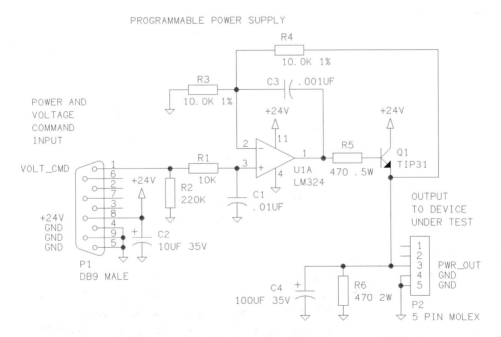

Figure 2-16   Schematic Redrawn with Improved Flow

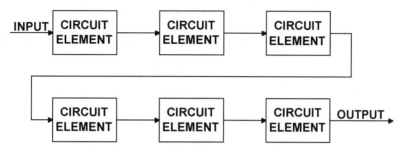

Figure 2-17   Schematic Flow in Rows

Signal Naming Conventions

Certain conventions should be observed for naming signals and power. As previously discussed, a backslash (\) following the signal name represents inverted signals or signals that are active low (logic function enabled or asserted at a zero logic level). Bus signals should be numbered in sequence, such as D0, D1, . . . D7. Data and address signals are always numbered starting from zero. For example, an eight bit data bus starts at D0 and ends at D7, not D1 and D8. Signal names containing D, DAT, or DATA are common for data lines and A or ADDR for address lines. Edge-triggered signals used to clock counters or flip-flops should contain CLK in the name, such as BUSCLK1. In general, signal names should be descriptive. The underline character (_) can be used to join segments of a signal name for clarity. For example, the signal name A2D_D0 (analog to digital converter data line 0) reads better than A2DD0. Avoid picking arbitrary signal names. If in doubt, construct an abbreviation from the plain language description of the signal.

Designs frequently utilize multiple power supplies and reference voltages. Choose appropriate names for power symbols. +5V is more descriptive than VCC or VDD. Unless you are designing battery powered vacuum tube equipment, do not use B+ as a power name. B+ is an archaic term for the "B" or plate supply battery. For battery powered portable equipment, varying battery voltages can be represented by adding BAT to the power name, for example +9VBAT. Reference voltages appear in analog circuits, especially digital to analog and analog to digital converters. Precision reference circuits used to generate a reference voltage are limited to a low current. The naming convention should preclude mistaking a reference for a power supply. A name such as +5.00VREF identifies a precise reference voltage that can be expected to vary less than .01V from the nominal +5.00V value.

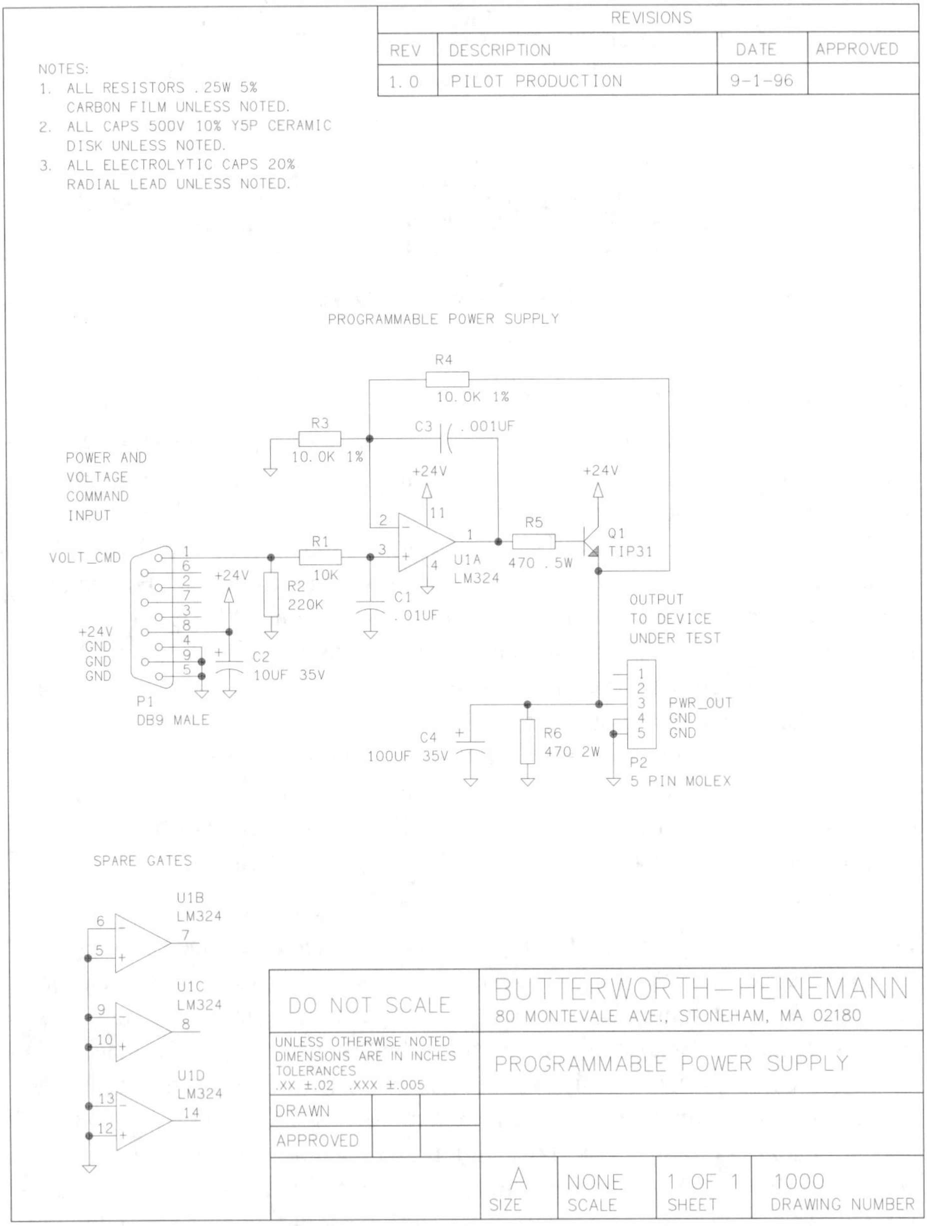

Figure 2-18   Finished Single Sheet Schematic

Title Block, Revision Block, and Notes

All schematic drawings should include a title block and revision block. Most schematics also require text notes to provide additional information and clarify certain details. Most organizations use predefined drawing formats that include the title block, revision block, and an area for text notes.

Figure 2-18 shows the complete version of the earlier schematic redrawn for improved flow. The title block in appears at the lower right corner and contains the following elements:

- **Company name and address**. Self explanatory.

- **Title**. The plain language description of the device or circuit.

- **Size**. Letter designators A-E are used for standard drawing sizes. Most schematics are now laser printed on A size paper (8.5 × 11 inches).

- **Scale**. The same title block is used for mechanical drawings, and a scale box appears in it. Since the concept of scale is not applicable to a schematic, the entry NONE is made in this box.

- **Sheet (number and number of sheets)**. Self explanatory.

- **Drawing number**. Most companies track documentation by means of a drawing number.

- **Tolerances.** The same title block is used for mechanical drawings, and a tolerance box appears in it. The tolerance box is not applicable to the schematic.

- **Date and signature.** Date and signature boxes are provided for the original draftsperson (DRAWN) and the checker (APPROVED). Initials are generally used in place of a full signature. This information can be entered as CAD text or handwritten on a paper copy. Courts have held that properly authorized electronic signatures are legally valid. The person signing the approval box is responsible for the integrity of the design. Certain designs, such as building fire protection systems, may require the signature of a licensed professional engineer. The author strongly recommends that for liability reasons, service bureaus and independent consultants never sign an approval box.

The revision block in Figure 2-18 appears at the upper right corner and includes:

- **Revision code**. Either a letter or number can be used. Decimal numbers are common in the electronics industry because of the rapid pace of changes. Development prototypes are given revision codes less than one, such as 0.9 for the final prototype. First production is usually revision 1.0. A major change such as a new circuit board causes the revision to jump to the next integer; for example, from 1.5 to 2.0. Minor changes, where by only a few component values are modified or jumpers and cuts are made on the board, cause the revision code to increment by .1, for example, from 2.0 to 2.1.

- **Description.** A brief textual description of the revision. The author suggests that if additional details are required, they be placed onto the drawing as text notes.

- **Date and approval signature**. The same considerations apply as with the date and signature boxes on the title block.

Text notes are generally placed in the top left corner of the drawing. In the case of text notes, too much detail is better than not enough. Back in the days of manual drafting on paper, editing text notes meant using an eraser. To avoid having to repeatedly erase and rewrite everything whenever a change or addition occurred, notes started at the bottom and ran in sequence going up. With the ease of CAD editing, this practice has become archaic. Notes are now written and numbered in normal sequence from top to bottom. Some of the items that should appear in the text notes include:

- Default values for components, such as resistor wattage rating and tolerance

- Preferred or approved vendors for critical or unique parts and any other important information not contained in the part descriptions

- Revision details, including compatibility of previous revisions

- Brief calibration and test instructions or a reference to a separate document

- Description of any required firmware

If a product requires extensive calibration or is likely to require field service, good practice dictates annotating the schematic with signal waveforms and voltage levels. Howard Sams Photofacts (third-party source for consumer products schematic and repair documentation) provide a good example of the type of information that should be included.

During the last decade, the trend for schematics has been away from large C, D, and E size pen-plotted or hand-drawn sheets. These large drawing sizes are cumbersome to handle and very expensive to reproduce. Products have become more complex, to the point that even several E size sheets will not suffice for the schematic of a new 68060 VME bus computer board. Multiple sheet A size schematics are the answer. They can be quickly run off on a laser printer and inexpensively reproduced on any copying machine. The only problem is providing some means of oversight and continuation between sheets. This problem is solved by use of the inter sheet signal symbols and sheet routing notes as shown in Figure 2-14.

Hidden IC Power Pins

Digital logic schematics are frequently drawn without visible power pins on the IC symbols. In this context power is understood to mean both the positive power connection(s) and ground. Figure 2-19 shows an example of a schematic with hidden IC power pins. The bypass capacitors (one per IC) are grouped together in the lower left corner, and a text note explains that all ICs use +5V power. Figure 2-20 shows the same schematic with visible power pins and the bypass capacitors located directly at each IC.

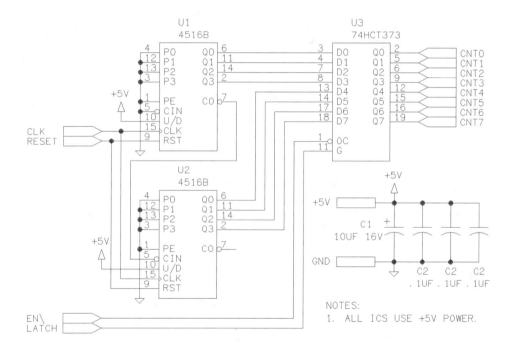

Figure 2-19   Digital Logic with Hidden Power Pins

Schematic clarity improves when clutter from power pins is eliminated. The use of hidden power pins originated back in the days before large surface mount device packages were common. Most digital ICs had power and ground on diagonal ends of the package and little guessing was involved. With the larger surface mount devices, this is not always the case. Hidden and thus unknown power pins can cause headaches when it comes to troubleshooting. A further and even more serious complication arises with designs that require multiple voltage levels. Multiple voltage designs, such as PC motherboards with 3.3V and 5V logic are now commonplace.

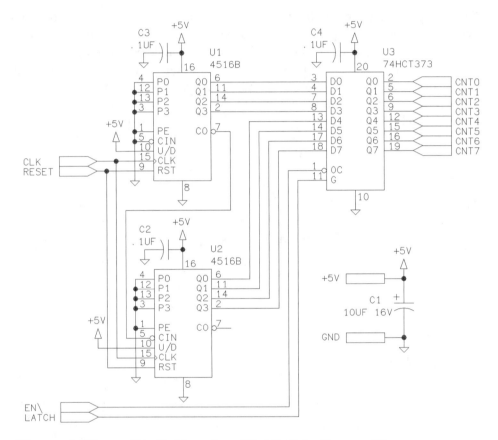

Figure 2-20   Digital Logic with Visible Power Pins

The author suggests that hidden power pins be used for all common digital logic on single power voltage designs. Complex parts with non-standard power and ground pin arrangements should show visible power pins. Visible power pins should be used for all devices on multiple power voltage designs. When hidden power pins are used, a text note should describe what power supply voltages are used and list pin numbers for any non-standard arrangements. Do not assume that the average technician or even fellow engineer will understand invisible power and ground pins without some explanation or that they can remember which pins are used on every possible device.

Schematic Organization and Planning

Two schools of though exist about how to plan and organize a schematic when using CAD tools. Younger engineers often prefer to start with an empty screen and try to organize their thoughts as they go along. They tend to use the CAD system as an electronic sketch pad. Older engineers, on the other hand, tend to view CAD as a drafting tool that is useful for preparing neat documentation at the completion of a design project.

Neither approach gives optimum results. Traditional desktop PCs and engineering workstations are not electronic sketch pads. Attempts to make PDAs (personal digital assistants) with stylus and handwriting recognition for use as electronic sketch pads have met with limited success — witness the limited success of the Apple Newton. A truly useful PDA is still years away. In the meantime, if you need a sketch pad, use an old-fashioned lab notebook.

Designs can be evolutionary or revolutionary. Products tend to evolve, and even an entirely new design may consist largely of recycled circuitry. Truly revolutionary designs starting with a clean slate are less common. If the so-called new design is merely a glorified engineering change, starting straight out in AutoCAD with the previous version of the schematic may be the best way to go. The more revolutionary the new design, the more planning and organization are required up front:

- Start with a clear design specification. The specification should include features and performance, interface requirements, physical characteristics (size, weight, appearance), operating environment (temperature, humidity, vibration), regulatory compliance (FCC, UL), and manufacturing cost target.

- List all integrated circuits and other specialized parts required for the design. Run copies of databook pages for all parts that will require creation of new schematic symbols.

- List signal names and buses. Interface signals are often established ahead of time from the design specification. The choice of processor will determine data, address, and bus control signals.

- Plan power usage and representation.

- Create symbol blocks for any required new parts.

- Sketch out a rough block diagram and use it to plan out the schematic. On multi-sheet schematics, carefully segment the design so that major circuit blocks will occupy individual pages.

- Draw the schematic and then add copious text notes. Run an initial check plot and review it for obvious errors.

- Extract the bill of materials information. Carefully examine this information, because it will often reveal subtle errors. Make corrections and run final plots.

- After the PCB design and board debugging are completed, go back and incorporate any engineering changes and other changes necessitated by PCB layout considerations.

Schematic Drafting Tutorial Exercise

This tutorial exercise shows you how to use AutoCAD to create a simple schematic and extract the bill of materials. Your task will be to create the programmable power supply schematic shown in Figure 2-18. You may want to run a copy of this figure and keep it handy for reference. To complete the tutorial, you will require access to a PC running AutoCAD Release 12 or 13 or AutoCAD LT Release 2 or higher.

The bill of materials section of the tutorial involves extracting part attributes from the AutoCAD drawing file. Extracted attribute information is then sorted and loaded into a spreadsheet program. While the exercise is based on the use of Microsoft Excel, you can use the same techniques with other spreadsheet programs such as Quattro Pro.

Files and utility programs required for the tutorial exercise are included on the floppy disk supplied with the book. The subdirectory TUTOR1 contains the files for this tutorial. FORMAT_A.DWG is an A size drawing format. SCH_LIB.DWG is the schematic parts library. BOM_EXT.TXT is the template file used to extract attributes for a bill of materials. BOM_SORT.EXE is a utility used to sort the bill of materials information extracted from AutoCAD. Create a TUTOR1 subdirectory on your hard drive. Copy the files listed above from the floppy disk onto the TUTOR1 subdirectory on your hard drive.

The floppy disk supplied with the book also contains a popular shareware text display utility, LIST.COM and a public domain font file, MONOSI.SHX. You can use the LIST.COM utility to examine template files and bill of materials files. Copy LIST.COM into your root or DOS directory, or other directory included in your PC's PATH statement. Refer to appendix D for more details, including shareware license and usage restrictions. MONOSI is a mono-spaced simplex font that gives highly legible results at the small text height settings required for schematics and PCBs. All the part symbols in the schematic library are defined with the MONOSI font. Copy MONOSI.SHX into your AutoCAD font subdirectory.

Drafting the Schematic

Start AutoCAD and open the A size drawing format, FORMAT_A.DWG. The drawing border, title block, and revision block will be displayed on the screen. All these entities are on the TITLEBLOCK layer. You will place all schematic entities on the SCHEMATIC layer. Use the LAYER command to create the SCHEMATIC layer and make this the current layer. Use white as the default color. Use the INSERT command to insert the file SCH_LIB.DWG. You need to type in the full file name. This loads all the schematic symbol blocks shown in Figures 2-1 through 2-14. The insertion location is not important, since SCH_LIB.DWG does not contain any drawing entities that will appear on the screen. The block entities in SCH_LIB.DWG are defined on the special AutoCAD layer 0. When you insert a schematic block, it will appear on the current layer.

Next, use the SAVE AS command from the FILE menu and save the drawing as TUTOR1.DWG. Note that AutoCAD automatically assigns the .DWG suffix. This leaves your original drawing format file FORMAT_A.DWG unchanged. All subsequent editing is done using TUTOR1.DWG.

The first step is to create any required new schematic symbols. For this exercise, you must create the 5 pin Molex connector P2. The schematic library loaded into the drawing contains a block for a 12 pin Molex connector named J_MLX_12. Use this existing part as a basis for your new 5 pin connector. Zoom into a small area of the drawing, leave GRID set to .1 inch and set SNAP to .025 inch. Insert J_MLX_12 on a .1 inch grid dot. When AutoCAD prompts for the REF (reference designator) and VAL (part value) attributes, just hit return. Once the block is inserted, use the EXPLODE command. After the block has been exploded, you can edit the individual entities. Note that the attribute tags, REF and VAL are now displayed instead of actual attribute values.

Edit the 12 pin connector. Erase pins 6 through 12 and the corresponding pin numbers. Then use the STRETCH command to shrink the body outline so that it is the correct size for a 5 pin connector. The pins for the 5 pin Molex must be on the left side. Note that all part pins are located on .1 inch grid locations. You can use either the MIRROR or MOVE commands to change the pin orientation. Then move the REF and VAL attributes up so that they are correctly aligned underneath the body outline. The 5 pin Molex connector should now appear the same as P2 in the schematic model (Figure 2-18). Use the BLOCK command to define a block for the 5 pin Molex. Use the name J_MLX_5. Use the left end of pin 1 as the insertion base point. Note that all parts in the schematic library use the end point of the upper left pin as the insertion base point. If a part has no pins on the left side, then the endpoint of the upper right pin is used instead. First select all the graphics entities (pins, body, and pin numbers). Then select the REF attribute. Select the VAL attribute last. The order in which you select attributes when defining a block determines the order in which AutoCAD prompts for attribute values when inserting the block. All parts in the library are defined so that REF is first, followed by VAL.

The J_MLX_5 block is now complete and you can start to insert the part symbols onto the sheet. Use the following block names:

- **Ceramic capacitors C1 and C3**: C

- **Electrolytic capacitors C2 and C4**: C_POL

- **Connectors P1 and P2**: P_DB9_MALE and J_MLX_5

- **Transistor Q1**: Q_NPN

- **Op amp U1**: U_OPA for U1A and U_OPA_ALT for U1B through U1D

Set SNAP to .10 while inserting the parts. Initially insert the parts to approximate locations on the sheet. Several of the resistors and C3 must be rotated. The attributes will then appear rotated. Use the ATTEDIT command to change the angle of these attributes back to zero (normal orientation). Later, once the parts are in final position, you can use ATTEDIT to change attribute locations so that they do not overlap parts.

After the parts have been inserted, draw lines for signal interconnections. Try to keep all lines on .10 grid locations for a neat appearance. You may need to move some parts for proper alignment. You will find that the STRETCH command is very useful for moving parts with attached signal lines. Insert junction (JUNC) and ground (GND) symbol blocks where required. Then insert the power (PWR) symbol blocks. Enter +24V for the power attribute.

As a final step, use the DTEXT command to enter notes, descriptive labels, pin numbers for U1, and signal name annotations at P1 and P2. Note that all part symbols use .065 text height. The text style for the A size drawing format, FORMAT_A.DWG, is set to MONOSI and .065 height. This gives good results when fitting text strings between signal lines or part pins on .1 inch grid locations. Set SNAP to .01 inch when placing text and zoom in close. Locate text about .02 inch above the lines or pins for best spacing.

Your first schematic drawing is now completed. Save the file and then print out the schematic. The hardcopy printout should appear similar to Figure 2-18. However, note that the scale of the drawing format in Figure 2-18 was adjusted to fit the page in the book.

Generating the Bill of Materials

AutoCAD uses a template file to determine what attribute information to extract from the drawing database and how to format this information. You should review this subject in your AutoCAD documentation. Template files are text files. You can use the LIST utility to examine the bill of materials template file, BOM_EXT.TXT. Exit to DOS and type:

CD\TUTOR1<ENTER>

LIST BOM_EXT.TXT<ENTER>

This changes to the TUTOR1 subdirectory used for this exercise and runs LIST.COM. The resulting screen display is shown in Figure 2-21. The first and last lines showing the file name and function key options are part of LIST.COM. Comprehensive on-line help is available. Press F1 and explore the features of LIST.COM.

```
LIST        1      3       09/01/1996 13:13 C:\ACAD12\TUTOR1\BOM_EXT.TXT
REF            C010000
VAL            C020000
→→→→→→→→→→→→→→→→→→→→→→→→→→→→→→→→→→→→→→→→→→→→→→→→→→→→→→→→→→→→→→→→→→→→→→→→→→→→→→→→→→→→
```

```
Command▶    *** End-of-file ***              Keys: ↑↓→← PgUp PgDn  F10=exit F1=Help
```

Figure 2-21   BOM_EXT.TXT Bill of Materials Template File

Note that BOM_EXT.TXT has two entries. The first entry causes AutoCAD to extract the REF attribute. The second entry is for the VAL attribute. The code C010000 formats the REF attribute information as ASCII text with a field width of 10 characters. Refer to your AutoCAD documentation for more details on template files. In summary, the BOM_EXT template file causes a separate line to be generated for each part. The reference designator appears in columns 1-10 and the part value in columns 11-30.

```
LIST        1       18      09/01/1996 13:16 C:\ACAD12\TUTOR1\TUTOR1.TXT
P1          DB9 MALE
U1A         LM324
R2          220K
R1          10K
R3          10.0K 1%
R4          10.0K 1%
R6          470 2W
R5          470 .5W
C1          .01UF
C3          .001UF
C2          10UF 35V
C4          100UF 35V
Q1          TIP31
P2          5 PIN MOLEX
U1B         LM324
U1D         LM324
U1C         LM324
→→→→→→→→→→→→→→→→→→→→→→→→→→→→→→→→→→→→→→→→→→→→→→→→→→→→→→→→→→→→→→→→→→→→→→→→→→→→→→→→→→→→

Command▶    *** End-of-file ***         Keys: ↑↓→← PgUp PgDn  F10=exit F1=Help
```

Figure 2-22   TUTOR1.TXT Unsorted Bill of Materials File

To extract the bill of materials, start AutoCAD and open the TUTOR1.DWG schematic drawing file. Use the ATTEXT command. Select SDF (space-delimited file) format. Then select the BOM_EXT.TXT template file. The bill of materials information will be written out to the file TUTOR1.TXT. Exit to DOS and use the LIST utility to examine TUTOR1.TXT. Your file should appear similar to that shown in Figure 2-22, except that the order of parts may differ. Note that AutoCAD outputs parts in the order that they appear in the database.

The next step is to sort the parts. The BOM_SORT.EXE utility can be used for this purpose. BOM_SORT automatically sorts parts by reference designator class and then by part value. The utility makes the following assumptions about the bill of materials file:

- **No header or extraneous information**. The file must contain only parts information. The file shown in Figure 2-22 has a suitable input format. At a minimum each line must contain a reference designator and a parts description. The line length must not exceed 79 characters. No blank lines are allowed.

- **Maximum of 399 lines**. This should suffice for most schematics drafted with AutoCAD. If you are attempting to draft more complex schematics, dedicated schematic capture software such as OrCAD should be investigated.

- **Reference designator starting in column 1**. BOM_SORT accepts reference designators with a one or two letter prefix, such as the standard prefixes listed in Table 2-1.

- **Part value starting in column 11**. BOM_SORT uses the first five characters (columns 11-15) of the part value to sort parts. The utility recognizes common electrical value multiplier prefixes (K, M, P, and U).

Use the BOM_SORT utility to sort the TUTOR1.TXT raw bill of materials file that you extracted from AutoCAD. At the DOS prompt, type:

CD\TUTOR1<ENTER>

BOM_SORT<ENTER>

BOM_SORT prompts for the name of the bill of materials input file and output file. The input file is not modified. Enter TUTOR1.TXT for the input filename and TUTOR1.BOM for the output filename. BOM_SORT exits back to DOS after completion. Use the LIST utility to examine TUTOR1.BOM. Your file should appear the same as that shown in Figure 2-23.

```
LIST        1       17      09/01/1996 13:32 C:\ACAD12\TUTOR1\TUTOR1.BOM
C3          .001UF
C1          .01UF
C2          10UF 35V
C4          100UF 35V
P2          5 PIN MOLEX
P1          DB9 MALE
Q1          TIP31
R5          470 .5W
R6          470 2W
R3          10.0K 1%
R4          10.0K 1%
R1          10K
R2          220K
U1A         LM324
U1B         LM324
U1D         LM324
U1C         LM324




Command►    *** End-of-file ***          Keys: ↑↓→← PgUp PgDn  F10=exit F1=Help
```

Figure 2-23   TUTOR1.BOM Sorted Bill of Materials File

Importing Bill of Materials Files into Microsoft Excel

Microsoft Excel is an excellent tool for managing and printing bills of materials. Other spreadsheet programs, such as Quattro Pro, can be used for the same purpose. Using a spreadsheet offers easy organization of data in columns and the capability of inserting and totaling cost information.

Use the following steps to import an AutoCAD generated bill of materials file into Excel.

- Extract the bill of materials by using the AutoCAD ATTEXT command. Select SDF format and use the BOM_EXT.TXT template file. Sort the extracted bill of materials using the BOM_SORT.EXE utility. Refer to the previous section for details. Note that BOM_EXT.TXT and BOM_SORT.TXT are in the TUTOR1 subdirectory of the floppy disk supplied with this book.

- Launch Excel and open the sorted bill of materials file. The Excel Text Import Wizard will appear because the file is not in Excel format. The Text Import Wizard consists of three steps, described in detail below.

- Text Import Wizard Step 1 — Select Data Type. This step selects the type of data to be imported. Select fixed width data, since the bill of materials file is organized into columns. You can also select the starting row. Select starting row 1. You must also select a file origin. Select DOS or Windows.

- Text Import Wizard Step 2 — Set Field Widths. This step sets the column breaks. The Excel Text Import Wizard will usually identify the correct column break between reference designator and part value data. It should place a break between columns 10 and 11. If required, you can override the Wizard's assignment.

- Text Import Wizard Step 3 — Set Data Format. This is the final step. You can set the data format for each column and skip selected columns. Set the reference designator and part value columns to text format.

Excel will import the raw bill of materials data into two columns. You can then edit the bill of materials and save it in spreadsheet format. Figure 2-24 shows the finished bill of materials. Use the following steps to edit and complete the bill of materials:

- Insert a column for quantity. Insert a row at the top and add column labels. Use bold text to make the labels stand out.

- Format column widths. The spreadsheet in Figure 2-24 uses column widths of 5, 25, 35, and 30 for quantity, reference designator, description, and vendor part number.

- Edit the bill of materials to combine parts with the same description on a single line and add the correct value in the quantity column.

- Complete the part descriptions and add vendor part numbers where applicable. Also add hardware items and parts such as the PCB, which do not appear on the schematic.

- Add blank lines to improve legibility.

- Save the finished spreadsheet. Caution! Make sure you select Excel format when you save your spreadsheet, otherwise some of the formatting information will be lost.

QTY	REFERENCE DESIGNATOR	DESCRIPTION	VENDOR PART NUMBER
1	C3	.001UF 500V 10% Y5P CERAMIC CAP	PANASONIC ECK-D2H102KB5
1	C1	.01UF 500V 10% Y5P CERAMIC CAP	PANASONIC ECK-D2H103KB5
1	C2	10UF 35V 20% ELECTROLYTIC CAP	PANASONIC ECE-A1VU100
1	C4	100UF 35V 20% ELECTROLYTIC CAP	PANASONIC ECE-A1VU101
1	P2	5 PIN STRAIGHT HEADER .156 CENTERS WITH LOCKING RAMP	MOLEX 26-48-1055
1	P1	9 PIN MALE D-SUB CONNECTOR RIGHT ANGLE PC MOUNT	AMP 747250-4
1	Q1	TIP31 TRANSISTOR	
1	R5	470 .5W 5% CARBON FILM RES	
1	R6	470 2W 5% METAL FILM RES	
2	R3,R4	10.0K .25W 1% RN-55 METAL FILM RES	
1	R1	10K .25W 5% CARBON FILM RES	
1	R2	220K .25W 5% CARBON FILM RES	
1	U1	LM324 IC	
1		PROGRAMMABLE POWER SUPPLY PCB REV 1.0	

Figure 2-24   TUTOR1 Bill of Materials Imported into Excel

Importing Schematic Graphics into Microsoft Word

Many companies use Microsoft Word to prepare technical documentation such as field service manuals. Schematics and other drawings generated in AutoCAD can easily be imported into Microsoft Word. The completed schematic in Figure 2-18 is an example of the quality that can be expected for an imported drawing. The recommended procedure is to plot HPGL (Hewlett-Packard Graphics Language) data from AutoCAD to a file and then import this file into Microsoft Word. Configure AutoCAD for an Hewlett-Packard pen plotter such as the HP7580B. Use the PLOT command and select Plot To File. To prevent clipping the drawing, select a paper size larger than the drawing or select Scaled To Fit. AutoCAD assigns the plot file the same name as the drawing except with the extension .PLT. Microsoft Word requires the extension .HGL to identify files containing HPGL data. You must rename the plot file with this .HGL extension before importing it into Microsoft Word. Most word-processing and desktop publishing programs accept HPGL format data. You can use the same procedure for importing AutoCAD drawings into these programs.

AutoCAD Release 12 and 13 also provide support for export of industry standard raster image file formats such as PCX and TIFF. The author has found the AutoCAD TIFF driver to be somewhat buggy, but export in PCX format appears to work well. Most of the figures in Chapter 1 were drawn in AutoCAD and then exported in PCX format.

Guidelines for Drawing Schematics with AutoCAD

Listed below are some general guidelines and suggestions for drawing schematics with AutoCAD:

- **Part symbol blocks**. Create parts with pins on .1 inch grid. This will make it easier to interconnect the parts later on. For ICs, use a rectangular outline on .1 inch centers.

- **Part library management**. Use a logical naming convention such as that introduced in this chapter in which the name starts with the default reference designator. Make up a master library drawing that shows all the parts in your library. Whenever you create a new part, make a backup copy of the library file onto floppy disk. If your library starts to get very large, you might want to split it into several files. You can use the PURGE command to remove unwanted blocks.

- **Data buses**. Use a .05 inch wide polyline to draw data buses. Refer to page 58 for recommended signal labels.

- **Text**. Use the suggested MONOSI text font at a height of .065 inch for maximum legibility when text must be fit between lines or pins on .1 inch grid locations. Set SNAP to .01 inch and place text about .02 inch above the line or pin.

- **Large designs**. Divide complex schematics for large designs into multiple A size sheets. Use the intersheet signal symbols shown in Figure 2-13 to show connections between sheets.

Conclusion

In this chapter you have learned background information on schematics and techniques for schematic drafting with AutoCAD. A clear understanding of this information is a helpful for successful use of AutoCAD to design PCBs. In subsequent chapters, the focus shifts to PCB design.

3

Single Sided PCB Design

In the previous chapter, you learned background information about electrical schematics and how to use AutoCAD for schematic drafting. The next three chapters are tutorial exercises intended to get you off to a fast start using AutoCAD for PCB design. In this chapter you will learn a structured approach and professional techniques by designing a small single sided PCB. The following chapters will extend these techniques for double sided PTH boards and SMT.

Single sided PCBs are still widely used for cost-sensitive, high-volume consumer products. Since only a single layer is available for routing, signal traces cannot cross over one another unless jumpers are used. While the use of multiple jumpers is not uncommon, the costs associated with jumper installation quickly exceed the potential cost savings of a single sided board versus double sided PTH boards. Single sided boards are generally manufactured in less-sophisticated facilities with a screen printed resist. The most commonly used design rule is a 50 mil grid and 25 mil traces. With a moderate amount of jumpers, the density limit for this type of design rule is about 1.25 square inch per chip equivalent (refer to the material in Chapter 1 on page 24).

Another limitation is that single sided PCBs should not be used in environments subject to vibration and shock. Components on single sided boards are supported only by the thin annular ring of copper pad material. Under repeated stress, the adhesive bond between the copper and board laminate can separate. The pad can come loose and break off from the associated circuit trace. Double sided PTH boards are much more rugged, since components are securely supported by the hole barrels that act like metal rivets.

Introduction to the Tutorial Design

The schematic for the single sided PCB design tutorial is shown in Figure 3-1. The circuit is for a simple handheld device used to test the tachometer in a race car. The unit is enclosed in a small die cast metal housing. The required board outline is given in Figure 3-2. The board mounts on four standoffs cast into the housing. A wire harness connects to a three pin Molex connector, J1.

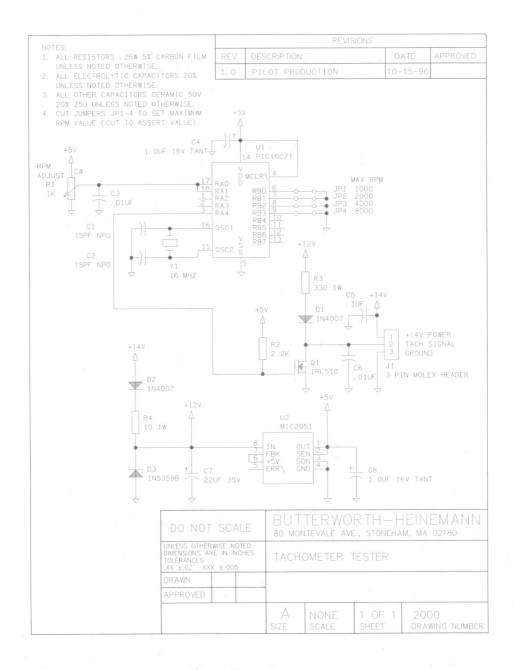

Figure 3-1   Schematic for the Single Sided PCB Tutorial

The only front panel control is a single turn potentiometer, R1, mounted in the middle of the board. Dimensions and required mounting locations are given in Figure 3-2. Note that only an approximate mounting location is given for the Molex connector. The exact location is left to the discretion of the PCB designer.

A bill of materials for the tachometer tester is given in Figure 3-3. The bill of materials as supplied to the PCB designer would typically include the first four columns: quantity, reference designator, part description, and vendor part number. The PCB designer adds the last column, which gives the names of the AutoCAD blocks representing the PCB pattern of each part. The original bill of materials would include only parts actually installed on the board. The PCB designer adds additional items such as jumpers, mounting holes, and spare component patterns.

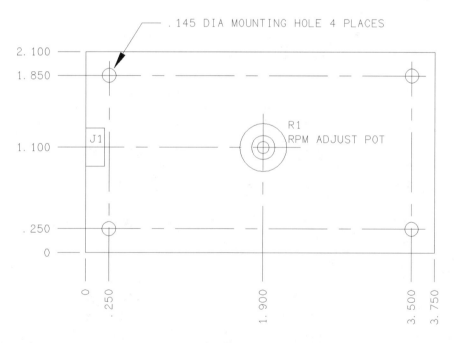

Figure 3-2   Board Outline for the Tutorial PCB

QTY	REFERENCE DESIGNATOR	DESCRIPTION	VENDOR PART NUMBER	PCB BLOCK
2	C1,C2	15PF 50V 5% NP0 CERAMIC CAP	PANASONIC ECC-F1H150JC	CAP_10LS
2	C3,C6	.01UF 50V 20% Z5U CERAMIC CAP	PHILLIPS A103M15Z5UFVVWA	CAP_40LS
1	C5	.1UF 50V 20% Z5U CERAMIC CAP	PHILLIPS A104M15Z5UFVVWN	CAP_40LS
2	C4,C8	1.0UF 16V 10% TANTALUM CAP	PANASONIC ECS-F1CE105K	ECAP_10LS20A
1	C7	22UF 35V 20% RADIAL ELEC CAP	PANASONIC ECE-A1VU220	ECAP_10LS25A
2	D1,D2	1N4007 DIODE		D_40LSA
1	D3	1N5359B DIODE		D_50LS15
1	J1	3 PIN HEADER .10 CENTERS FRICTION LOCK	MOLEX 22-23-2031	SIP_3P
4	JP1,JP2,JP3,JP4			JP_10LS
1	Q1	IRL510 MOSFET	IR	TO220_DNA
1	R4	10 1W 5% CARBON FILM RESISTOR		R_60LS
1	R3	330 1W 5% CARBON FILM RESISTOR		R_60LS
1	R1	1K .5W CONDUCTIVE PLASTIC POT	CLAROSTAT 392JA-102	VRES_50D
1	R2	2.2K .25W 5% CARBON FILM RESISTOR		R_40LS
1	U2	MIC2951 IC	MICREL	DIP_8
1	U1	PIC16C71 IC W/ TACH TESTER REV 1.0 FIRMWARE	MICROCHIP	DIP_18
1	Y1	16 MHZ HC-49/US CRYSTAL	ECS-160-20-4	XTAL_HC18UP
1		TACHOMETER TESTER PCB REV 1.0		
4		.145 DIA MOUNTING HOLE		PAD_250R145

Figure 3-3   Bill of Materials for the Tutorial PCB

As the first step in the design tutorial, calculate the chip equivalents (CE), useable board area, and board density (see Chapter 1, page 23).

CE is calculated by adding up all the device pins. You can use the bill of materials listing or schematic. Include the jumpers, JP1-4, but not the mounting holes. A simple trick is to first add up all the two lead components (such as capacitors, diodes, jumpers, and resistors) and multiply by two. Then add up all the three lead components (transistors, pots) and multiply by three. Then add any remaining components such as ICs. You should come up with a total of 73 pins for the tutorial design, or 5.2 CE.

The useable board area does not include the area taken up by the mounting holes. These holes are located .25 inch from the board edges. General practice is to use large diameter pads for all mounting holes and then connect these pads to ground. The only exceptions are products for which high voltage or other safety concerns dictate an isolated board. 6-32 hardware is commonly used for board mounting.

A .25 inch pad and .145 inch diameter hole size is a good match for a standard 6-32 screw head.

To allow for the mounting hole pads, an area of .375 × .375 inch (.14 square inch) becomes unusable at each of the four corners of the board. Given the overall board dimensions of 3.75 × 2.1 inch, the useable board area is reduced to 7.3 square inches. The calculated board density is 1.4 square inch per CE. This is greater than the suggested minimum of 1.25 given in Table 1-1, so you should be able to place and interconnect the parts within the available board area.

Structured Design Approach

Achieving professional PCB design results with AutoCAD requires a structured design approach. This design approach includes the use of AutoCAD layers, blocks, and attributes and conversion of AutoCAD data into the Gerber and Excellon data required by board manufacturers.

Before continuing, you might spend some time reviewing layer, block, and attribute concepts in your AutoCAD documentation. The layer assignments used for PCB design are shown in Table 3-1.

Table 3-1   AutoCAD Layers for PCB Design

LAYER NAME	COLOR	PEN	SIZE	NOTES
SILK_COMP	WHITE	2	.01	
TRACE_COMP	BLUE	1	.005	
TRACE_SOLDER	RED	1	.005	
PADS	GREEN	127	N/A	DISPLAY ONLY
	YELLOW	3	.02	FILL PATTERN
VIAS	GREEN	127	N/A	DISPLAY ONLY
	YELLOW	3	.02	FILL PATTERN
MASK_COMP	WHITE	2	.01	
MASK_SOLDER	WHITE	2	.01	
OUTLINE	WHITE	2	.01	
DRILL	WHITE	2	.01	
ASSEMBLY	WHITE	2	.01	
TITLEBLOCK	WHITE	2	.01	

Each layer has an associated color, pen number, and pen width. With the exception of polylines, AutoCAD does not allow direct association of a line width parameter with graphic entities. The technique used to control and specify different line widths is use of color. Different line widths are represented by colors. A particular pen is then assigned to each color for plotting. In turn, each pen has a defined pen width.

Let's examine the layer assignments in Table 3-1 in more detail. Please note that terminology can be somewhat confusing. For example, the term *solder mask* refers to the artwork used for screening green solder resist on the PCB surface. Boards can have both a solder side and component side solder mask. Also note that most artwork is created by plotting a composite of multiple layers. For example, the solder side artwork consists of the OUTLINE, PADS, and TRACE_SOLDER layers.

- **SILK_COMP**. This layer contains component outlines and legends (reference designators) that are silk-screened with white ink on the top side of the PCB. The silkscreen outlines and legends are displayed in white and plotted with pen 2, which is assigned a width of .01 inch. This is an industry standard width that gives good results with the silk-screening process.

- **TRACE_COMP**. This layer contains all circuit traces and other copper patterns on the component side of the PCB. Since the component side of the PCB is not used for trace routing in single sided boards, this layer is empty. The component side will be used in subsequent tutorials. The component side is displayed in blue and plotted with pen 1, which is assigned a width of .005 inch. Circuit traces and solid copper areas are drawn as polylines. The AutoCAD plot driver strokes the pen back and forth to fill in polylines. Using a fine pen width such as .005 inch allows narrow polylines down to about .012 inch.

- **TRACE_SOLDER**. This layer contains all circuit traces and other copper patterns on the solder side of the PCB. For a single sided board, all circuit traces are on the solder side. The solder side is displayed in red and plotted with pen 1, which is assigned a width of .005 inch. The same plotting considerations as noted above for the component side also apply to the solder side.

- **PADS**. This layer contains pads for through hole components. In all the tutorial exercises, pads for through hole parts are identical on both the component and solder side of the PCB. Two colors are used for pads. Green is used to display the outline of the pad for design and checking purposes. A nonexistent pen number 127 is assigned to green to prevent this color from plotting. Yellow is used for the fill pattern. This yellow fill pattern is plotted with pen 3, which is assigned a width of .02 inch.

- **VIAS**. This layer contains pads for vias. In all other respects, this layer is treated the same as the PADS layer. The use of a separate VIAS layer allows a solder mask artwork to be generated without clearance areas for vias. Since vias are not used with single sided boards, this layer is empty. The VIAS layer will be used in subsequent tutorials

- **MASK_COMP.** This layer contains any special solder mask patterns required for the top (component) side of the board. The tutorial exercises in this book do not require special solder mask patterns. When the solder mask artwork is plotted, oversize component pads are plotted along with any special patterns on this layer. The oversize pads are created by changing the pen number of the yellow fill pattern on the PADS layer to pen 4, which is then plotted with a width of .03 inch. The resulting pads are .01 inch oversize as customary for a solder mask artwork.

- **MASK_SOLDER**. This layer contains any special solder mask patterns required for the back (solder) side of the board.

- **OUTLINE.** This layer contains cut marks, scribe lines, and other features that define the board outline. These features are displayed in white and plotted with pen 2, which is assigned a width of .01 inch. The board manufacturer uses the outline features to depanelize individual boards by means of shearing or NC routing operations.

- **DRILL**. This layer contains drill size symbols and attributes associated with the pads of through hole components and vias. The DRILL layer also contains manufacturing notes. Drill size attributes are extracted and converted to Excellon format NC drill data. The drill size symbols and manufacturing notes appear in the drill detail drawing, which is part of the documentation required for PCB manufacturing.

- **ASSEMBLY**. This layer contains notes and details that will appear in the PCB assembly drawing.

- **TITLEBLOCK**. This layer contains the drawing border, titleblock, and revision block used for manufacturing documentation.

At first glance, the number of required layers may seem overwhelming and confusing. In fact, the use of a structured approach with artwork defined by multiple layers greatly simplifies the design process.

Pad Blocks

AutoCAD blocks are used for all pads on the PCB. Pad blocks are in turn nested within part blocks representing the components on the PCB. Individual pads can also appear by themselves. Examples include vias, the connections between layers on double sided boards, and mounting holes.

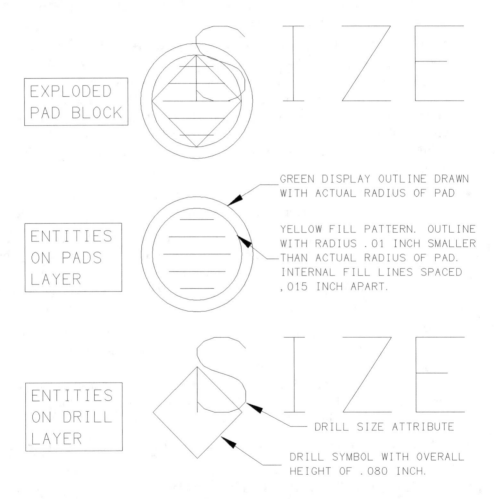

Figure 3-4   Detail of Round Pad Block

Figure 3-4 shows a typical round pad block. The pad block consists of entities on two layers: PADS and DRILL. The insertion base point is the center of the pad. For conventional single and double sided boards using through hole components, only a single pad layer is required since identical pads are used on both sides of the board. Surface mount components require a pad on only one layer.

Entities on the PADS layer consist of a green display outline and a yellow fill pattern. The green display outline is used during the design process and printing of check plots on a laser printer. It represents the outer boundary of the pad and allows a quick visual determination of clearances to adjacent pads and traces. For final artwork, plotting of the green outline is suppressed by means of assigning the color green to a nonexistent pen number.

The yellow fill pattern must be drawn so that the pad has the correct outline on the final artwork plot. Enough overlap must exist between adjacent fill lines to assure that the interior of the pad is plotted as a solid area without clear streaks. A .02 inch pen width is used for plotting the pads as they appear on the component and solder side of the PCB. The outline of the fill pattern must be offset by 1/2 the pen width. Thus the yellow outline must be created with a radius .01 inch less than the actual radius of the pad. Internal fill lines are spaced .015 inch apart, resulting in an overlap of .005 inch. The internal fill lines extend to within about .01 inch of the yellow outline.

Entities on the DRILL layer consist of a drill size symbol and attribute. Drill symbols appear on the PCB manufacturing drawing (also referred to as the *drill detail drawing*). A unique symbol is used for each drill size. Thus both round and square pads with a .037 inch drill hole would use the same drill symbol. Some industry standards exist for drill symbols:

- **Size**. Since the most common hole spacing is on .1 inch centers, drill symbols are usually drawn so that they will fit into a .08 × .08 inch box. This assures that adjacent symbols do not overlap. In some cases holes are closer together and some overlap will occur, but the .08 × .08 drill symbol size is a good compromise. Smaller symbols would reduce legibility.

- **Symbol**. The most common drill symbol is a cross (+). Drill symbols should clearly identify the center of the pad and be symmetric about the pad centerline. Note that the drill symbol in Figure 3-4 has a line drawn from the top of the box to the center of the pad.

AutoCAD attributes are used to associate drill size information with the pad block. The drill size attribute along with the X and Y coordinates for each pad on the board can then by extracted with the ATTEXT command and written to a file. The information in this file can in turn be converted into Excellon format NC drill data for the board manufacturer.

Drill size is a preset, invisible attribute with prompt and tag set to SIZE. The attribute value is preset to the required drill hole size. Since the drill size attribute is defined as an invisible attribute, it is not displayed unless the ATTDISP parameter is set to *on*. The drill size attribute does not normally need to be displayed during PCB design operations or plotted. It is only used to extract information when creating the Excellon NC drill data. Note that the tag SIZE, not the preset value, is shown in Figure 3-4, since the pad block in the figure has been exploded. When attributes are created, they are drawn in the current text style. The font and height of an invisible attribute are not critical. A convenient insertion point for the drill size attribute is the center of the pad. The choice of this location is arbitrary, it does not affect the NC drill data. The X and Y coordinates extracted for NC drill data refer to the insertion point of the pad block itself. This is not clearly explained in the AutoCAD documentation.

The suggested sequence of steps for creating a pad block can be summarized as follows:

1.   Set up the PADS and DRILL layers.

2.   Draw the green pad outline on the PADS layer.

3.   Draw the yellow fill pattern on the PADS layer.

4.   Draw the drill symbol on the DRILL layer.

5.   Define the drill size attribute on the DRILL layer.

6.   Use the BLOCK command to define the pad block.

A logical naming convention is used for pad blocks (and part blocks) throughout the examples and tutorial exercises in this book. Pad names are of the form:

PAD_60R37 or PAD_80S45

The first set of numbers is the pad size or diameter in mils (60 means .06 inch), the letter identifies the shape (R for round, S for square), and the last set of numbers is the drill size in mils. Thus PAD_60R37 is a .06 inch diameter round pad with a .037 inch drill size.

An example of a square pad block is shown in Figure 3-5. Pad blocks are easy to create; the process is covered in detail in Chapter 4.

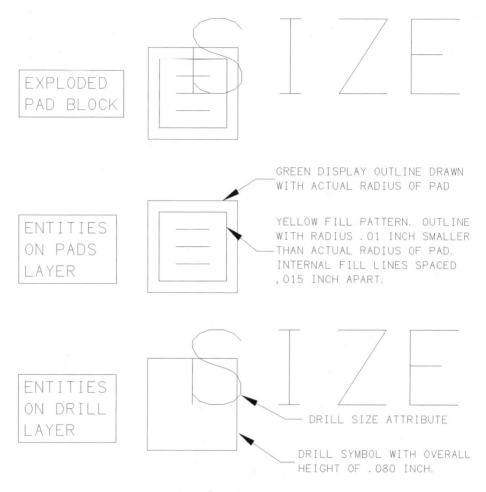

EXPLODED PAD BLOCK

ENTITIES ON PADS LAYER

GREEN DISPLAY OUTLINE DRAWN WITH ACTUAL RADIUS OF PAD

YELLOW FILL PATTERN. OUTLINE WITH RADIUS .01 INCH SMALLER THAN ACTUAL RADIUS OF PAD. INTERNAL FILL LINES SPACED .015 INCH APART.

ENTITIES ON DRILL LAYER

DRILL SIZE ATTRIBUTE

DRILL SYMBOL WITH OVERALL HEIGHT OF .080 INCH.

Figure 3-5   Detail of Square Pad Block

Part Blocks

AutoCAD blocks are used for all parts (components) on the PCB. Figure 3-6 shows a typical part block. Pad blocks are nested within the part block definition. The part block consists of entities on three layers. These layers include the two layers used for the pads (PADS and DRILL) and the SILK_COMP layer. The center of the upper left pad is generally used as the insertion point. For front panel components such as switches and potentiometers, the center of the mounting hole is a more logical insertion point.

All entities on the SILK_COMP layer are drawn in white. These entities consist of the part outline and the reference designator. The part outline is generally drawn to correspond to the dimensions of the part body and may include orientation and polarity symbols (for example a diode symbol or + symbol for an electrolytic capacitor).

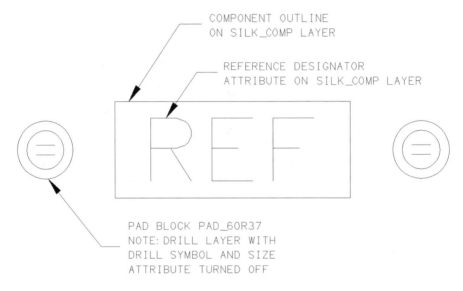

Figure 3-6   Detail of a Part Block

AutoCAD attributes are used to associate a reference designator with the pad block. One could just use plain text, but an attribute has certain advantages. Attributes in blocks can easily be edited, including the attribute text location and angle. This editing capability is important for PCB design. The reference designator attribute is a preset, visible attribute with prompt and tag set to REF. The attribute value is preset to a generic value, such as C? for a capacitor or R? for a resistor. When the part block is inserted, AutoCAD displays this generic preset value and prompts for the actual value to be used on the board.

Note that the tag REF, not the preset value, is shown in Figure 3-6 since the part block in the figure has been exploded. When attributes are created, they are drawn in the current text style. The MONOSI font, a monospaced sans serif font, is recommended for optimum legibility. The recommended height is .065 inch. The insertion point for the reference designator attribute is the part center.

The suggested sequence of steps for creating a part block can be summarized as follows:

1. Define the required pad blocks.

2. Setup the SILK_COMP layer and make this the current layer.

3. Insert the required pad blocks.

4. Draw the part outline.

5. Define the reference designator attribute.

6. Use the BLOCK command to define the part block.

As with pad blocks, a logical naming convention is used for the part blocks throughout the examples and tutorial exercises in this book. Part names are of the form:

D_50LS15 or DIP_8 or XTAL_HC18UP

The first set of letters is either the reference designator (D for diode) or an obvious abbreviation for the part package (DIP for dual inline IC or XTAL for a crystal). The information after the underscore character is the package size and orientation. D_50LS15 refers to a diode with .50 inch lead spacing and .15 inch body diameter. Dimensions are always given in mils. DIP_8 is an 8 pin dual inline package. XTAL_HC18UP is an HC18 crystal package oriented standing up.

An extensive part block library is included on the disk supplied with this book. These predefined part blocks will be used for the tutorial exercises. Part blocks are easy to create; the process is covered in detail in Chapter 4. Appendix D contains a complete listing and description of the pad and part blocks including on the disk.

Starting the Tutorial Exercise

This tutorial exercise shows you how to use AutoCAD to design a simple single sided PCB and generate the required manufacturing documentation and artwork. Your task will be to design a PCB for the tachometer tester schematic shown in Figure 3-1 using the board outline shown in Figure 3-2 and the bill of materials in Figure 3-3. You may want to run copies of these figures and keep them handy for reference.

To complete the tutorial, you will require access to a PC running AutoCAD Release 12 or 13. AutoCAD LT does not currently support the special AutoCAD binary ADI plot file format required for generation of Gerber format files for photoplotting PCB artwork.

An alternative technique that can be used with AutoCAD LT for Windows 95 is discussed in Chapter 10. This is based on conversion of HPGL (Hewlett-Packard Graphics Language) plot files to Gerber format. If you are using AutoCAD LT for Windows 95, you can complete the tutorial exercise in this chapter up to the point of generating board artwork and then skip to Chapter 10.

Files and utility programs required for the tutorial exercise are included on the floppy disk supplied with the book. The design-related files for this tutorial are in the subdirectory TUTOR2. FORMAT_A.DWG is an A size drawing format. PCB1_LIB.DWG is the PCB parts library. File conversion utilities required to generate Gerber and Excellon format data are in the AUTOPADS subdirectory. The use of these utilities is explained later in the chapter. For now, create a TUTOR2 subdirectory on your hard drive. Copy the files from the TUTOR2 subdirectory on the floppy disk to the TUTOR2 subdirectory on your hard drive.

The floppy disk supplied with the book also contains a popular shareware text display utility, LIST.COM, and a public domain font file, MONOSI.SHX. You can use the LIST.COM utility to examine template files and bills of materials files. Copy LIST.COM into your root or DOS directory, or other directory included in your PC's PATH statement. Refer to Appendix D for more details, including shareware license and usage restrictions. MONOSI is a mono-spaced simplex font that gives highly legible results at the small text height settings required for schematics and PCBs. All the part symbols in the library are defined using the MONOSI font. Copy MONOSI.SHX into your AutoCAD font subdirectory.

Setting Up Layers

Start AutoCAD and open the A size drawing format, FORMAT_A.DWG. The drawing border, title block, and revision block will be displayed on the screen. Use the INSERT command to insert the file PCB1_LIB.DWG. You need to type in the full file name. This loads all the required PCB pad and part blocks. The insertion location is not important, since PCB1_LIB.DWG does not contain any drawing entities that will appear on the screen. Next, use the SAVE AS command from the FILE menu and save the drawing as TUTOR2.DWG. Note that AutoCAD automatically assigns the .DWG suffix. This leaves your original drawing format file FORMAT_A.DWG unchanged. All subsequent editing is done using TUTOR2.DWG.

Open TUTOR2.DWG and then use the LAYER command to define the required layers. These layers are listed in Table 3-2. The layers listed in Table 3-2 are a subset of those listed in Table 3-1. Component side trace and mask layers are not required for this single sided PCB tutorial. Some of the layers will already exist, since you started with the drawing format file FORMAT_A.DWG and then loaded the PCB1_LIB.DWG library.

Table 3-2   Required AutoCAD Layers

LAYER NAME	COLOR
SILK_COMP	WHITE
TRACE_SOLDER	RED
PADS	YELLOW
OUTLINE	WHITE
DRILL	WHITE
ASSEMBLY	WHITE
TITLEBLOCK	WHITE

Drawing the Board Outline

Use the LAYER command to set OUTLINE as the current layer. Set all layers to *on* except DRILL and ASSEMBLY. Use the ATTDISP command to set attribute display to normal. This inhibits display of invisible attributes, such as drill hole size. Use the GRID and SNAP commands to select a .1 inch grid and .025 inch snap.

Starting from a grid point, draw the board outline shown in Figure 3-7 using the dimensions given in Figure 3-2. The outline consists of cut marks at each corner of the board. The length of the cut marks is not critical. General practice is to make the cut marks about .1 to .25 inch long.

Next, use the UCS and ORIGIN commands to set the origin point for the drawing to the lower left hand corner of the board. This will facilitate subsequent component insertion and dimensioning.

Placing Components

Set SILK_COMP as the current layer. First, place the components that have defined locations. Refer to Figure 3-1, 3-2, and 3-3. The mounting holes, J1, and R1 have defined locations.

Keeping track of your work is an important part of the design process. Use a red pencil to mark off components on the schematic and bill of materials as you place them on the board.

Use the INSERT command to place the mounting holes. The part block name is PAD_250R145. Since the origin point is set the same as in Figure 3-2, you can directly enter the coordinates for the mounting holes. The mounting holes do not require rotation or scaling, so accept the default values. Note that pads such as those used for mounting holes (or vias on double sided boards) do not have reference designators.

Next insert J1 and R1. Use the part block names listed on the bill of materials in Figure 3-3. The exact location of J1 is not critical; use Figure 3-7 as a rough guide. Unless a precise location is required, always place components on grid. Use the .1 inch grid for initial component placement. After inserting a component you can always use the MOVE or ROTATE commands to change the location or orientation. After you insert the component, AutoCAD will prompt for the reference designator attribute; enter J1.

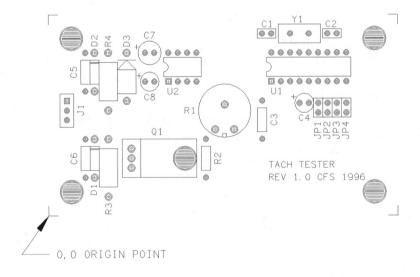

Figure 3-7   Board Outline and Component Placement

Finish the component placement by placing the remaining components, again using Figure 3-7 as a rough guide. Many of the components will have to be rotated 90 or 270 degrees during insertion. The resistors, jumpers, and non-polarized capacitors can be rotated so that the reference designators are oriented as shown in the figure. This saves editing time later on. Polarized parts such as diodes and electrolytic capacitors must be inserted with the proper rotation.

Optimum component placement is critical to the success of a PCB design. Take a moment to compare the component placement on the board to the schematic. Note the overall strategy of placing components in rows and how related components are grouped together to maintain signal flow. Note how all the pads on the top row are aligned in a straight line.

After inserting all the components, use the ATTEDIT command to orient and locate the reference designator attributes as shown in Figure 3-7. You can also use ATTEDIT to correct or change the value of reference designators. Using ATTEDIT can be somewhat clumsy. For optimum productivity, you should zoom into a section of the board and select about a half dozen reference designators at a time for editing. In some cases, ATTEDIT may fail to catch an attribute in the selection set. Setting a smaller snap, such as .01, will help.

Standard practice is to move reference designators outside the component outline so that they will still be visible when the board is assembled. However, this is not always possible on very dense boards.

After completing the component placement, add text legends to identify the board, revision level, designer's initials (use your own), and date as shown in the lower right corner of Figure 3-7. Use text style MONOSI with a height of .065 inch.

Zoom in so that your screen resembles Figure 3-7. Save the drawing and then print out a hardcopy to use as a check plot. You can use PLOT DISPLAY at 2:1 scale. It is good practice always to make check plots as large as possible. For larger PCBs, you can rotate the plot 90 degrees and use a scale factor such as 1.5:1 to fill the page. The use of a color inkjet printer is highly recommended, but you can also use a laser printer. Note that the pads do not appear filled on the screen or on paper hardcopy. At this point, the fill lines are not plotted with the correct width. The green outline represents the boundary of the pads. Later, when a Gerber format photoplotter data file is generated, the fill lines will have the correct width, and the pads will appear filled.

This is also a good time to save a backup copy of the drawing to floppy disk. You should make a backup copy whenever a major stage in the design process has been completed.

Trace Routing

After the components have been placed, signal traces are routed on the solder side. Two approaches to trace routing are possible when using AutoCAD for PCB design. Many designers prefer to use a paper hardcopy of the board layout with component outlines and pads and manually draw the trace routing. Colored pencils are usually used for this purpose. These designers find it easier to visualize the layout and experiment with various routing strategies on a sheet of paper. One can make several copies of the layout and then route small sections of the design. After the design has been routed on paper, the traces are drawn in AutoCAD.

Other designers prefer to work on-screen from the start. Either approach can work, but starting with a paper hardcopy is probably advisable for the novice designer. In either case, use a red pencil to "red line" signal traces on the schematic as you draw them on the board layout.

Use the 50 mil grid and 25 mil trace design rule for the tutorial board. This design rule is explained in detail in Chapter 1, page 25. The smallest trace, used for signal connections, is 25 mils. Traces cannot run between pads located on .1 inch centers. Wider traces are commonly used for ground distribution. Closely examine the suggested trace routing in Figure 3-9. A heavy 100 mil wide ground trace is run around the periphery of the board. This heavy trace connects the pads for the mounting holes. Additional 50 mil wide traces distribute ground to J1, Q1, and various components grouped around U1 and U2. The remaining ground connections and all power and signal connections are made with 25 mil wide traces. General practice is to always route ground traces first, followed by power and signal traces.

The ground distribution around the periphery of the board is typical. Today, many boards also have large ground plane areas to reduce noise susceptibility and radiation. A minimum clearance is required from the edge of the board to the copper pattern. The suggested minimum clearance is .025 inch.

You must have detailed information about component pin assignments to route the board. This is an area where errors can easily creep into the design. Industry standards exist for pin assignments on many common parts. If you are not absolutely certain about a particular part, obtain a copy of the manufacturer's data sheet. Distributors' catalogs are also a useful source of information. Most of the parts used in the tutorial exercises in this book appear in the Digi-Key catalog. Digi-Key is an outstanding source for fast delivery of electronic components. You can obtain their catalog by calling 1-800-DIGI-KEY.

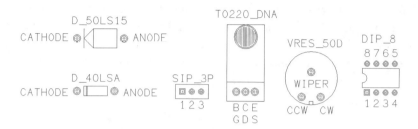

Figure 3-8   Typical Pin Assignments

Refer to Figure 3-8 and the general guidelines below for more information about pin assignments (all components are viewed from the top side):

- **ICs**. Pin 1 is identified on the PCB layout with a square pad. If the orientation notch in the package is facing up, pin 1 is the upper left pin. Pins are numbered in rows, with the last pin opposite pin 1.

- **Polarized capacitors**. The + symbol on the PCB layout is self explanatory.

- **Diodes.** The cathode is identified with a thick bar or diode symbol on the PCB layout.

- **LEDs**. There is no standard for assigning the cathode or anode pin to the flat side. Always check the particular manufacturer's data sheet.

- **Transistors**. Pin assignments vary widely, especially for smaller devices. Most TO-220 and TO-247 power transistors use the pin assignment BCE (base, collector, emitter) or equivalent GDS (gate, drain, source) for MOSFETs when oriented as shown in Figure 3-8.

- **Connectors**. Pin 1 is usually identified on the PCB layout with a square pad. Refer to the data sheet for details. D-Sub connectors often cause confusion.

- **Potentiometers and switches**. These cause the most trouble. One of the corollaries of Murphy's law states that toggle switches and pots will always be backwards. When a toggle switch handle is up, the switch connection is made to the bottom pin. Carefully check manufacturer's data sheets to identify the CW (clockwise) and CCW (counter-clockwise) terminals on potentiometers. Some manufacturers show the pinout viewed from the bottom, which is a mirror image of the board layout viewed from the top.

Draw the traces using the suggested routing in Figure 3-9. Set TRACE_SOLDER as the current layer. Set the grid and snap to .05 inch. Use the POLYLINE command to draw traces. You must draw a continuous polyline from pad to pad. If you end a polyline at a corner and then draw another polyline, a chunk will appear to be missing at the corner as shown in Figure 3-10. If this happens, you can use the PEDIT (polyline edit) command and JOIN option to join the polylines together again.

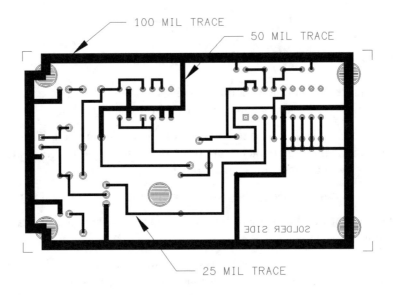

Figure 3-9   Trace Routing on Solder Side

After completing the trace routing, add a text legend to identify the solder side as shown in the lower right corner of Figure 3-9. This is especially important on double sided boards. The author has seen boards manufactured with the solder and component sides reversed because the artwork was not clearly identified. Use text style MONOSI with a height of .065 inch. Remember that you are viewing the design from the component side. You must mirror any text appearing on the solder side so that the text will appear right reading on the actual artwork. Use the MIRROR command to mirror text strings.

Save the drawing. Turn on the SILK_COMP layer and then print out a hardcopy to use as a check plot. This will show components, pads, and trace routing. Check each trace against the schematic, red lining both the schematic and check plot as you proceed. Correct any errors, save the final drawing to your hard drive, and save a backup copy to floppy disk.

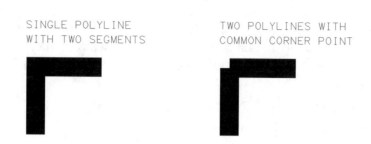

SINGLE POLYLINE
WITH TWO SEGMENTS

TWO POLYLINES WITH
COMMON CORNER POINT

Figure 3-10   Polyline Corners

The PCB design is now complete, and the next task is to generate manufacturing documentation and artwork.

Introduction to the AutoPADS Utilities

The AutoPADS utilities are used to convert AutoCAD data to Gerber format photoplotter data and Excellon format NC drill data, both of which are industry standards for PCB manufacturing. Information about photoplotting artwork and numerically controlled board drilling is given in Chapter 1 starting on page 17. For detailed information about Excellon and Gerber format, refer to Appendixes A and B.

The AutoPADS utility programs are included on the floppy disk supplied with this book. AutoPADS consists of the main AutoPADS (AutoCAD to Gerber) conversion utility, the AutoDRIL (AutoCAD to Excellon) conversion utility, and various support files. Create an AUTOPADS subdirectory on your hard drive. Copy all the files from the AUTOPADS subdirectory on the floppy disk to the AUTOPADS subdirectory on your hard drive.

Manufacturing Documentation

Manufacturing documentation consists of the Excellon format NC drill data, drill detail drawing, and board assembly drawing.

Extracting NC Drill Data

The drill size attribute associated with pad blocks is used to extract NC drill data from AutoCAD. This raw data is then converted to Excellon format by means of the AutoDRIL conversion utility.

AutoCAD uses a template file to determine what attribute information to extract from the drawing database and how to format this information. You should review this subject in your AutoCAD documentation. Template files are text files. You can use the LIST utility to examine the NC drill data template file, NC_EXT.TXT. This is one of the AutoPADS support files you copied onto your hard drive. Exit to DOS and type:

CD\AUTOPADS<ENTER>

LIST NC_EXT.TXT<ENTER>

This changes to the AUTOPADS subdirectory and runs LIST.COM. The resulting screen display is shown in Figure 3-11. The first and last lines showing the file name and function key options are part of LIST.COM. Comprehensive on-line help is available. Press F1 and explore the features of LIST.COM.

```
LIST        1      4      07/07/1990 09:21 C:\AUTOPADS\NC_EXT.TXT
SIZE          N007004
BL:X          N007004
BL:Y          N007004
>>>>>>>>>>>>>>>>>>>>>>>>>>>>>>>>>>>>>>>>>>>>>>>>>>>>>>>>>>>>>>>>>>>>>>




Command▶   *** End-of-file ***        Keys: ↑↓→← PgUp PgDn  F10=exit F1=Help
```

Figure 3-11   NC_EXT.TXT NC Drill Data Template File

Note that NC_EXT.TXT has three entries. The first entry causes AutoCAD to extract the SIZE attribute. The second and third entries extract the X and Y coordinates for the pad. The code N007004 formats the attribute information as numeric data with a field width of seven digits and four digits after the decimal point. Refer to your AutoCAD documentation for more details on template files. In summary, the NC_EXT template file causes a separate line to be generated for each pad with the pad size and X,Y coordinates.

To extract the NC drill data, start AutoCAD and open the TUTOR2.DWG PCB drawing file. Use the ATTEXT command. Select CDF (comma-delimited file) format. Then select the NC_EXT.TXT template file. The raw NC drill data will be written out to a file in CDF format. Use the filename DRILL.TXT.

At this point a minor AutoCAD bug enters the picture. AutoCAD has a World Coordinate System (WCS) and a User Coordinate System (UCS). The origin of the UCS was moved to the lower left corner of the PCB. Coordinates displayed in AutoCAD are based on this new UCS origin. Unfortunately, the X,Y block coordinates extracted via the ATTEXT command are **always based on the WCS**. These coordinates will appear to be offset from the expected UCS value. This offset must be corrected during the conversion to Excellon format, since the board manufacturer will expect the origin (0,0) location to be the lower left corner of the PCB.

You must know the actual WCS coordinates of the lower left corner of the board. Use the UCS command and the WORLD option. This restores the WCS origin. Press F6 to enable dynamic (continuously updated) coordinate display. Move the cursor to the intersection of the two cut marks at the lower left corner of the PCB. Write down these X and Y coordinates for use as offsets in the next part of this exercise. Then use the UCS command and ORIGIN option to move the UCS origin back to the lower left corner of the PCB.

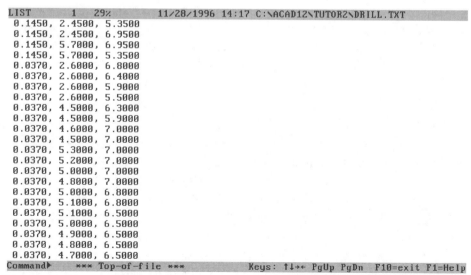

Figure 3-12   DRILL.TXT CDF File with NC Data

Exit to DOS and use the LIST utility to examine DRILL.TXT. Your file should appear similar to that shown in Figure 3-12, except that the order in which pad attributes appear may differ. Note that AutoCAD outputs attributes in the order that they appear in the database.

Running AutoDRIL to Generate Excellon Data

The AutoDRIL program requires that all AutoCAD extract files have filenames with a .TXT extension, according to AutoCAD naming conventions. AutoDRIL generates Excellon format NC drill data files with a .CNC extension and tool usage report files with a .DAT extension. The path and filename are retained. The AutoCAD extract file is not modified. The new files are written to the same drive and subdirectory.

To run the AutoDRIL program, exit to DOS and type:

CD\AUTOPADS <ENTER>

AUTODRIL <ENTER>

The copyright notice screen appears, and you can hit any key to continue and run the conversion program.

Throughout the AutoDRIL program, you can navigate the various menu options by pressing the Tab key to go forward or the Shift + Tab keys to go back to the previous choice. When you are prompted for a parameter value or filename, enter the information and then press the Enter key. When you "tab" to menu options such as OK (means continue) or QUIT (stop program), the selected menu option will become highlighted. You can then execute the menu option by pressing the Enter key.

AutoDRIL Conversion Options

The first screen gives you the option of listing the conversion results to an attached printer. The conversion results listing is a three column table consisting of tool number, tool size, and quantity. Tools are consecutively numbered, starting at one for the smallest tool size (same as drill hole size). The quantity refers to the number of pads found for the particular tool size.

The second conversion option screen gives you the option of adding a tool information header to the Excellon format file. Select this option. The tool header option writes a three column table with tool number, tool size, and quantity at the beginning of the Excellon format file. If you respond NO for the header option, a separate file with the tool information will be created and given the extension .DAT.

Note that the PCB manufacturer must have tool information, either as a header, as a separate file, or as a printed listing. Otherwise they will have no way of knowing the size of the tools called out in the Excellon file. Excellon format only provides for a tool number and does not include any size information.

X and Y Offset Entry

This screen allows entry of X and Y axis offsets. The default offsets are zero. If you enter new offset values, these will be added to the X and Y drill location coordinates read in from AutoCAD. In general, you want the origin point (X=0 and Y=0) of the Excellon data that you send the board manufacturer to be at the lower left corner of the PCB. Because of the AutoCAD bug discussed on page 101, this may not be the case. The AutoDRIL X and Y offset function allows you to output correct Excellon data. Recall the X,Y coordinate values you wrote down from page 101. Use the **negative** of these values, for example –X and –Y, as offsets when running AutoDRIL.

CDF Filename Entry

The filename entry screen will prompt you for the name of the CDF file that contains the extracted NC drill data. You can specify a drive and path as part of the filename, just as you would with any other DOS command. But you must not include an extension. The program assumes the extension .TXT for the CDF file and uses the same drive, path, and name with a .CNC extension for the Excellon output file it creates.

After you have entered the filename, the conversion process will start. During the conversion process, you can stop the program and return to the DOS prompt by pressing the Esc key. Any partially converted CNC file will be deleted. Please note that the Esc key works only while the conversion screen is displayed.

After the conversion process is completed, you can select one of two options. You can CONTINUE to convert another file or you can QUIT the program. If you elect to continue, you will be asked for another CDF filename.

AutoDRIL first sorts the NC drill data extracted from AutoCAD, according to tool (drill) size and X and Y coordinates. As mentioned earlier, the smallest tool size is output first. Following industry standards, sorting on X and Y coordinates is done in channels approximately .40 inches wide along the X axis. This minimizes the total motion of the drill spindle. After all the data has been sorted, it is converted into Excellon format.

AutoDRIL Error Messages

If an error occurs, AutoDRIL will display an appropriate error message. Most of the error messages are self-explanatory. The most common errors relate to entry of improper drive, path, or filenames, or printer off-line. Remember that the path is relative to the subdirectory from which AutoDRIL is running. Thus if AutoDRIL is running from the C:\AUTOPADS subdirectory and the file that you want to convert, for example DRILL.TXT , is loaded into the C:\TUTOR2 subdirectory, you must enter C:\TUTOR2\DRILL as the path and filename on the filename entry screen.

AutoDRIL Limitations

AutoDRIL supports only English inch units. This means that the NC data extracted from AutoCAD must be in inch units. All X and Y coordinates must be within the range of zero to 32 inches. Tool sizes must be within the range of .001 to .999 inch. Values outside these ranges will cause an error message to be displayed, and the program will halt. To increase conversion speed, AutoDRIL sorts all data in RAM. This places a limitation on the number of drill holes. If AutoDRIL encounters a file with more than 1999 holes, an error message will be displayed, and the program will halt.

AutoDRIL may not run correctly if memory resident programs or print/plot spoolers are loaded. The program is not intended to be run from within AutoCAD either as a menu selection or by use of the SHELL command. You must quit AutoCAD (or any other program) before running AutoDRIL. AutoDRIL will run from a DOS window in Windows.

Examining the Excellon NC Drill Data File

Exit to DOS and use the LIST utility to examine the tool information header and Excellon format data in DRILL.CNC. This is the file converted by AutoDRIL. Your file should appear similar to that shown in Figure 3-13, except for the order in which data appears.

Print the screen listing by pressing the Alt + P keys. This will give you hardcopy of the tool information header, which gives the drill sizes and quantities. This information is required for the drill detail drawing.

```
LIST        1    31%      11/30/1996 00:58 C:\ACAD12\TUTOR2\DRILL.CNC
TOOL      SIZE      QUANTITY
  1       .037        57
  2       .045        16
  3       .145         5
EXCELLON DATA FOLLOWS
T1
X004Y004
X004Y008
X002Y01
X002Y011
X002Y012
X004Y013
X004Y017
X0105Y014
X0115Y014
X013Y014
X014Y014
X0105Y017
X0115Y017
X013Y017
X014Y017
X015Y017
X016Y017
Command▶    *** Top-of-file ***      Keys: ↑↓→← PgUp PgDn  F10=exit F1=Help
```

Figure 3-13   DRILL.CNC File with Excellon Format Data

Drill Detail Drawing

Start AutoCAD and load the TUTOR2 drawing. Use the LAYER command to set the DRILL, OUTLINE, and TITLEBLOCK layers on, with DRILL as the current layer. Use the STYLE command to set MONOSI with a height of .075 inch as the current text style.

Use Figure 3-14 as a guide. First, complete the board outline by drawing lines between the cut marks. Make sure that the UCS origin is the lower left corner of the board. Use ordinate dimensioning to add the dimensions as shown in Figure 3-14. Note that ordinate dimensioning is preferred for PCBs, since all features are NC drilled and NC routed based on an origin point. Ordinate dimensioning also produces less drawing clutter than conventional dimensioning. If you are not familiar with ordinate dimensioning in AutoCAD, refer to your AutoCAD documentation.

The next step is to insert the drill table (also referred to as the *drill chart*). The file DRL_TABL contains the drill table. This file should be in your TUTOR2 subdirectory. Use the INSERT command to insert the DRL_TABL file. Place the drill table in the lower left corner of the drawing. Then use the DTEXT command to insert the required quantity and tool number data.

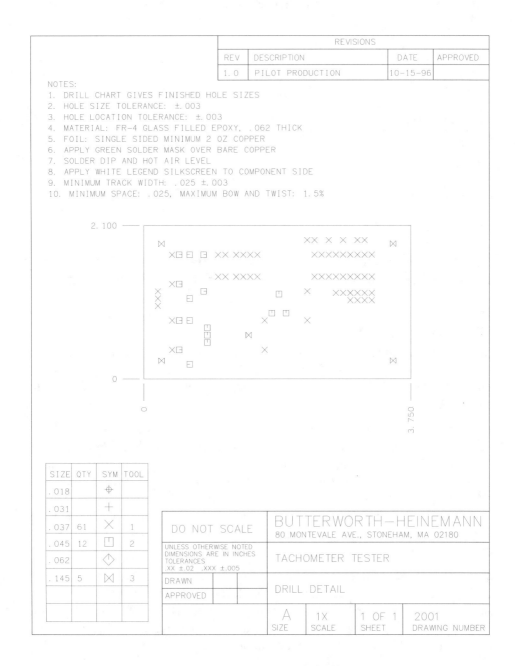

Figure 3-14   Finished Drill Detail Drawing

Next, add the text notes shown in Figure 3-14 near the top of the drawing. Take a moment to examine these notes. They are generic notes for manufacturing a single sided PCB using SMOBC (solder mask over bare copper).

The last step is to add the required text information to the revision block and title block. This includes the drawing title, scale factor, sheet number, drawing number, revision code, description, and date. Use Figure 3-14 as a guide.

The drill detail drawing is now complete. Save the drawing and then print out a hardcopy.

Assembly Drawing

The assembly drawing is the final piece of manufacturing documentation. Use the LAYER command to set the ASSEMBLY, OUTLINE, SILK_COMP, and TITLEBLOCK layers on, with ASSEMBLY as the current layer.

Use Figure 3-15 as a guide. First, complete the board outline by drawing lines between the cut marks. Next, add the text notes shown in Figure 3-15 near the top of the drawing. The last step is to add the required text information to the revision block and title block. This includes the drawing title, scale factor, sheet number, drawing number, revision code, description, and date.

The PCB assembly drawing is now complete. Save the drawing and then print out a hardcopy. This is also a good time to save another backup copy of the drawing to floppy disk.

Board Artwork

The artwork required to manufacture the board includes the component legend silkscreen, solder side pattern, and solder mask pattern. As explained in Chapter 1, board manufacturers generally do not want artwork per se, but rather the Gerber photoplotter data for the various artwork layers. Your task will be to generate this data.

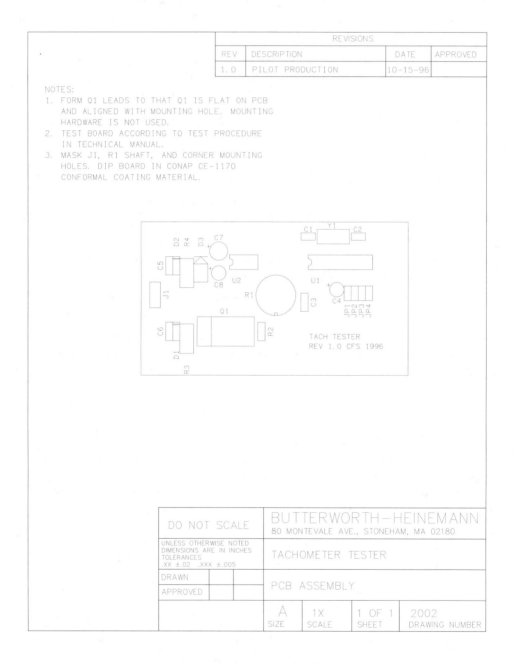

NOTES:
1. FORM Q1 LEADS TO THAT Q1 IS FLAT ON PCB
   AND ALIGNED WITH MOUNTING HOLE. MOUNTING
   HARDWARE IS NOT USED.
2. TEST BOARD ACCORDING TO TEST PROCEDURE
   IN TECHNICAL MANUAL.
3. MASK J1, R1 SHAFT, AND CORNER MOUNTING
   HOLES. DIP BOARD IN CONAP CE-1170
   CONFORMAL COATING MATERIAL.

TACH TESTER
REV 1.0 CFS 1996

DO NOT SCALE	BUTTERWORTH—HEINEMANN			
	80 MONTEVALE AVE., STONEHAM, MA 02180			
UNLESS OTHERWISE NOTED DIMENSIONS ARE IN INCHES TOLERANCES .XX ±.02 .XXX ±.005	TACHOMETER TESTER			
DRAWN	PCB ASSEMBLY			
APPROVED				
	A SIZE	1X SCALE	1 OF 1 SHEET	2002 DRAWING NUMBER

Figure 3-15   Finished PCB Assembly Drawing

AutoCAD Configuration

The AutoPADS utility converts binary plot data files generated by the Autodesk Device Interface (ADI) into Gerber format photoplotter files. Before you can use AutoPADS, you must configure your AutoCAD program for the binary file ADI plot driver. The following instructions are for Release 13, but the same general procedure can also be used for Release 12.

1. Load AutoCAD. Select Configure from the pulldown menu.

2. Select option 5, Configure Plotter, from the Configuration Menu.

3. At the plotter configuration menu, select the option to add a plotter configuration.

4. Next, select AutoCAD file output formats (Pre 4.1).

5. Select the Binary Plotter File output format.

6. Release 13 asks for level 1 or 2 compatibility. AutoPADS supports both levels. Previous AutoCAD releases output data at level 1.

7. AutoCAD asks: Does the plotter have multiple pens? Answer Y (yes).

8. How many pens? Answer 127.

9. Does the plotter have multiple dash line styles? Answer N (no).

10. Is the plotter speed variable? Answer N.

11. Some releases of AutoCAD may ask about multiple pen widths. Answer N.

12. Next you will be asked to specify the maximum plot size and plotter steps per inch. The values given below are appropriate for most applications. For more information, refer to the section on limitations and units.

13. AutoCAD asks: Specify plot size in millimeters? Answer N.

14. Maximum horizontal (X) plot size in inches? Answer 16.

15. Plotter steps per inch in the horizontal (X) direction? Answer 2000.

16. Maximum vertical (Y) plot size in inches? Answer 16.

17. Plotter steps per inch in the vertical (Y) direction? Answer 2000.

18. Do you want to change anything? Answer Y.

19. Skip over the pen and color assignment menu for now.

20. Would you like to calibrate the plotter? Answer N.

21. Size units? Answer I (inches).

22. Plot origin? Answer 0,0.

23. Standard values for plotting sizes. Enter the size or width? Answer MAX.

24. Rotate plots clockwise degrees? Answer 0.

25. Some releases of AutoCAD may ask for a pen width. Answer .005.

26. Adjust area fill for pen width? Answer Y.

27. Remove hidden lines? Answer N.

28. Next, you are asked to specify the scale factor for plotting. Answer by entering 1=1.

29. Finally, enter a description for the plotter configuration. Use a name such as BINARY ADI 2000 DPI.

30. Exit back to the Main Menu and answer Y to keep configuration changes.

AutoCAD is now configured to support a binary ADI plot driver at 2000 DPI resolution with a maximum plot size of 16 × 16 inches.

AutoCAD Limitations

The AutoCAD binary ADI plot driver is the fastest plot driver available. It is also very easy to use. If you follow a few simple rules, you will always obtain photoplots that exactly represent the PCB design that you created in AutoCAD.

The binary ADI plot driver uses 16 bit binary numbers. The total number of plotter steps cannot exceed 32767 in the positive X or Y direction. Plotter steps mean the same thing as DPI on a laser photoplotter. If you select 1000 DPI, the maximum plot size is approximately 32 × 32 inches. At 2000 DPI the maximum plot size decreases to 16 × 16 inches. At 4000 DPI the maximum plot size is only 8 × 8 inches. This is an intrinsic limitation of AutoCAD. Plotting at 2000 DPI gives excellent results for most types of artwork. This allows a 16 × 16 inch plot size that is adequate for all but the largest PCBs.

AutoCAD also is one of the few CAD programs that do not directly associate widths with lines in the drawing. Polylines do have a defined width, but they are plotted by means of stroking (moving the pen back and forth). When you define a pen width (e.g. .005 inch) for plotting, AutoCAD uses the information to calculate the amount of stroking required to fill polylines and other solid areas. If you made the selection to adjust area fill boundaries for pen width during the configuration process, the pen is offset by half its width while stroking polylines and solids.

Please note that the pen widths on the plot menu in AutoCAD only determine how AutoCAD will fill wide polylines. These pen widths **do not** directly control the width of lines. **The pen number is what determines the line width in the actual plotting device.** It is very important to clearly understand this distinction.

AutoCAD Binary ADI Plotting Considerations

Before you proceed, you may want to review the material on plotting in your AutoCAD Reference Manual. To generate a binary ADI plot file from AutoCAD, use the PLOT menu. Next, set up your pen assignments. A color table will be displayed and you will have the option of selecting pen numbers for each color. Pen 127 is used for colors that you don't want to plot (e.g., the green pad display outline). You should always select line type 0 (continuous line). Pen speed is ignored.

After you have completed the pen assignments, you can set up the area you want to plot. In most cases you will want to select the plot EXTENTS option. After you have selected the area of the drawing that you want to plot, you can enter the filename for the plot file. The filename must include the drive and path to the subdirectory that you have created for your plot data.

Once you have properly configured AutoCAD, you can keep current plotting values, such as pen assignments, for subsequent plots. Be careful not to change the adjust area setting (yes) or plot scale (always 1=1).

Plot origin sometimes causes confusion. You should create all your designs with the drawing origin (X=0 and Y=0) at the lower left-hand corner. No entities should be placed at negative X or Y coordinates. The plot origin also should be X=0 and Y=0, which is the default. This will prevent negative X and Y coordinates from appearing in the Gerber data and ensure compatibility with all laser photoplotters.

Gerber Output from AutoPADS

You should read Appendix A for a discussion of Gerber data format and an overview of photoplotting technology. You will usually be sending the converted Gerber data files to a service bureau or board manufacturer for photoplotting. The Gerber format output by AutoPADS is the most commonly used in the industry: 2.4 decimal format, absolute coordinates, inch units, leading zero suppression, and * as the end of block character. Note that 2.4 format means six total digits and four digits after the decimal point. This allows steps as small as .0001 inch.

Aperture Assignments

AutoPADS automatically assigns a Gerber aperture D code for each AutoCAD pen number. AutoCAD pen numbers 1 to 126 are converted to Gerber D codes 11 to 136 (Gerber D codes start at number 10). Pen number 127 is ignored. This is useful for data that you do not want to convert.

Plotting and Conversion Considerations

Traces on the PCB are drawn using AutoCAD polylines with some defined width. Assign pen 1 to all colors used for polylines. Assign a size of .005 inch to pen 1. AutoPADS converts pen 1 to aperture D11 in the Gerber file. D11 could then be assigned the same size of .005 inch when photoplotting the Gerber file. However, slight clear streaks may appear on the photoplotted artwork owing to insufficient overlap of lines in filled areas and wide traces. For this reason, you should assign a .006 inch size for aperture D11. This will result in some overlap and should eliminate any clear streaks in the photoplotted artwork. The photoplotted traces will be .001 inch wider than the AutoCAD polylines. If greater accuracy is required for specialized applications, you can compensate by reducing the width of the polylines .001 inch. For example, if you want precise .013 inch wide photoplotted traces (a common design rule for double sided PCBs), use .012 inch wide polylines. Note that fill mode must be turned on and adjust area fill selected when plotting any polylines or other filled objects.

Solid areas (also called *fills* or *ground planes*) with an irregular shape are often required. The AutoCAD SOLID command is quite versatile for this purpose. The same considerations that apply to polylines apply to solids. They should be drawn in the same color as the polylines on a given layer.

Photoplotted lines include component outlines, cut marks, and text on the PCB. These types of lines are usually photoplotted at .010 inch width. This width gives good results for graphics that are to be silkscreened on the PCB with an epoxy ink. AutoCAD line entities are used for these types of lines. Use the color white for lines. Then assign pen 2 to the color white. AutoPADS converts pen 2 to aperture D12. Assign a .010 inch size to aperture D12 for photoplotting.

Pads are created as AutoCAD blocks. An overview is presented on page 86. More detailed information, including an exercise that involves creating new pads from scratch is presented in the next chapter. In summary, a pad consists of a green display outline and yellow fill pattern. The green display outline shows the actual outer dimension of the pad. This green outline is assigned pen 127, which is ignored by AutoPADS.

Only the yellow pad fill pattern is photoplotted. The dimensions of the fill pattern are adjusted to compensate for the aperture width so that the pad is photoplotted at the correct size. Pen 3 is assigned to the yellow pad fill pattern. AutoPADS converts pen 3 to aperture D13. For a normal pad on the component or solder side artwork layers, assign a size of .020 inch to aperture D13.

Efficient fill patterns as shown on page 86 are not difficult to create. You might be tempted to use AutoCAD's DONUT command. This does not generate an efficient fill pattern. The donut shape is more like an oversized * (asterisk) with a rough outline.

Photoplotting oversized solder mask pads is very easy. Change the pen assignment for the yellow pad fill pattern to pen 4. AutoPADS converts pen 4 to aperture D14. By assigning a larger size to aperture D14, the pads can be photoplotted oversize. For .010 inch oversize pads, use a size of .030 inch for aperture D14. Likewise, if you require any special solder mask clearance areas, you can create solid patterns on the MASK_SOLDER layer.

Generating the Binary ADI Plot Files

Make sure that you have properly configured AutoCAD for the binary ADI plot driver as explained on page 109. Then start AutoCAD and load the TUTOR2 drawing file. For plotting and converting the PCB artwork, use the layer, color, pen, and Gerber D code assignments shown in Table 3-3. The layer combinations will make more sense as you read further.

Table 3-3   Layer Assignments for Single Sided PCB Artwork

ARTWORK	LAYER USAGE	COLOR	PEN	/SIZE	D CODE	/SIZE
SILK_CMP	SILK_COMP	WHITE	2	.01	D12	.01
	OUTLINE	WHITE	2	.01	D12	.01
ART_SOL	TRACE_SOLDER	RED	1	.005	D11	.006
	PADS	YELLOW	3	.02	D13	.02
		GREEN	127	.01	NOT PLOTTED	
	OUTLINE	WHITE	2	.01	D12	.01
MASK_SOL	MASK_SOLDER	WHITE	2	.01	D12	.01
	PADS	YELLOW	4	.02	D14	.03
		GREEN	127	.01	NOT PLOTTED	
	OUTLINE	WHITE	2	.01	D12	.01

Silkscreen Artwork

Silkscreen artwork consists of two AutoCAD layers: SILK_COMP and OUTLINE. Use the LAYER command to turn on these layers. Turn off all the other layers in the drawing. Only the component outlines, silkscreen text including reference designators, and board cut marks should be displayed. All these entities should be white.

Next, plot this silkscreen layer. Make sure fill mode is turned on and you have done a AutoCAD regen. Click on the plot menu, select the 2000 DPI binary ADI plot driver, and set up the required pen assignments. For each color, assign the appropriate pen number and size, as given in Table 3-3. Red and blue are both pen 1 with size .005, white is pen 2 with size .010, yellow is pen 3 with size .020, and green is pen 127 (not converted by AutoPADS, but use size .010). Remember that pen 127 is used for colors that are for display only. Note that not all these pen assignments are immediately used. Make sure you select plot extents and adjust area fill on. Tell AutoCAD to write the plot data to a file. Use the filename SILK_CMP.

Solder Side Artwork

The solder side artwork consists of three AutoCAD layers: TRACE_SOLDER, PADS, and OUTLINE. The TRACE_SOLDER layer contains all the copper traces. The PADS layer contains the pads. Pads are drawn in two colors. Yellow is used for a fill pattern. This is what is photoplotted. Green is used as an outline of the pad for display purposes. The green color is assigned pen number 127 so that it will be ignored by AutoPADS. Use the LAYER command to turn on the TRACE_SOLDER, PADS, and OUTLINE layers. Turn off all other layers in the drawing. Only the green/yellow pads, red solder side traces, and white board cut marks should now be displayed. Plot the solder side artwork. Keep the same pen assignments you previously set up. Make sure that adjust area fill is turned on for all artwork plots. Tell AutoCAD to write the plot data to a file. Use the filename ART_SOL.

Solder Mask Artwork

The solder mask artwork is handled slightly differently. You want the solder mask pads to be .010 inch oversize. This can easily be done with a .010 inch larger aperture to photoplot the pad fill pattern. Solder mask artwork sometimes contains ground planes (solid filled areas). These are also easily handled with the same technique.

The solder mask artwork consists of three AutoCAD layers: MASK_SOLDER, PADS, and OUTLINE. The MASK_SOLDER layer contains any solid areas or special patterns (not used in this tutorial). Use the LAYER command to turn on the PADS and OUTLINE layers. Turn off all other layers in the drawing. Only the green/yellow pads and white board cut marks should now be displayed Plot the solder mask artwork. You will need to change one pen assignment in the color table; assign yellow to pen 4 with size .020. Later, the solder mask pads will be photoplotted oversize. Tell AutoCAD to write the plot data to a file. Use the filename MASK_SOL.

You have now generated binary ADI plot files for the three pieces of PCB artwork. The next step is to use AutoPADS to convert these files to Gerber format.

Running AutoPADS to Generate Gerber Data

AutoCAD will automatically assign a .PLT extension to any binary ADI plot files that you create. When you run AutoPADS, it will assign a .GBR extension to the converted Gerber file. The path and filename are retained. The original AutoCAD plot file will remain unchanged. The new files are written to the same drive and subdirectory.

To run the AutoPADS program, exit to DOS and type:

CD\AUTOPADS<ENTER>

AUTOPADS<ENTER>

The copyright notice screen appears, and you can hit any key to continue and run the conversion program.

Throughout the AutoPADS program, you can navigate the various menu options by pressing the Tab key to go forward or the Shift + Tab keys to go back to the previous choice. When you are prompted for a parameter value or file name, enter the information and then press the Enter key. When you "tab" to menu options such as OK (means continue) or QUIT (stop program), the selected menu option will become highlighted. You can then execute the menu option by pressing the Enter key.

ADI Resolution Setup

This screen prompts you for the ADI resolution in steps per unit. The default is 2000 DPI. The value you enter must be the same as that for which you configured AutoCAD.

Binary ADI Plot Filename Entry

The filename entry screen will prompt you for the name of the AutoCAD binary ADI plot file that you are going to convert. You can specify a drive and path as part of the filename, just as you would with any other DOS command. But you must not include an extension. The program assumes the extension .PLT for the AutoCAD file and uses the same drive, path, and name with a .GBR extension for the Gerber output file it creates.

After you have entered the filename, the conversion process will start. During the conversion process, you can stop the program and return to the DOS prompt by pressing the Esc key. Any partially converted GBR file will be deleted. Please note that the Esc key works only while the conversion screen is displayed.

When the conversion is completed, the number of Gerber draws that were processed are displayed. Note that AutoPADS outputs only Gerber draw commands since these are the only kind of data found in the AutoCAD binary ADI plot file. Solid patterns such as PCB pads and targets are not converted into Gerber flash commands as is done in most PCB design software. AutoCAD automatically fills these solids with many stroked lines (these become Gerber draws), just as it does with a conventional pen plotter.

After the conversion is completed, you can select one of two options. You can CONTINUE to convert another file or you can QUIT the program.

AutoPADS Error Messages

If an error occurs, AutoPADS will display an appropriate error message. Most of the error messages are self-explanatory. The most common errors relate to entry of improper drive, path, filenames, or printer off-line. Remember that the path is relative to the subdirectory from which AutoPADS is running. Thus if AutoPADS is running from the C:\AUTOPADS subdirectory and the file that you want to convert, for example SILK_CMP.PLT, is loaded into the C:\TUTOR2 subdirectory, you must enter C:\TUTOR2\SILK_CMP on the entry screen.

AutoPADS may not run correctly if memory resident programs or print/plot spoolers are loaded. The program is not intended to be run from within AutoCAD either as a menu selection or by using the SHELL command. You must quit AutoCAD (or any other program) before running AutoPADS.

Converting the Plot Files with AutoPADS

Run AutoPADS and convert the three AutoCAD binary ADI files that you created (SILK_CMP.PLT, ART_SOL.PLT, and MASK_SOL.PLT). Use the default ADI resolution (2000 DPI). When you are finished, exit AutoPADS and use the DOS DIR command to check the files in your TUTOR2 subdirectory. You should see the three original .PLT files and three new .GBR files. These are your artwork files.

Sending Files to a Service Bureau

Now that your first design is completed, you may want to send the files to a service bureau or PCB manufacturer. If you have a company with which you already do business, you might be able to persuade them to plot the files on a trial basis. If not, service bureaus that offer Gerber photoplotting service are located in most major metropolitan areas.

Files can be transferred on floppy disk or on-line via modem to an electronic bulletin board system (BBS). Most service bureaus and PCB manufacturers maintain a 24 hour BBS with a dedicated phone line. For on-line transfer, you will require communications software. PROCOMM PLUS (by Quarterdeck Corporation, 13160 Mindanao Way, Marina del Rey, CA 90292, Phone: 310-309-3700) is highly recommended and widely used for this purpose. A communications protocol such as ZMODEM is used within the communications software to assure error-free file transfer. ZMODEM automatically detects and corrects any errors.

The PCB manufacturer will require the files listed in Table 3-4.

Table 3-4   Files Required for PCB Manufacturing

FILENAME	DESCRIPTION
SILK_CMP.GBR	Top side legend silkscreen artwork
ART_SOL.GBR	Solder side artwork
MASK_SOL.GBR	Back side solder mask artwork
DRILL.PLT or DRILL.GBR	Drill detail drawing
DRILL.CNC	Excellon drill data and tool header
README.DOC	Text file including information on apertures and the Gerber format

If you are having a service bureau plot the artwork, the drill detail drawing and Excellon drill data files can be omitted.

Drill Detail Drawing File

The PCB manufacturer requires the information on the drill detail drawing. In most cases this drawing is electronically transferred along with the Gerber artwork and Excellon NC drill data.

Most PCB manufacturers can accept the drill detail drawing in HPGL or Gerber format. Not very many companies will accept AutoCAD drawing files (DWG or DXF). Check with your manufacturer to find out what format they prefer.

HPGL is the original data format used by Hewlett-Packard pen plotters. There is also a newer HPGL/2 version, but this is not widely accepted and therefore not recommended. To generate an HPGL file for your drill detail drawing, you must first configure AutoCAD for a Hewlett-Packard plotter. Configure AutoCAD for a model 7580 plotter. This is a large 22 × 34 inch plotter, so any conceivable drill detail drawing should fit within the available plot area. Start AutoCAD, load the drill detail drawing, and use the PLOT command. Select the 7580 plotter device. Pen assignments are not critical. You can select pen 1 for all colors and use a .01 inch pen width. Next, select the Plot to File option. You can specify a filename, such as DRILL.PLT. AutoCAD automatically assigns the .PLT extension to all plot files.

The other option is to generate Gerber data for your drill detail drawing. Follow the same basic procedure as for the silkscreen artwork, except use the layers appropriate for the drill detail drawing (i.e., DRILL, OUTLINE, and TITLEBLOCK). Plot binary ADI data to a file. Use the filename DRILL.PLT. Then use AutoPADS to convert this file to Gerber format. In this case, you would include the Gerber file DRILL.GBR with the data submitted to the PCB manufacturer.

PCB README.DOC File

The README.DOC file is an ASCII text file that contains important information about the data that you are sending to the service bureau or PCB manufacturer. You can use a text editor or word-processing software in non-document mode to create the README.DOC file. EDIT.COM, the text editor supplied with DOS is ideal for this purpose. If you use a Windows program such as Microsoft Word, use a non-proportional font such as Courier or set tabs so that text will line up in columns. Make sure you save the file in ASCII text only format.

A sample README.DOC file is in the TUTOR2 subdirectory on the floppy disk included with this book. The contents of the file are listed on the following page. You can use this as a guideline for creating your own README.DOC file.

PCB ARTWORK DATA README FILE:
    PCB NAME: TACHOMETER TESTER
    REV CODE: 1.0
    PART NUMBER: 7100-1110-010
    ZIP FILE: TUTOR2.ZIP

SERVICES REQUIRED:
    FABRICATE 10 PROTOTYPE BOARDS WITH
    1 WEEK TURNAROUND. SHIP UPS RED.
    CALL FOR PURCHASE ORDER BEFORE
    PROCEEDING.

CONTACT:
    CHRIS SCHROEDER
    BUTTERWORTH-HEINEMANN
    80 MONTEVALE AVE.
    STONEHAM, MA 02180
    PH: 617-555-5555

DATA FILES:

FILENAME	DESCRIPTION
SILK_CMP.GBR	TOP SIDE LEGEND SILKSCREEN ARTWORK
ART_SOL.GBR	SOLDER SIDE ARTWORK
MASK_SOL.GBR	SOLDER MASK ARTWORK
DRILL.PLT	DRILL DETAIL DRAWING (HPGL)
DRILL.CNC	EXCELLON FORMAT N/C DRILL
	DATA WITH TOOL SIZE HEADER

GERBER FORMAT NOTES:
    ENGLISH (INCH) UNITS
    ABSOLUTE COORDINATES
    XX.XXXX (2.4) DIGIT FORMAT
    LEADING ZERO SUPPRESSION
    * END OF BLOCK CHARACTER
    M02* END OF PLOT

APERTURE LIST AND NOTES:
    POSITIONS ARE GERBER D-CODES. ALL
    APERTURES ARE ROUND WITH DIAMETERS
    IN MILS (I.E. 50 MILS = .05 INCH)

POSITION	SIZE
11	6
12	10
13	20
14	30

Compressing Files with PKZIP

Since Gerber files can get quite large and multiple files are required for a given board design, general practice is to compress all the required files into a single file with file compression software. The PKZIP utilities are the industry standard for file compression. If you do not already have the PKZIP utilities, a shareware version is included on the floppy disk supplied with this book. The filename is PK204G.EXE. This is a self-extracting file. Refer to appendix D for more details, including shareware license and usage restrictions. Load the PKZIP utilities into a UTILS subdirectory on your hard drive. You can do this by copying the PK204G.EXE file into the UTILS subdirectory and then running it to extract the individual PKZIP utilities and documentation. Make sure that your PC's path statement includes the UTILS subdirectory.

The compressed file that contains all the data files is called an archive (or ZIP) file and is assigned a .ZIP extension. When the service bureau or PCB manufacturer receives a ZIP file on floppy disk or on their BBS, they assume that it was compressed with PKZIP. They will decompress the ZIP file to recover the individual files. Next, they will look for a text file with a name like README.DOC that contains further information about the job.

A convenient approach to generating the ZIP file is to load all the required files listed in Table 3-3 into a temporary subdirectory and then run the PKZIP program from that subdirectory. For example, if you loaded all the files in Table 3-4 into a subdirectory named TEMP, you would generate the ZIP file by typing:

CD\TEMP<ENTER>

PKZIP -A TUTOR2.ZIP *.*<ENTER>

This instructs PKZIP to "add" all files in the TEMP subdirectory to an archive file named TUTOR2.ZIP.

Conclusion

You have now learned the basic techniques for designing a PCB with AutoCAD, generating manufacturing data, and sending this data to a PCB manufacturer. The next chapters extend these basic techniques to double sided plated through hole boards and surface mount technology.

4

Double Sided PCB Design

In the previous chapter, you learned how to design a single sided PCB using AutoCAD and to generate the required manufacturing documentation and artwork. The basic techniques you learned for a single sided PCB can easily be extended for the more widely used double sided PTH boards. In this chapter you will design a double sided PCB. You will also learn how to create pad and part blocks required for new components that are not in an existing library.

Double sided PTH boards account for about one half of the total square footage of boards manufactured worldwide. Double sided PTH boards can be found in almost every imaginable type of automotive, computer, consumer, industrial, and even military product. Since two layers are available for routing and via holes can connect traces between layers, signal traces can easily cross over one another without the use of jumpers. Much higher component densities can be achieved on a double sided PTH board than on a single sided board.

Double sided PTH boards are generally manufactured in facilities with a relatively high level of automation. Screen printed plating resists are still used, but most resists are now photoimaged with a dry film or liquid photoresist. The photoimaging process allows a much finer trace width. All commercial facilities can manufacture boards using a 25 mil grid and 13 mil trace design rule. Most facilities can accommodate 16.7 mil grid and 8 mil trace design rules without any significant cost penalties. Density limits for these design rules are given in Table 1-1 on page 24.

Components on double sided PTH boards are securely supported by the hole barrels, which act like metal rivets. These boards can be used in severe environments where they are subjected to high levels of vibration and shock.

Introduction to the Tutorial Design

The schematic for the double sided PCB design tutorial is shown in Figure 4-1. The tachometer calibrator is for an improved version of the simple tachometer tester from the previous tutorial.

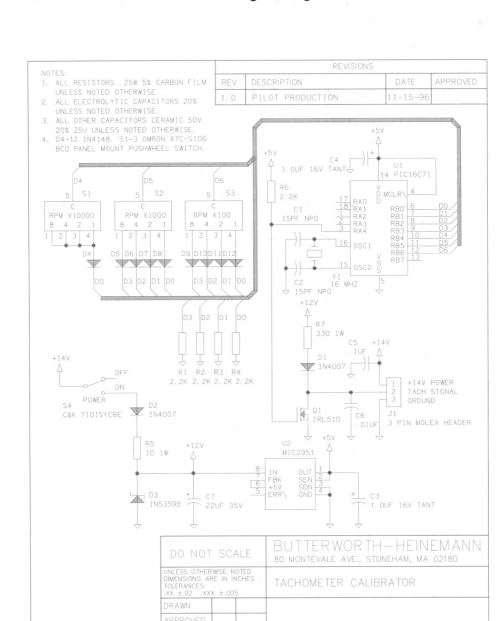

Figure 4-1   Schematic for the Double Sided PCB Tutorial

The tachometer calibrator is a handheld device used to calibrate the tachometer in a race car. Three pushwheel switches allow setting a precise rpm level from 100 to 19,900 rpm in 100 rpm increments. The unit is enclosed in a small die cast metal housing. The required board outline is given in Figure 4-2. The board mounts on four standoffs cast into the housing. A wire harness connects to a three pin Molex connector, J1.

The front panel controls include the three pushwheel switches and a power on/off switch. Dimensions and required mounting locations are given in Figure 4-2. The dimensions represent the insertion points of the part blocks. In the real world, the PCB designer would probably have to calculate these dimensions based on a front panel drawing. This is an important part of the planning process required before starting on the actual PCB design and it is usually not a trivial task. Note that only an approximate mounting location is given for the Molex connector. The exact location is left to the discretion of the PCB designer.

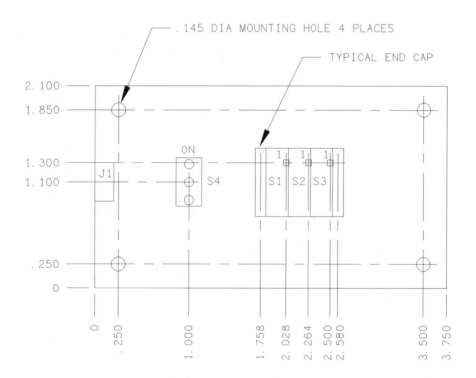

Figure 4-2   Board Outline for the Tutorial PCB

QTY	REFERENCE DESIGNATOR	DESCRIPTION	VENDOR PART NUMBER	PCB BLOCK
2	C1,C2	15PF 50V 5% NP0 CERAMIC CAP	PANASONIC ECC-F1H150JC	CAP_10LS
1	C6	.01UF 50V 20% Z5U CERAMIC CAP	PHILLIPS A103M15Z5UFVVWA	CAP_40LS
1	C5	.1UF 50V 20% Z5U CERAMIC CAP	PHILLIPS A104M15Z5UFVVWN	CAP_40LS
2	C3,C4	1.0UF 16V 10% TANTALUM CAP	PANASONIC ECS-F1CE105K	ECAP_10LS20A
1	C7	22UF 35V 20% RADIAL ELEC CAP	PANASONIC ECE-A1VU220	ECAP_10LS25A
2	D1,D2	1N4007 DIODE		D_40LSA
9	D4,D5,D6,D7,D8,D9,D10,D11 D12	1N4148 DIODE		D_40LS
1	D3	1N5359B DIODE		D_50LS15
1	J1	3 PIN HEADER .10 CENTERS FRICTION LOCK	MOLEX 22-23-2031	SIP_3P
1	Q1	IRL510 MOSFET	IR	TO220_DNA
1	R5	10 1W 5% CARBON FILM RESISTOR		R_60LS
1	R7	330 1W 5% CARBON FILM RESISTOR		R_60LS
5	R1,R2,R3,R4,R6	2.2K .25W 5% CARBON FILM RESISTOR		R_40LS
1	S4	SPDT SWITCH	C&K 7101SYCBE	SW_SPDT
3	S1,S2,S3	BCD PUSHWHEEL SWITCH	OMRON A7C-S106	SW_BCD_A7C
1		END CAP PAIR FOR PUSHWHEEL SWITCH	OMRON A7C-1M	SW_END_A7C
1	U2	MIC2951 IC	MICREL	DIP_8
1	U1	PIC16C71 IC W/ TACH CALIBRATOR REV 1.0 FIRMWARE	MICROCHIP	DIP_18
1	Y1	16 MHZ HC-49/US CRYSTAL	ECS-160-20-4	XTAL_HC18UP
1		TACHOMETER CALIBRATOR PCB REV 1.0		
4		.145 DIA MOUNTING HOLE		PAD_250R145

Figure 4-3   Bill of Materials for the Tutorial PCB

A bill of materials for the tachometer calibrator is given in Figure 4-3. The bill of materials as supplied to the PCB designer would typically include the first four columns: quantity, reference designator, part description, and vendor part number. The PCB designer adds the last column, which gives the names of the AutoCAD blocks representing the PCB pattern of each part. The original bill of materials would include only parts actually installed on the board. The PCB designer adds additional items such as jumpers, mounting holes, and spare component patterns.

As the first step in the design tutorial, calculate the CE, useable board area, and board density (see Chapter 1, page 23).

CE is calculated by adding up all the device pins. You can use the bill of materials listing or schematic. Do not include the mounting holes. A simple trick is to first add up all the two lead components (such as capacitors, diodes, jumpers, and resistors) and multiply by two. Then add up all the three lead components (transistors, pots) and multiply by three. Then add any remaining components such as ICs and switches. You should come up with a total of 104 pins for the tutorial design, or 7.4 CE.

The useable board area does not include the area taken up by the mounting holes. These holes are located .25 inch from the board edges. General practice is to use large-diameter pads for all mounting holes and then connect these pads to ground. The only exceptions are products with which high voltage or other safety concerns dictate an isolated board. 6-32 hardware is commonly used for board mounting. A .25 inch pad and .145 inch diameter hole size is a good match for a standard 6-32 screw head.

To allow for the mounting hole pads, an area of .375 × .375 inch (.14 square inch) becomes unusable at each of the four corners of the board. Given the overall board dimensions of 3.75 × 2.1 inch, the useable board area is reduced to 7.3 square inch. The calculated board density is just under 1.0 square inch per CE. This is greater than the suggested minimum of .70 given in Table 1-1 for the 25 mil grid and 13 mil trace design rule. You should be able to comfortably place and interconnect the parts within the available board area using this design rule.

Structured Design Approach

The layer assignments used for the double sided PCB are the same as those introduced in the previous chapter. Refer back to the material on pages 83-91 in Chapter 3. For this tutorial, you will use the same layer assignments as given in Table 3-1 on page 83. The only difference is that the TRACE_COMP and VIAS layers are used for the double sided board in this tutorial, whereas these layers were not required for the single sided board in the previous tutorial.

Double sided boards generally do not require two pieces of solder mask artwork. If the pads are the same on both sides, a single piece of solder mask artwork is used for both sides of the board. In this case the solder mask artwork is created from the PADS layer as with a single sided board. Recall that if special artwork features are not required on the solder mask, the MASK_COMP and MASK_SOLDER layers are not required and only the PADS layer is used to create the solder mask artwork.

Starting the Tutorial Exercise

This tutorial exercise shows you how to use AutoCAD to design a moderate density double sided PTH board and generate the required manufacturing documentation and artwork. Your task will be to design a PCB for the tachometer calibrator schematic shown in Figure 4-1 using the board outline shown in Figure 4-2 and the bill of materials in Figure 4-3. You may want to run copies of these figures and keep them handy for reference.

Files and utility programs required for the tutorial exercise are included on the floppy disk supplied with this book. The design-related files for this tutorial are in the subdirectory TUTOR3. FORMAT_A.DWG is an A size drawing format. PCB1_LIB.DWG is the PCB parts library. File conversion utilities required to generate Gerber and Excellon format data are in the AUTOPADS subdirectory. The use of these utilities was explained in detail in Chapter 3 on pages 99-117.

For now, create a TUTOR3 subdirectory on your hard drive. Copy the files from the TUTOR3 subdirectory on the floppy disk to the TUTOR3 subdirectory on your hard drive.

The floppy disk supplied with the book also contains a popular shareware text display utility, LIST.COM, and a public domain font file, MONOSI.SHX. If you have already loaded these, you can skip ahead. If not, refer to page 92 in Chapter 3 for further instructions.

Start AutoCAD and open the A size drawing format, FORMAT_A.DWG. The drawing border, title block, and revision block will be displayed on the screen. Use the INSERT command to insert the file PCB1_LIB.DWG. You need to type in the full filename. This loads all the required PCB pad and part blocks. The insertion location is not important, since PCB1_LIB.DWG does not contain any drawing entities that will appear on the screen. Next, use the SAVE AS command from the FILE menu and save the drawing as TUTOR3.DWG. Note that AutoCAD automatically assigns the .DWG suffix. This leaves your original drawing format file FORMAT_A.DWG unchanged. All subsequent editing is done with TUTOR3.DWG.

At this point, the drawing file is set up and you are ready to start on the design. Most designs will require one or more new pads and parts that are not available in the library. You must create a new part block for S4, the SPDT power on/off switch, since this part is not in the PCB1_LIB library. Figure 4-4 gives dimensions for the C&K 7101SYCBE part used for S4. This figure is typical of what you would find on a manufacturer's data sheet.

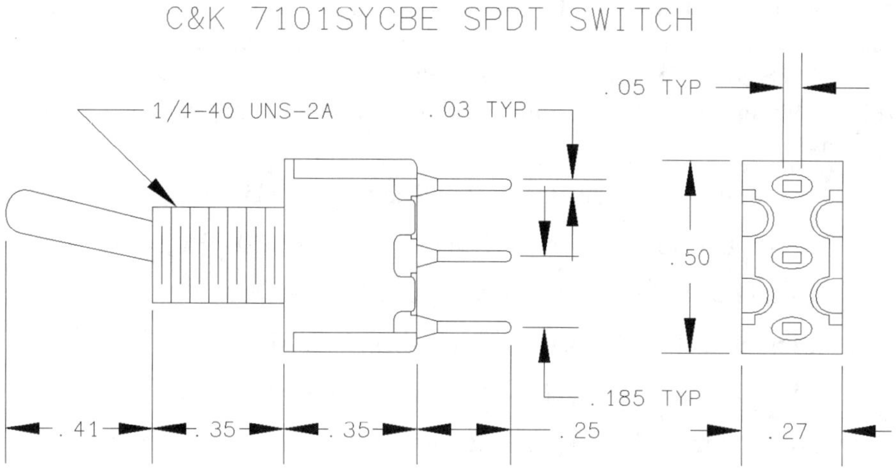

C&K 7101SYCBE SPDT SWITCH

Figure 4-4   Dimensions for C&K SPDT Switch

Rules for Lead Spacing, Hole Diameter, and Pad Size

Certain rules and standards exist for component lead spacing, hole diameters, and pad sizes.

Lead spacing is given on the manufacturer's data sheet for most connectors, ICs, front panel components, and radial lead components. A fixed lead spacing is specified by the manufacturer since these devices do not have leads that require bending prior to insertion in the PCB.

Axial lead components such as resistors require lead bending prior to insertion. Use the following simple formula to find the minimum lead spacing (inch units):

Minimum Lead Spacing = Part Body Length + .120

Use this formula to calculate the minimum lead spacing and then round up to the nearest .025 or .05 inch grid value. For example, a common .25 watt resistor has a body length of about .26 inch. The minimum lead spacing would be .38, which rounds up to .40 inch. This simple formula can be used for most low-power components when the lead diameter is less than .05 inch. For larger components, use the following formula and again round up to the nearest grid value:

Minimum Lead Spacing = Part Body Length + (8 × Lead Diameter)

The hole diameter affects insertion and soldering operations. If the hole is too small, insertion will be difficult, and automatic insertion equipment may fail. A small hole results in a tight fit around the lead. In an extreme case, solder may not wick into the hole. If the hole is excessively large, solder may also fail to wick into the hole. Minimum and maximum hole diameters (inch) are given by the following formulas:

Minimum Hole Diameter = Lead Diameter + .005 + Hole Size Tolerance

Maximum Hole Diameter = Lead Diameter + .020 – Hole Size Tolerance

With a typical finished hole size tolerance of ±.003 inch, these formulas reduce to:

Minimum Hole Diameter = Lead Diameter + .008

Maximum Hole Diameter = Lead Diameter + .017

Thus, a hole size range is acceptable for any given lead diameter. In practice, a limited number of different hole sizes are used to accommodate a wide range of lead sizes. For example, .037, .045, and .062 inch holes would accommodate any lead diameter from .020 to .054 inch.

Many component leads have square or rectangular cross sections. In this case, the diameter of circle that is circumscribed around the lead is used to calculate the required hole size. The diameter of the circumscribed circle is the same as the diagonal across the lead. This can easily be calculated by using the Pythagorean theorem, as shown in Figure 4-5 for the case of the C&K switch lead. The .03 × .05 inch switch lead is circumscribed by a circle of .058 inch.

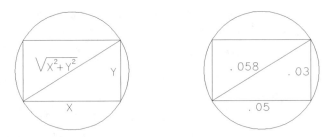

Figure 4-5   Switch Lead and Circumscribed Circle

Holes smaller than given by the formula on the preceding page can be used with square and rectangular leads, as long as the hole diameter (with allowance for tolerance) exceeds that of the circumscribed circle. Even if the corners of the lead contact the hole, large spaces are still present on the sides to allow solder wicking. For example, .037-.041 inch diameter holes are commonly used for parts with .025 inch square pins, which includes wire wrap sockets and many common connectors. For a typical finished hole size tolerance of ±.003 inch, the minimum hole diameter is given by:

$$\text{Minimum Hole Diameter} = \text{Diameter of Circumscribed Circle} + .003$$

Significantly larger hole diameters should be avoided. Oversized holes are more readily tolerated on axial lead components, since the part body rests on the board and the leads are usually clinched. If a radial lead part such as a switch is inserted into oversized holes, the part may not stay straight during soldering. Bending the part to straighten it after soldering is not recommended, as the leads may crack.

The minimum hole diameter for the C&K switch lead would be .061 inch (.058 +.003). Round this up to .062 inch diameter.

The minimum pad size is a function of the hole diameter. Round pads represent the worst case as only a thin annular ring remains once the hole is drilled. Standard IPC-D-300G for Class B (standard) calls for a minimum .010 inch annular ring on unplated holes and a minimum .006 inch annular ring on PTH. For example, a via with a .031 inch diameter hole should have a minimum pad diameter of .051 inch. The C&K switch would require pads with a minimum diameter of .082 inch (.062 + 2 × .010). No limitation exists as far as a maximum pad size, other than clearance to adjacent features.

Since the C&K switch will be soldered to the PCB and secured to the front panel by means of the switch bushing, significant stress can be expected on the switch leads, and large pads are highly desirable. The lead spacing is given as .185 inch. Pads with a .15 inch diameter will provide good support and adequate clearance.

Creating a New Pad Block

Verify that the drawing contains the required layers. Figure 4-6 shows the minimum layers for pad and part blocks. These layers should already exist, since you loaded the PCB1_LIB.DWG library. For a detailed explanation of how these layers are used, refer to the material in Chapter 3 starting on page 83. The procedure for creating a new pad block is explained on pages 86-89. Review this material before proceeding.

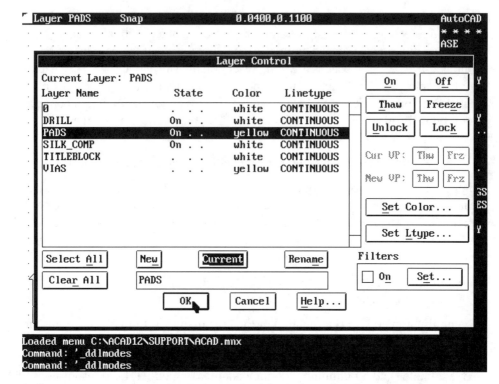

Figure 4-6   AutoCAD Layers for Pad and Part Blocks

Turn on all the layers shown in Figure 4-6 and set PADS as the current layer. Set the grid to .01 inch and the snap to .005 inch. Set the text style to MONOSI with a height of .065 inch. Set ATTDISP on. Zoom into a small area so that the grid dots are clearly visible and you can easily move the cursor in .005 snap increments. Set the UCS origin to a grid dot near the center of the screen. Use this origin point as the center of the pad.

Start by drawing the green pad outline. Refer to Figure 4-7. Use the CIRCLE command to draw a .15 inch diameter (.075 inch radius) circle, then change the color to green. Next, draw the yellow fill pattern. The outline of the yellow fill pattern must be offset by half the pen width. Since a .02 inch wide pen is used for plotting the yellow fill pattern, the radius of the yellow outline circle must be .065 inch (.075 actual pad radius – .02 pen width/2). Draw a yellow circle with .065 inch radius.

Complete the fill pattern by drawing the internal fill lines. These lines are spaced .015 inch apart, resulting in an overlap of .005 inch. The internal fill lines should extend to within .01 inch of the yellow outline circle.

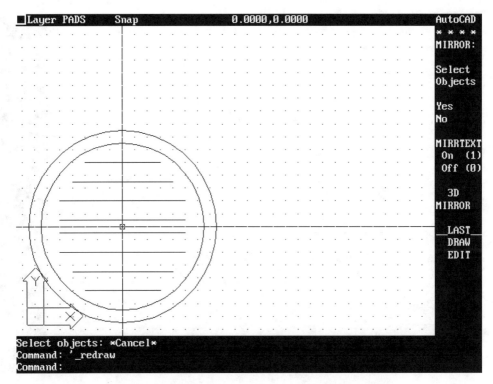

Figure 4-7   New Pad with Outline and Fill Pattern

Start at the top and draw the first three fill lines. The third fill line will be near the center of the pad. Use the MIRROR command. Select the three fill lines and mirror them about the X axis crossing through the center of the pad. Select the "do not delete" option to retain the original three lines. You should now have the fill pattern as it appears in Figure 4-7. Since pads are usually symmetrical, using the MIRROR command saves time in drawing fill patterns. Note that the two fill lines near the center of the pad are spaced only .01 inch apart. Having fill lines closer together than the nominal .015 inch spacing is not a problem. The PADS layer is now complete.

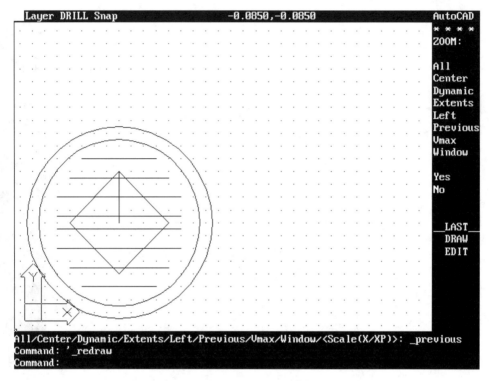

Figure 4-8   New Pad with Drill Symbol Added

The next step is to draw the drill symbol and create the drill size attribute. These entities appear on the DRILL layer. Set DRILL as the current layer. Draw the drill symbol as shown in Figure 4-8. The drill symbol is drawn to fit within a .08 × .08 inch box. This reduces the likelihood that drill symbols will overlap, even on dense boards. Note the line going to the center of the pad. Drill symbols should always have some feature to identify the center. While clearly established industry standards do not exist for drill symbols, five common symbols are shown in the drill table in Figure 3-14. If more symbols are required, a common practice is to use the cross (+) symbol in conjunction with an identifying letter such as A, B, C, and so on. The cross identifies the pad center and the letter is placed to the immediate right just above the centerline of the cross, for example +[A].

Before creating the drill size attribute, make sure that the text style has been correctly set to MONOSI and .065 inch height and that ATTDISP is set on. Use the ATTDEF command to create the drill set attribute definition. Select the invisible and preset options. Use SIZE for both the attribute tag and prompt.

Enter the selected hole size, .062, as the default attribute value. Use the center of the pad as the starting point for the attribute text. When you are finished, the pad with drill symbol and size attribute should appear as in Figure 4-9. Note that the attribute tag (SIZE) appears, not the default attribute value.

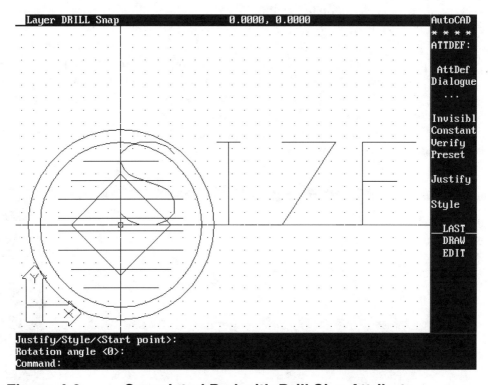

Figure 4-9   Completed Pad with Drill Size Attribute

The final step is to create the actual pad block. Leave DRILL as the current layer and make sure all other layers are on. Use the BLOCK command. Enter the pad block name, PAD_150R62. This follows the naming convention introduced in Chapter 3 for a .15 inch diameter round pad with a .062 inch diameter drill hole size. Select the center of the pad as the insertion base point. Then select all the entities that make up the pad. Your first pad block is now complete. This pad block will be nested within the part block that you will create for the switch.

Creating a New Part Block

The procedure for creating a new part block was explained in detail on pages 89-91 in the previous chapter. Please take a few minutes to carefully review this material before proceeding.

Make sure you have set up the required AutoCAD layers as shown in Figure 4-6. Turn all layers on and set SILK_COMP as the current layer. You will now work at a larger scale, so set the grid to .1 inch and the snap to .025 inch. Make sure the text style is still set to MONOSI with a height of .065 inch. Set ATTDISP to normal. This turns off the display of invisible attributes. Zoom into a small area so that the grid dots are clearly visible and you can easily move the cursor in .025 snap increments. Set the UCS origin to a grid dot near the center of the screen. Use this origin point as the center of the first pad. It will later be used as the insertion base point of the part block.

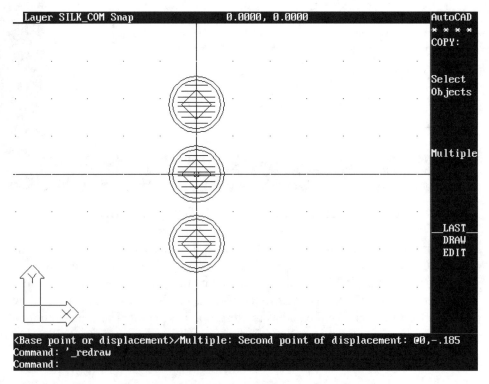

Figure 4-10   New Part with Pad Blocks Inserted

For round front panel controls such as toggle switches, LEDs, phone jacks, and potentiometers, the center of the shaft or panel opening is generally used as the insertion base point. For other devices such as ICs, the part is oriented with pin 1 at the top. Pin 1 is used as the insertion base point. Pin 1 is generally on the left side. Discrete two lead parts such as capacitors, diodes, and resistors are oriented horizontally along the X axis, and the left pin is used as the insertion base point.

Refer to Figure 4-10. Start by inserting the three pads. Use the PAD_150R62 pad block you just finished creating. Use the INSERT command. Place the first pad at the center origin point. Once you have inserted the first pad, you can use the COPY command for the remaining two pads. Copy the center pad and use displacements of ±.185 inch along the Y axis (@0,.185 and @0,−.185). The three pads along with drill symbols should now appear on the screen as shown in Figure 4-10.

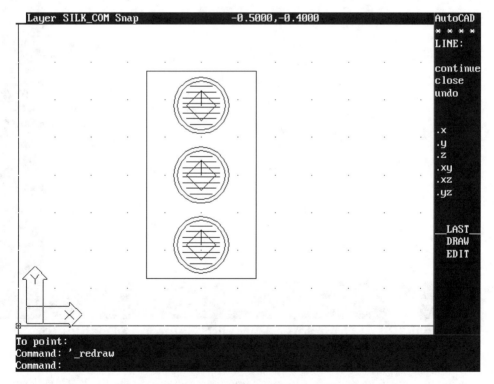

Figure 4-11   New Part with Component Outline

The next step is to draw the component outline as shown in Figure 4-11. Make sure that SILK_COMP is set as the current layer. The actual switch outline dimensions are given as .27 inch wide and .5 inch high in Figure 4-4.

Good practice dictates keeping the component outline on a .025 grid. Component outlines can be drawn slightly larger, but must never be smaller than the actual part dimensions. To stay on grid, the outline width must be increased to .3 inch. If the .5 inch dimendsion were used for the outline height, the outline would pass through the upper and lower pads. Good practice dictates keeping the component outline clear of any pads. If the board was manufactured with epoxy ink silkscreened onto a pad, some of the ink could wick into the PTH barrels and cause serious soldering problems. To stay clear of the pads, the switch outline height is increased to .55 inch. Draw the switch outline on the SILK_COMP layer as shown in Figure 4-11.

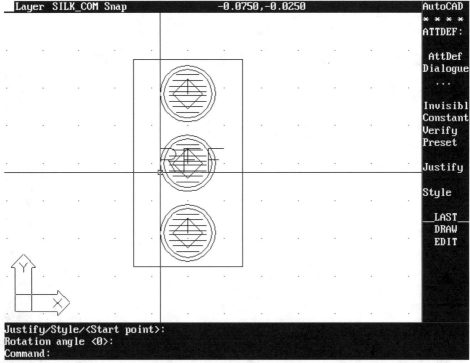

Figure 4-12   Completed Part with Reference Designator

The next step is to create the reference designator attribute. The reference designator attribute appears with the component outline on the SILK_COMP layer. Use the ATTDEF command to create the reference designator attribute definition. Select the visible options. Note that the reference designator attributes is **not** preset as was the case for the drill size attribute. Use REF for both the attribute tag and prompt. Use SW? as the default attribute value. Since the attribute is not preset, the default value will be displayed and you will be prompted for a new value whenever you insert the part block. Select a starting point for the attribute text so that it is centered in the component outline as shown in Figure 4-12. Note that the reference designator attribute will be moved outside the component outline and properly oriented after the part block has been inserted on the board. Letting the reference designator overlap the center pad does not create a problem during the initial part block definition.

The final step is to create the actual part block. Leave SILK_COMP as the current layer and make sure all other layers are on. Use the BLOCK command. Enter the part block name, SW_SPDT. Select the previously set origin point (center of the middle pad) as the insertion base point. Then select all the entities that make up the part.

Your first part block is now complete and you are ready to continue the design process with the component placement. This is also a good time to save a backup copy of the drawing to floppy disk. You should make a backup copy whenever a major stage in the design process has been completed.

Setting Up Layers

Open TUTOR3.DWG and then use the LAYER command to define any required layers. These layers are listed in Table 4-1. Most of these layers should already exist, since you started with the drawing format file FORMAT_A.DWG and then loaded the PCB1_LIB.DWG library.

Table 4-1   Required AutoCAD Layers

LAYER NAME	COLOR
SILK_COMP	WHITE
TRACE_COMP	BLUE
TRACE_SOLDER	RED
PADS	YELLOW
VIAS	YELLOW
OUTLINE	WHITE
DRILL	WHITE
ASSEMBLY	WHITE
TITLEBLOCK	WHITE

Drawing the Board Outline

Use the LAYER command to set OUTLINE as the current layer. Set all layers to *on* except DRILL and ASSEMBLY. Use the ATTDISP command to set attribute display to normal. This inhibits display of invisible attributes, such as drill hole size. Use the GRID and SNAP commands to select a .1 inch grid and .025 inch snap.

Starting from a grid point, draw the board outline as shown in Figure 4-13 using the dimensions given in Figure 4-2. The outline consists of cut marks at each corner of the board. The length of the cut marks is not critical. General practice is to make the cut marks about .1 to .25 inch long.

Next, use the UCS and ORIGIN commands to set the origin point for the drawing to the lower left hand corner of the board. This will facilitate subsequent component insertion and dimensioning.

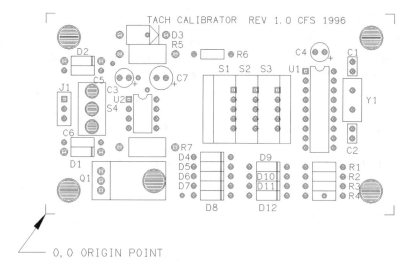

Figure 4-13   Board Outline and Component Placement

Placing Components

Set SILK_COMP as the current layer. First, place the components that have defined locations. Refer to Figures 4-1, 4-2, and 4-3. The mounting holes, J1, S1-4, and the switch endcaps have defined locations.

Keeping track of your work is an important part of the design process. Use a red pencil to mark off components on the schematic and bill of materials as you place them on the board.

Use the INSERT command to place the mounting holes. The part block name is PAD_250R145. Since the origin point is set the same as in Figure 4-2, you can directly enter the coordinates for the mounting holes. The mounting holes do not require rotation or scaling, so accept the default values. Note that pads such as those used for mounting holes and vias do not have reference designators. Parts that do not have an electrical function, such as the switch end caps, are also defined without reference designators.

Next insert J1, S1-4, and the switch end caps. Use the part block names listed on the bill of materials in Figure 4-3. The exact location of J1 is not critical. Use Figure 4-13 as a rough guide. Unless a precise location is required, always place components on grid. Use the .1 inch grid for initial component placement. After inserting a component you can always use the MOVE or ROTATE commands to change the location or orientation. After you insert the component, AutoCAD will prompt for the reference designator attribute; enter J1.

The switch end caps represent a special case. The OMRON pushwheel switches, like most panel mounted thumbwheel or pushwheel switches, snap together in a row. The end caps snap on each end of the switch row. The end caps do not have any pins or PCB mounting tabs, but room must be allotted for them on the board so that they do not interfere with other components.

The pushwheel switches are defined with pin 1 as the insertion point. The end caps are defined with an insertion point that lines up with pin 1 on an adjacent switch. The dimensions given on Figure 4-2 are the coordinates of these insertion points. Note that the OMRON switches are metric parts. This is why some of the switch coordinates in Figure 4-2 on not on grid. Only pin 1 of S3 is on grid. When traces are routed to metric parts with pins off grid, the general technique is stay on grid and end each trace at a grid location closest to the center of the pad. Avoid running traces off grid.

The C&K toggle switch S4 is defined with the center pin (also centerline of the mounting bushing) as the insertion point. Note that Figure 4-2 shows the ON position at the top. It is customary to orient toggle switches so that the switch handle is up when a function is turned on. However, the internal construction of all toggle switches is such that a connection is made to the pin opposite the handle. The pin corresponding to ON is the bottom pin. The author has lost count of how many prototype boards he has seen where the PCB designer made a mistake in this area.

Finish the component placement by placing the remaining components, again using Figure 4-13 as a rough guide. Many of the components will have to be rotated 90 or 270 degrees during insertion. The resistors and non-polarized capacitors can be rotated so that the reference designators are oriented as shown in the figure. This saves editing time later. Polarized parts such as diodes and electrolytic capacitors must be inserted with the proper rotation.

Optimum component placement is critical to the success of a PCB design. Take a moment to compare the component placement on the board with the schematic. Note the overall strategy of placing components in rows and how related components are grouped together to maintain signal flow. Note how all the pads on the top row are aligned in a straight line.

After inserting all the components, use the ATTEDIT command to orient and locate the reference designator attributes as shown in Figure 4-13. You can also use ATTEDIT to correct or change the value of reference designators. Using ATTEDIT can be somewhat clumsy. For optimum productivity, you should zoom into a section of the board and select about a half dozen reference designators at a time for editing. In some cases, ATTEDIT may fail to catch an attribute in the selection set. Setting a smaller snap, such as .01 will help.

Standard practice is to move reference designators outside the component outline so that they will still be visible when the board is assembled. However, this is not always possible on very dense boards.

After completing the component placement, add text legends to identify the board, revision level, designer's initials (use your own), and date as shown in the upper right corner of Figure 4-13. Use text style MONOSI with a height of .065 inch.

Your screen should closely resemble Figure 4-13. Save the drawing and then print a hardcopy. You can use PLOT EXTENTS at 1:1 scale. The use of a laser or inkjet printer is recommended. Note that the pads do not appear filled on the screen or on paper hardcopy. At this point, the fill lines are not plotted with the correct width. The green outline represents the boundary of the pads. Later, when a Gerber format photoplotter data file is generated, the fill lines will have the correct width and the pads will appear filled.

This is also a good time to save a backup copy of the drawing to floppy disk. You should make a backup copy whenever a major stage in the design process has been completed.

Trace Routing

After the components have been placed, signal traces are routed on the both the TRACE_COMP and TRACE_SOLDER layers. Via pads are inserted where signals cross between layers. Via pads are inserted just like the mounting hole pads. The name of the via pad block in the library is VIA.

Two approaches to trace routing are possible when using AutoCAD for PCB design. Many designers prefer to use a paper hardcopy of the board layout with component outlines and pads and manually draw the trace routing. Colored pencils are usually used for this purpose with red for the solder side and blue for the component side. Designers who use this approach find it easier to visualize the layout and experiment with various routing strategies on a sheet of paper. One can make several copies of the layout and then route small sections of the design. After the design has been routed on paper, the traces are drawn in AutoCAD.

Other designers prefer to work on-screen from the start. Either approach can work, but starting with a paper hardcopy is probably advisable for the novice designer. In either case, use a red pencil to "red line" signal traces on the schematic as you draw them on the board layout.

Use the 25 mil grid and 13 mil trace design rule for the tutorial board. This design rule is explained in detail in Chapter 1, page 26. The smallest trace, used for signal connections, is 13 mils. One 13 mil trace can run in between pads located on .1 inch centers. Wider traces are commonly used for ground distribution. Closely examine the suggested trace routing in Figures 4-15 and 4-16. Ground and +5V power is distributed with a bus pattern similar that that shown in Figure 1-20 in Chapter 1 on page 32. A heavy 100 mil wide ground trace is run around the periphery of the board on the solder side. This heavy ground bus connects the pads for the mounting holes. Additional 50 mil wide traces distribute ground to J1, Q1, and various components grouped around U1 and U2. The remaining ground connections are made with 25 mil wide traces. Power (+5V) is also run around the periphery of the board, but on the component side. A 50 mil trace is used for the +5V power bus; 50 mil power and ground traces run in parallel between the rows of pin on U1. General practice is always to route ground traces first, followed by power and signal traces.

As explained in Chapter 3 on page 112, traces are photoplotted 1 mil oversize. This is not a major factor with 25 mil or wider traces on generous grid spacings, but you must compensate for the smaller 13 mil traces. Use a 12 mil polyline in AutoCAD for traces that are to be plotted at 13 mils on the final artwork.

The power and ground distribution around the periphery of the board is typical. Today, many boards also have large ground plane areas to reduce noise susceptibility and radiation. A minimum clearance is required from the edge of the board to the copper pattern. The suggested minimum clearance is .025 inch.

As explained in the previous tutorial, the designer must have detailed information about component pin assignments to route the board. This is an area where errors can easily creep into the design. If you are not absolutely certain about a particular part, obtain a copy of the manufacturer's data sheet.

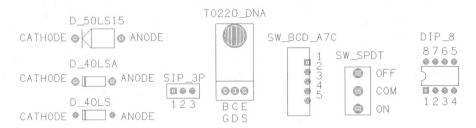

Figure 4-14   Typical Pin Assignments

Refer to Figure 4-14 and the general guidelines below for more information about pin assignments (all components are viewed from the top side):

- **ICs**. Pin 1 is identified on the PCB layout with a square pad. If the orientation notch in the package is facing up, pin 1 is the upper left pin. Pins are numbered in rows, with the last pin opposite pin 1.

- **Polarized capacitors**. The + symbol on the PCB layout is self explanatory.

- **Diodes**. The cathode is identified with a thick bar or diode symbol on the PCB layout.

- **LEDs**. There is no standard for assigning the cathode or anode pin to the flat side. Always check the particular manufacturer's data sheet.

- **Transistors**. Pin assignments vary widely, especially for smaller devices. Most TO-220 and TO-247 power transistors use the pin assignment BCE (base, collector, emitter) or equivalent GDS (gate, drain, source) for MOSFETs when oriented as shown in Figure 4-14.

- **Connectors**. Pin 1 is usually identified on the PCB layout with a square pad. Refer to the data sheet for details. D-Sub connectors often cause confusion.

- **Potentiometers and switches**. These cause the most trouble. One of the corollaries of Murphy's law states that toggle switches and pots will always be backwards. When a toggle switch handle is up, the switch connection is made to the bottom pin. Carefully check manufacturer's data sheets to identify the

CW (clockwise) and CCW (counter-clockwise) terminals on potentiometers. Some manufacturers show the pinout viewed from the bottom, which is a mirror image of the board layout viewed from the top.

Draw the traces using the suggested routing in Figures 4-15 and 4-16. Set the grid and snap to .025 inch. Use the POLYLINE command to draw traces. You must draw a continuous polyline from pad to pad. If you end a polyline at a corner and then draw another polyline, a chunk will appear to be missing at the corner as shown in Figure 3-10 in Chapter 3, page 99. If this happens, you can use the PEDIT (polyline edit) command and JOIN option to join the polylines together again. To start a trace on the solder side, set TRACE_SOLDER as the current layer. Change the current layer and insert vias as necessary to route the traces.

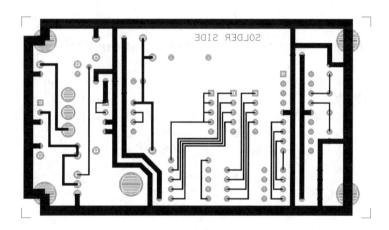

Figure 4-15   Trace Routing on Solder Side

After completing the trace routing, add text legends to identify the solder side and component sides as shown near the upper right corner of Figures 4-15 and 4-16. This is especially important on double sided boards. The author has seen boards manufactured with the solder and component sides reversed because the artwork was not clearly identified. Use text style MONOSI with a height of .065 inch. Remember that you are viewing the design from the component side. You must mirror any text appearing on the solder side so that the text will appear right reading on the actual artwork. Use the MIRROR command to mirror text strings.

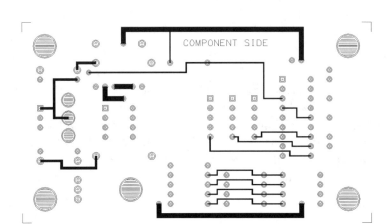

Figure 4-16   Trace Routing on Component Side

Save the drawing. Turn on the SILK_COMP layer and then print out a hardcopy to use as a check plot. This will show components, pads, and trace routing. Check each trace against the schematic, red lining both the schematic and check plot as you proceed. Correct any errors, save the final drawing to your hard drive and save a backup copy to floppy disk.

The PCB design is now complete, and the next task is to generate manufacturing documentation and artwork.

Using the AutoPADS Utilities

The AutoPADS utilities are used to convert AutoCAD data to Gerber format photoplotter data and Excellon format NC drill data, both of which are industry standards for PCB manufacturing. Information about photoplotting artwork and numerically controlled board drilling is given in Chapter 1 starting on page 17. For detailed information about Excellon and Gerber format, refer to Appendixes A and B.

The AutoPADS utility programs are included on the floppy disk supplied with the book. AutoPADS consists of the main AutoPADS (AutoCAD to Gerber) conversion utility, the AutoDRIL (AutoCAD to Excellon) conversion utility, and various support files.

Detailed instructions on loading AutoPADS, configuring AutoCAD, and using AutoPADS are given in Chapter 3 starting on page 99. The same procedures, as explained in Chapter 3 for a single sided board, will be used for the double sided board in this tutorial exercise. The only significant difference is that an additional artwork layer is required for the component side.

Manufacturing Documentation

Manufacturing documentation consists of the Excellon format NC drill data, drill detail drawing, and board assembly drawing.

Extracting NC Drill Data and Running AutoDRIL

Follow the same procedure as explained in Chapter 3 on pages 99-104, except substitute the appropriate subdirectory and filenames for the current tutorial, TUTOR3. When you have completed extracting and converting the NC drill data, exit to DOS and use the LIST utility to examine the tool information header in the Excellon data file DRILL.CNC. Print out the screen listing by pressing the Alt + P keys. This will give you hardcopy of the tool information header, which gives the drill sizes and quantities. This information is required for the drill detail drawing.

Drill Detail and Assembly Drawings

Start AutoCAD and load the TUTOR3 drawing. Then follow the same procedure as explained in Chapter 3 on pages 105-107.

Use Figure 4-17 as a guide for the drill detail drawing. Use the text notes shown in this figure. Take a moment to examine these notes for a double sided PTH PCB using SMOBC. Compare these notes with the notes for a single sided PCB as shown in Figure 3-14 on page 106. Save the drawing file and then print out a hardcopy of the drill detail drawing.

Use Figure 4-18 as a guide for the PCB assembly drawing. Use the text notes shown in this figure. Save the drawing file and then print out a hardcopy of the PCB assembly drawing. This is also a good time to save another backup copy of the drawing file to floppy disk.

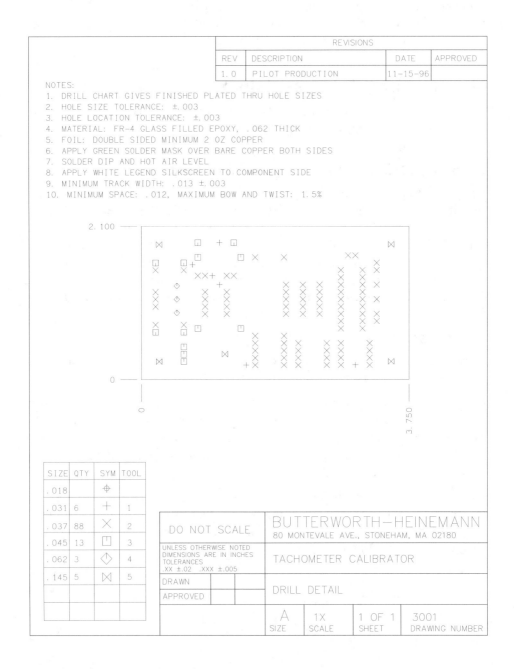

Figure 4-17   Finished Drill Detail Drawing

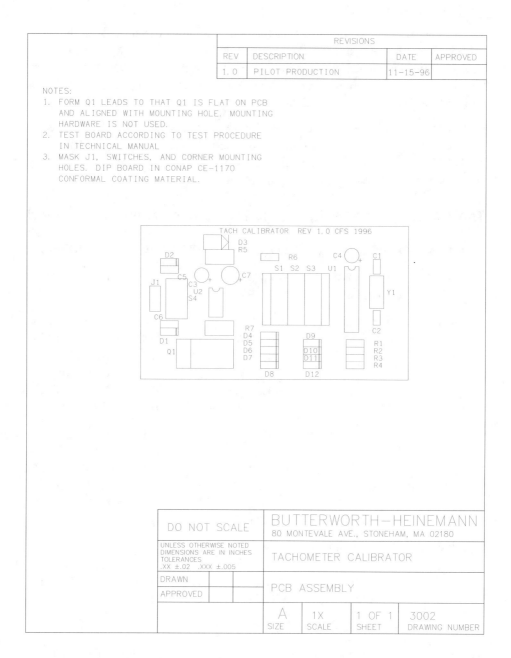

REVISIONS			
REV	DESCRIPTION	DATE	APPROVED
1.0	PILOT PRODUCTION	11-15-96	

NOTES:
1. FORM Q1 LEADS TO THAT Q1 IS FLAT ON PCB
   AND ALIGNED WITH MOUNTING HOLE. MOUNTING
   HARDWARE IS NOT USED.
2. TEST BOARD ACCORDING TO TEST PROCEDURE
   IN TECHNICAL MANUAL
3. MASK J1, SWITCHES, AND CORNER MOUNTING
   HOLES. DIP BOARD IN CONAP CE-1170
   CONFORMAL COATING MATERIAL.

TACH CALIBRATOR REV 1.0 CFS 1996

DO NOT SCALE

BUTTERWORTH-HEINEMANN
80 MONTEVALE AVE., STONEHAM, MA 02180

UNLESS OTHERWISE NOTED
DIMENSIONS ARE IN INCHES
TOLERANCES
.XX ±.02 .XXX ±.005

TACHOMETER CALIBRATOR

DRAWN

APPROVED

PCB ASSEMBLY

A SIZE	1X SCALE	1 OF 1 SHEET	3002 DRAWING NUMBER

Figure 4-18   Finished PCB Assembly Drawing

Board Artwork

The artwork required to manufacture the board includes the component legend silkscreen, component side pattern, solder side pattern, and solder mask pattern. As explained in Chapter 1, board manufacturers generally do not want artwork per se, but rather the Gerber photoplotter data for the various artwork layers. Your task will be to generate this Gerber data.

Follow the same procedure as explained in Chapter 3 on pages 107-117, except substitute the appropriate subdirectory and filenames for the current tutorial, TUTOR3. For plotting and converting the various pieces of artwork, use the layer, color, pen, and Gerber D code assignments shown in Table 4-2.

Table 4-2   Layer Assignments for Double Sided PCB Artwork

ARTWORK	LAYER USAGE	COLOR	PEN/SIZE		D CODE/SIZE	
SILK_CMP	SILK_COMP	WHITE	2	.01	D12	.01
	OUTLINE	WHITE	2	.01	D12	.01
ART_CMP	TRACE_COMP	BLUE	1	.005	D11	.006
	PADS	YELLOW	3	.02	D13	.02
		GREEN	127	.01	NOT PLOTTED	
	VIAS	YELLOW	3	.02	D13	.02
		GREEN	127	.01	NOT PLOTTED	
	OUTLINE	WHITE	2	.01	D12	.01
ART_SOL	TRACE_SOLDER	RED	1	.005	D11	.006
	PADS	YELLOW	3	.02	D13	.02
		GREEN	127	.01	NOT PLOTTED	
	VIAS	YELLOW	3	.02	D13	.02
		GREEN	127	.01	NOT PLOTTED	
	OUTLINE	WHITE	2	.01	D12	.01
MASK_SOL	MASK_SOLDER	WHITE	2	.01	D12	.01
	PADS	YELLOW	4	.02	D14	.03
		GREEN	127	.01	NOT PLOTTED	
	OUTLINE	WHITE	2	.01	D12	

The layer combinations are the same as those used for the single sided board in Table 3-3 on page 113, except that the component side artwork and vias layers have been added.

Generate the Gerber file for the component side artwork using the same procedure as for the solder side (explained on page 114), except substitute the layers TRACE_COMP, PADS, VIAS, and OUTLINE. Use the filename ART_CMP for the component side artwork

Run AutoPADS to convert the four AutoCAD binary ADI files that you created (SILK_CMP.PLT, ART_CMP.PLT, ART_SOL.PLT, and MASK_SOL.PLT). Then exit to DOS and use the DOS DIR command to check the files in your TUTOR3 subdirectory. You should see the four original .PLT files and four new .GBR files. These are your Gerber artwork files.

Preparing Files for a Service Bureau

If you want to send the files for your completed double sided PCB to a photoplotting service bureau or board manufacturer, you can use the procedures explained in Chapter 3 on pages 117-120.

The PCB manufacturer will require the files listed in Table 4-3.

Table 4-3   Files Required for PCB Manufacturing

FILENAME	DESCRIPTION
SILK_CMP.GBR	Top side legend silkscreen artwork
ART_CMP.GBR	Component side artwork
ART_SOL.GBR	Solder side artwork
MASK_SOL.GBR	Solder mask artwork (use for both sides)
DRILL.PLT or DRILL.GBR	Drill detail drawing
DRILL.CNC	Excellon drill data and tool header
README.DOC	Text file including information on apertures and the Gerber format

If you are having a service bureau plot the artwork, the drill detail drawing and Excellon drill data files can be omitted.

The README.DOC file for a double sided board also requires an additional entry for the component side artwork. A sample README.DOC file suitable for a double sided board is in the TUTOR3 subdirectory on the floppy disk included with the book. The contents of the file are listed on the following page. You can use this as a guideline for creating your own README.DOC file.

PCB ARTWORK DATA README FILE:
    PCB NAME: TACHOMETER CALIBRATOR
    REV CODE: 1.0
    PART NUMBER: 7100-1120-010
    ZIP FILE: TUTOR3.ZIP

SERVICES REQUIRED:
    FABRICATE 10 PROTOTYPE BOARDS WITH
    1 WEEK TURNAROUND. SHIP UPS RED.
    CALL FOR PURCHASE ORDER BEFORE
    PROCEEDING.

CONTACT:
    CHRIS SCHROEDER
    BUTTERWORTH-HEINEMANN
    80 MONTEVALE AVE.
    STONEHAM, MA 02180
    PH: 617-555-5555

DATA FILES:

FILENAME	DESCRIPTION
SILK_CMP.GBR	TOP SIDE LEGEND SILKSCREEN ARTWORK
ART_CMP.GBR	COMPONENT SIDE ARTWORK
ART_SOL.GBR	SOLDER SIDE ARTWORK
MASK_SOL.GBR	SOLDER MASK ARTWORK (USE FOR BOTH SIDES)
DRILL.PLT	DRILL DETAIL DRAWING (HPGL)
DRILL.CNC	EXCELLON FORMAT N/C DRILL
	DATA WITH TOOL SIZE HEADER

GERBER FORMAT NOTES:
    ENGLISH (INCH) UNITS
    ABSOLUTE COORDINATES
    XX.XXXX (2.4) DIGIT FORMAT
    LEADING ZERO SUPPRESSION
    * END OF BLOCK CHARACTER
    M02* END OF PLOT

APERTURE LIST AND NOTES:
    POSITIONS ARE GERBER D-CODES. ALL
    APERTURES ARE ROUND WITH DIAMETERS
    IN MILS (I.E. 50 MILS = .05 INCH)

POSITION	SIZE
11	6
12	10
13	20
14	30

Conclusion

You have now learned the basic techniques for designing a double sided, plated through hole PCB with AutoCAD. The next chapter extends these basic techniques to surface mount technology.

5

Surface Mount PCB Design

In the previous chapters, you learned how to design single sided and double sided PCBs using conventional through hole components. While these types of boards are still widely used, today most new designs are based on SMT. The basic techniques you learned for a single and double sided PCBs can be adapted for the design of SMT boards. In this chapter you will design a small, but complex SMT board. This board has SMT and conventional through hole components mounted on both sides. This chapter will also introduce some of the basic concepts related to SMT.

Most new automotive, computer, consumer, and industrial products utilize SMT. Double sided and multi-layer PTH boards are generally used for SMT designs. Very high densities can be obtained since two layers are available for both component mounting and signal traces. True SMT only boards are still rare outside the computer industry. The major reason is that power devices with high current or voltage levels do not readily lend themselves to SMT. Heat transfer from SMT semiconductors is also a problem. For now, the designer must deal with mixed technology boards.

Double sided PTH boards for SMT are generally manufactured in facilities with a high level of automation and fine tuned process controls. Plating resists are primarily photoimaged with a dry film or liquid photoresist. The photoimaging process allows the relatively fine trace width and precise pad shapes required for SMT. Most SMT boards are based on a 16.7 mil grid and 8 mil trace design rule. The practical density limit is about .25 sq-inch/CE for each side (see Table 1-1 on page 24).

The use of SMT results in additional advantages besides the obvious size reduction. The small size of the components and short lead lengths greatly improve resistance to shock and vibration in severe environments. Robotics equipment used in assembly reduces the likelihood of errors. The author's experience with SMT in automotive applications has shown that overall product quality increases and that reduced life cycle costs more than compensate for the slightly higher cost of the SMT components.

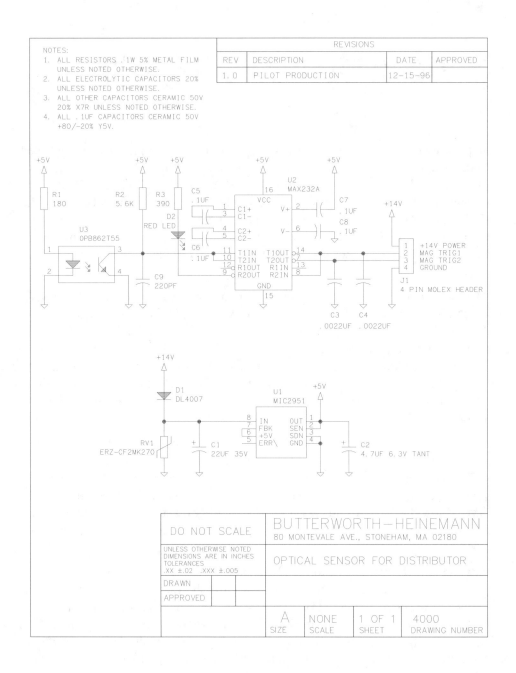

Figure 5-1   Schematic for the Surface Mount PCB Tutorial

Introduction to the Tutorial Design

The schematic for the SMT design tutorial is shown in Figure 5-1. This optical sensor board was designed by the author for use in a special distributor for circle track racing. The overall construction of the distributor is similar to precision optical encoders. A thin stainless steel disk with precise photochemically etched slots is attached to the distributor shaft. An infrared light beam generated by U3, a slotted optical switch, is interrupted by the disk. When a slot in the disk rotates through U3, a trigger signal is generated. U2 converts the signal from U3 to the bipolar (±7V) signal level required to trigger an ignition system. U2 is a MAXIM RS-232 interface IC with a built-in charge pump that operates from a single +5V supply. While primarily intended for a computer interface application, the MAXIM IC proved ideal for this automotive application.

U3 mounts on an aluminum base plate. The PCB is located about 1/8 inch above the base plate. The required board outline and critical component mounting locations are given in Figure 5-2. Note that only approximate locations are given for D2 and J1. The four leads from U3 attach to the back side of the PCB and are soldered from the top. The remaining through hole components, D2 and J1, are mounted on the top side of the PCB. Surface mount devices are mounted on both sides. The limited spacing from the base plate dictates that only low-profile parts such as chip resistors and capacitors be mounted on the back side of the PCB. The assembly is completed with a potting shell that surrounds the PCB and attaches to the base plate. After a final test, the assembly is encapsulated with an epoxy material.

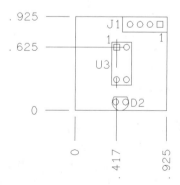

Figure 5-2   **Board Outline for the Tutorial PCB**

QTY	REFERENCE DESIGNATOR	DESCRIPTION	VENDOR PART NUMBER	PCB BLOCK
1	C9	220PF 50V 10% X7R CERAMIC 805 SMD CAP	PANASONIC ECU-V1H221KBN	CAP_805_SMD
2	C4	.0022UF 50V 10% X7R CERAMIC 805 SMD CAP	PANASONIC ECU-V1H222KBN	CAP_805_SMD
4	C6	.1UF 50V +80/-20% Y5V CERAMIC 1206 SMD CAP	ROHM MCH315F104ZP	CAP_1206_SMD
1	C2	4.7UF 6.3V 20% TANTALUM 3216 SMD CAP	PANASONIC ECS-TOJY475R	ECAP_3216_SMD
1	C1	22UF 35V 20% ELECTROLYTIC SMD CAP	PANASONIC ECE-V1VA220P	ECAP_30SQ_SMD
1	D1	DL4007 LL-41 MELF DIODE	TAITRON	D_LL41_SMD
1	D2	RED LED	PANASONIC LN263CPP	LED_10LS15
1	J1	4 PIN HEADER .10 CENTERS FRICTION LOCK	MOLEX 22-24-2031	SIP_4P
1	R1	180 .1W 5% METAL FILM 805 SMD RESISTOR	PANASONIC ERJ-6GEY	R_805_SMD
1	R3	390 .1W 5% METAL FILM 805 SMD RESISTOR	PANASONIC ERJ-6GEY	R_805_SMD
1	R2	5.6K .1W 5% METAL FILM 805 SMD RESISTOR	PANASONIC ERJ-6GEY	R_805_SMD
1	U2	MAX232A SOIC	MAXIM	DIP_16SO
1	U1	MIC2951-03BM SOIC	MICREL	DIP_8SO
1	U3	SLOTTED OPTICAL SWITCH	OPTEK OPB862T55	OPB_32LS
1	RV1	ERZ-CF2MK270 SMD SURGE ABSORBER	PANASONIC	RV_3224_SMD
1		OPTICAL PICKUP PCB REV 1.0		

Figure 5-3   Bill of Materials for the Tutorial PCB

A bill of materials for the optical sensor is given in Figure 5-3. The bill of materials as supplied to the PCB designer would typically include the first four columns: quantity, reference designator, part description, and vendor part number. The PCB designer adds the last column, which gives the names of the AutoCAD blocks that represent the PCB pattern of each part.

As the first step in the design tutorial, calculate the CE, useable board area, and board density (see Chapter 1, page 23).

The CE is calculated by adding up all the device pins. You can use the bill of materials listing or a schematic. Add up all the two lead components (such as capacitors, diodes, and resistors) and multiply by two. Then add any remaining components, including the ICs. You should come up with a total of 62 pins for the tutorial design, or 4.4 CE.

Assume that a clearance of about .025 inches is required between the board edge and the nearest components. Given the overall board dimensions of .925 inches square, the useable board area works out to about .77 square inches. The calculated board density is just under .175 square inch per CE. This is less than the suggested minimum of .25 given in Table 1-1 for the 16.7 mil grid and 8 mil trace design rule. Consequently, parts must be mounted on both sides of the board, and trace routing will be a significant challenge.

Structured Design Approach for SMT

Additional layer assignments, beyond those introduced in the previous tutorials, are required for SMT devices. Even though SMT parts may be soldered to both sides of the PCB, the top side will continue to be referred to as the "component" side and the back side as the "solder" side.

Table 5-1   AutoCAD Layers for SMT PCB Design

LAYER NAME	COLOR	PEN	SIZE	NOTES
SILK_COMP	WHITE	2	.01	
SILK_SOLDER	WHITE	2	.01	
TRACE_COMP	BLUE	1	.002	
TRACE_SOLDER	RED	1	.002	
PADS	GREEN	127	N/A	DISPLAY ONLY
	YELLOW	3	.02	FILL PATTERN
PADS_COMP	CYAN	1	.002	SMT DEVICES ONLY
PADS_SOLDER	MAGENTA	1	.002	SMT DEVICES ONLY
VIAS	GREEN	127	N/A	DISPLAY ONLY
	YELLOW	3	.02	FILL PATTERN
MASK_COMP	WHITE	2	.01	
MASK_SOLDER	WHITE	2	.01	
OUTLINE	WHITE	2	.01	
DRILL	WHITE	2	.01	
ASSEMBLY	WHITE	2	.01	
TITLEBLOCK	WHITE	2	.01	

Each layer has an associated color, pen number, and pen width. As with previous tutorial exercises, the technique used to control and specify different line widths is the use of color. Different line widths are represented by colors. A particular pen is then assigned to each color for plotting. In turn, each pen has a defined pen width. Note that the smallest pen width is now .002 inch instead of the .005 inch previously used. Since the design rule calls for fine .008 inch traces and SMT devices require small precisely defined pads, a smaller pen width is used to create the fill pattern. The small pen width results in sharper corners.

Let's examine the layer assignments in Table 5-1 in more detail. As with the previous tutorials, artwork is created by means of plotting a composite of multiple layers. For example, the solder side artwork consists of the OUTLINE, PADS, PADS_SOLDER, VIAS, and TRACE_SOLDER layers.

- **SILK_COMP**. This layer contains the top side component outlines and legends (reference designators) generally silk screened with white ink on the PCB. The silkscreen outlines and legends are displayed in white and plotted with pen 2, which is assigned a width of .01 inch.

- **SILK_SOLDER**. This layer contains the back side component outlines and reference designators. It is displayed and plotted the same as the top silk layer.

- **TRACE_COMP**. This layer contains all circuit traces and other copper patterns on the component side of the PCB, except pads and vias. The component side is displayed in blue and plotted with pen 1, which is assigned a width of .002 inch. Circuit traces and solid copper areas are drawn as polylines. The AutoCAD plot driver strokes the pen back and forth to fill in polylines. The .002 inch pen width allows narrow polylines down to .006 inch.

- **TRACE_SOLDER**. This layer contains all circuit traces and other copper patterns on the solder side of the PCB, except component pads. The solder side is displayed in red and plotted with pen 1, which is assigned a width of .002 inch. The same plotting considerations as noted for the component side also apply to the solder side.

- **PADS**. This layer contains pads for through hole components. In all the tutorial exercises, pads for through hole parts are identical on both the component and solder side of the PCB. Two colors are used for pads. Green is used to display the outline of the pad for design and checking purposes. A nonexistent pen number 127 is assigned to green to prevent this color from plotting. Yellow is used for the fill pattern. This yellow fill pattern is plotted with pen 3, which is assigned a width of .02 inch.

- **PADS_COMP**. This layer contains pads for SMT components mounted on the top side of the PCB. SMT pads, which are always rectangular or square patterns, are drawn with short polyline segments. A separate outline is not used. Cyan is used for the top side SMT pads. The cyan fill pattern is plotted with pen 1, which is assigned a width of .002 inch to assure sharp corners.

- **PADS_SOLDER**. This layer contains pads for SMT components mounted on the back side of the PCB. Magenta is used for the back side SMT pads. The magenta fill pattern is plotted with pen 1 and a width of .002 inch.

- **VIAS**. This layer contains pads for vias. In all other respects, it is treated the same as the PADS layer. Vias on SMT boards are usually covered with solder mask, so via features do not appear on the solder mask artwork. Using a separate layer for vias allows turning off this layer before the solder mask artwork is plotted.

- **MASK_COMP**. This layer contains any special solder mask patterns required for the top (component) side of the board. The tutorial exercise does not require special solder mask patterns. When the solder mask artwork is plotted, oversize component pads are plotted along with any special patterns on this layer. The oversize pads are created by changing the pen number of the color assigned to the fill pattern on the appropriate pad layers. The artwork is then plotted with a larger pen size to generate .01 inch oversize pads.

- **MASK_SOL**. This layer contains any special solder mask patterns required for the back (solder) side of the board.

- **OUTLINE**. This layer contains cut marks, scribe lines, and other features that define the board outline. These features are displayed in white and plotted with pen 2, which is assigned a width of .01 inch. The board manufacturer uses the outline features to depanelize individual boards via shearing or NC routing.

- **DRILL**. This layer contains drill size symbols and attributes associated with the pads of through hole components and vias. The DRILL layer also contains manufacturing notes. Drill size attributes are extracted and converted to Excellon format NC drill data. The drill size symbols and manufacturing notes appear in the drill detail drawing.

- **ASSEMBLY**. This layer contains notes and details that will appear in the PCB assembly drawing.

- **TITLEBLOCK**. This layer contains the drawing border, titleblock, and revision block used for manufacturing documentation.

For SMT boards with components mounted only on the top side of the PCB, the SILK_SOLDER and PADS_SOLDER layers are not required.

Limitations of AutoCAD become apparent in the design of SMT boards. Since AutoCAD does not provide a direct means of changing multiple layers on blocks, separate top and back side SMT part blocks must be created. Most dedicated PCB design software packages allow an SMT part block to be inserted on either side of the board. Small SMT pad details require the use of a narrow line width for plotting. Manually creating the fill pattern as with through hole pads is not practical. Polyline segments are used to create SMT pads, and AutoCAD does a considerable amount of stroking to generate the fill pattern. The plot files quickly become unmanageable. AutoCAD is not a practical design tool for SMT boards larger than about 10 square inches.

SMT Pads

AutoCAD blocks are used for pads of through hole components to allow an easy means of associating and later extracting NC drill data. Since SMT pads do not require drill holes, no reason exists for using pad blocks. The pads are directly drawn within the part block definitions for the SMT components.

For through hole components, the size of the pad is determined by the lead diameter. More complex relationships exist for SMT pads. SMT pad shapes are determined by the dimensions of the SMT part and the soldering process used.

Somewhat different pad sizes are used for reflow and wave soldering. Most SMT assembly is now done with a reflow soldering process, and all pad relationships given in this text apply to reflow soldering. However, the designer must be aware of the applicable considerations. Figure 5-4 shows SMT pad to part dimension relationships. In general, the X dimension is smaller and the Y dimension is larger when a wave soldering process is used.

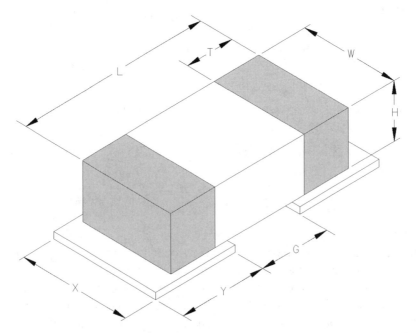

Figure 5-4   SMT Pad to Part Dimension Relationships

Passive SMT components such as resistors and capacitors come in EIA standardized sizes. A four-digit size code is commonly used for chip components. For example, the most common chip resistor sizes are 0805, 1206, and 1210, corresponding to .0625 watt, .125 watt, and .25 watt. The first two digits give the length and the last two digits give the width in units of hundreds of an inch, e.g., a 1206 resistor is .12 × .06 inches. Similar size codes are used for ceramic chip capacitors. Molded tantalum capacitors also use a four-digit code, but the units are in tenths of a millimeter, e.g., a 3216 tantalum capacitor is 3.2 × 1.6 mm. Diodes are commonly found in a cylindrical MELF package. Two common MELF diode sizes are the DO-35/DL-35 and DO-41/LL-41. Various SOT (small outline transistor) packages, such as the SOT-23 and SOT-223 are used for transistors and MOSFETs. Common ICs with gull wing shaped leads are offered in SOIC packages. While a detailed discussion of all SMT packages and pad shapes is beyond the scope of this text, references are given at the end of Chapter1 on page 35. Some guidelines for pad shapes are given below, but in most cases the designer should refer to the manufacturer's data sheet for specific recommendations. Production process considerations also may dictate some adjustments to the pad shapes.

The following approximate formulas give recommended relationships between pad and part dimensions for common chip components when a reflow soldering process is used (refer to Figure 5-4):

$$X = W + .01$$

$$Y = H/2 + T + .01$$

$$G = L - 2T - .01$$

Where all dimensions are in inches and

X = Pad width

Y = Pad length

G = Gap between pads

W = Part width

H = Part height

L = Part length

T = Metallized termination length

These formulas break down for small 0805 size components. The figures and tables on the following pages give specific recommendations for common SMT components.

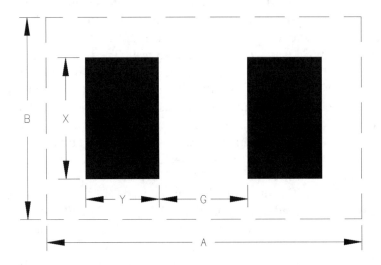

Figure 5-5   Pad Dimensions for Two Terminal SMT Parts

Recommended pad dimensions for common chip resistors and capacitors, molded tantalum capacitors, and MELF diodes are given in Figure 5-5 and Table 5-2. All dimensions are in inches. A reflow soldering process is assumed. Note that A and B represent the dimensions of the component outline on the silkscreen. These dimensions also represent the minimum spacing between components.

Table 5-2   Pad Dimensions for Two Terminal SMT Parts

PACKAGE STYLE	A	B	G	X	Y
0805 CHIP	.175	.075	.025	.060	.055
1206 CHIP	.200	.100	.065	.080	.055
1210 CHIP	.225	.150	.065	.120	.055
2010 CHIP	.300	.150	.155	.120	.055
2512 CHIP	.350	.175	.195	.135	.055
3216 TANTALUM CAP	.225	.100	.065	.080	.055
7243 TANTALUM CAP	.400	.250	.150	.150	.100
DL-35 MELF DIODE	.250	.125	.075	.055	.065
LL-41 MELF DIODE	.325	.175	.115	.070	.085

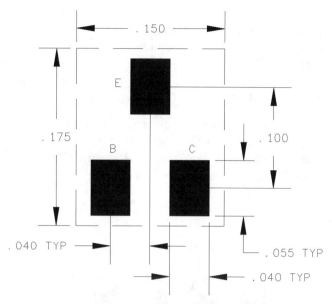

Figure 5-6   Pad Dimensions for SOT-23 Parts

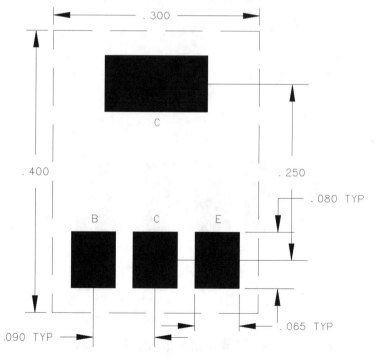

Figure 5-7   Pad Dimensions for SOT-223 Parts

Recommended pad dimensions for common SMT transistors are shown in Figures 5-6 and 5-7. Many popular TO-92 (through hole) transistors are available as SMT devices in the SOT-23 package. Devices with higher current and power dissipation ratings are offered in the SOT-223 package. MOSFETS, voltage regulators, and zener diodes are also available in the SOT-23 package.

Figure 5-8 gives parametric dimensions for common 8, 14, 16, 18, and 20 pin SOIC packages. The variable N in the overall length formula represents the number of pins. Standard 8 to 16 pin SOIC devices utilize the narrow width. Some 16 and most 18 to 28 pin devices are supplied in the wide style, also referred to as an *SOL (small outline large)* package.

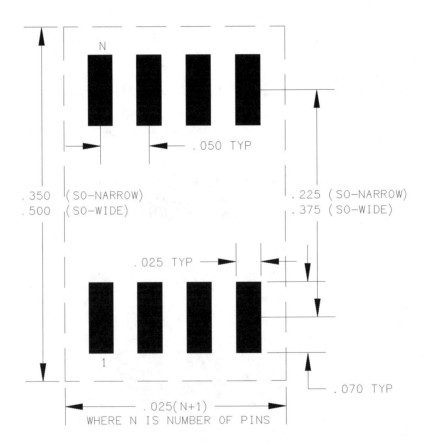

Figure 5-8   Pad Dimensions for SOIC Parts

SMT pads are easily drawn with AutoCAD polylines. As mentioned before, separate top and back side SMT part blocks are required for designs in which SMT components are mounted on both sides of the PCB. Top side part blocks would use pads drawn in cyan on the PADS_COMP layer. Back side part blocks would use pads drawn in magenta on the PADS_SOLDER layer. Cyan and magenta give reasonable contrast with blue and red signal traces.

Polylines used to represent SMT pads are drawn with pen number 1 and a width of .002 inch (refer to Table 5-1). Remember that AutoCAD automatically offsets the pen position by half the pen width while stroking polylines so that the plotted width is correct. When the AutoCAD plot file is later converted to Gerber format, a slightly larger .003 inch aperture is used to photoplot the pads. This is the same oversized plotting technique introduced in previous chapters for photoplotting signal traces. The .001 inch oversize aperture assures a good fill pattern without streaks. Pad dimensions will be oversize by .001 inch, which generally does not cause any problems.

For solder mask artwork that requires oversized clearance pads, a different pen number (such as pen 5) is assigned to the cyan and magenta colors used for the SMT pads. In AutoCAD, the same pen width of .002 inch is used for generating a plot file. When this AutoCAD plot file is later converted to Gerber format, a .012 inch aperture is used to plot the solder mask clearance pads. The resulting solder mask artwork will have pads precisely .010 inch oversize, which is the recommended industry standard.

SMT Part Blocks

SMT part blocks are created similar to part blocks for conventional through hole components except that nested pad blocks are not used. SMT part blocks consist of entities on two layers. Top side SMT part use the PADS_COMP and SILK_COMP layers. Back side SMT parts use the PADS_SOLDER and SILK_SOLDER layers. The center of the part or the center of pin 1 is generally used as the insertion point.

As explained earlier, pads are drawn with polylines. For SOICs, a single pad could be drawn and then copied. Entities on the silkscreen layer are drawn in white. These entities consist of the part legend and the reference designator. The part outline is not used, since the part legend is generally somewhat larger than the actual component outline. AutoCAD attributes are used for the reference designator. The same techniques are used as with part blocks for through hole components.

Recommended SMT Design Practices

Figure 5-9 shows preferred SMT PCB design practices related to trace routing and via holes. Three SMT pad patterns are shown. Vias connect to the left pads, and traces connect to the right pads. The upper and lower right pads connect to a wide trace such as might be used for a power bus.

The upper SMT pattern in Figure 5-9 shows the preferred design practice. Traces are brought into the SMT pads at right angles and on the pad centerlines. The connection to the power bus is made with a narrow trace. In general, traces routed to SMT pads should not be wider than about .015 inch and should run for a minimum of .025 inch prior to a transition to a wider trace, power bus, or via pad. Vias and traces are not located underneath components.

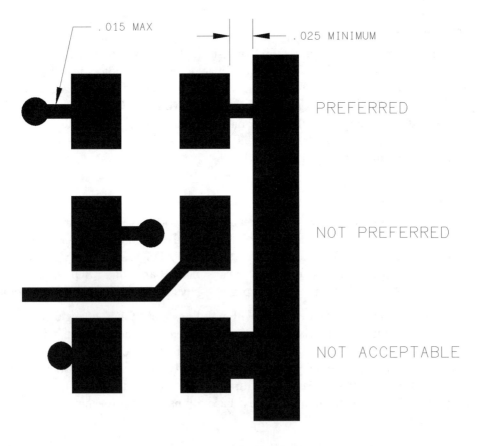

Figure 5-9   Recommended SMT Design Practices

Dense SMT boards may require the somewhat relaxed design practices shown in the middle pattern on Figure 5-9. Vias may be located underneath components, but still separated from the SMT pads by a short trace. Traces can enter SMT pads at 45 degree angles and may run in proximity beside or between the pads.

Via holes placed underneath SMT chip components must be plugged or "tented" with solder mask. Consequently, clearance pads for via holes must not appear on the solder mask artwork. As explained in the previous section, this is accomplished by means of turning the VIAS layer off when the solder mask artwork is plotted.

The lower SMT pattern in Figure 5-9 shows design practices that are clearly unacceptable and would lead to serious manufacturing problems. A wide trace directly connects to the right pad, and a via directly contacts the left pad. Both the wide trace and via tend to draw heat and solder away from the SMT pads during the reflow soldering process, causing potential soldering defects.

Spacing between adjacent SMT components must meet certain requirements. Preferred pad-to-pad spacing is .050 inch for most components. A minimum spacing of .025 inch is acceptable for dense boards. At least .100 inch spacing is recommended for fine pitch components (pads on less than .040 centers). Closer spacing may result in difficulty applying solder paste with a stencil during board assembly.

Component keep-out zones are required at the board edge. Preferred component keep-out clearance is .200 inch. Very dense boards may require a zero clearance, with component pads as close as .050 inch from the board edge. This can be accomplished if the board is part of a larger panel that provides the required clearance.

Automated equipment for component placement also imposes certain requirements on the board design. Individual board patterns are generally stepped and repeated onto a panel. Maximum panel sizes range from 14 × 18 inch to 18 × 20 inch. Individual board outlines are partially NC routed with small breakaway tabs left to hold the boards in place on the panel. Tooling holes and fiducial targets used by machine vision systems on automated assembly equipment can be located at the edges of the panel.

The PCB designer must maintain close communication with both the board manufacturer and board assembly house during the design process. Since AutoCAD places limits on practical board size, the task of stepping and repeating the board artwork and adding tooling features is best left to the board manufacturer. However, the PCB designer should maintain responsibility and coordinate the process.

Starting the Tutorial Exercise

This tutorial exercise shows you how to use AutoCAD to design a high-density board with SMT components on both sides. You will also learn to generate the required manufacturing documentation and artwork. Your task will be to design a PCB for the optical sensor shown in Figure 5-1 using the board outline shown in Figure 5-2 and the bill of materials in Figure 5-3. You may want to run copies of these figures and keep them handy for reference.

Files and utility programs required for the tutorial exercise are included on the floppy disk supplied with this book. The design-related files for this tutorial are in the subdirectory TUTOR4. FORMAT_A.DWG is an A size drawing format. PCB2_LIB.DWG is the PCB parts library that includes SMT devices. File conversion utilities required to generate Gerber and Excellon format data are in the AUTOPADS subdirectory (refer to Chapter 3 pages 99-117 for details).

For now, create a TUTOR4 subdirectory on your hard drive. Copy the files from the TUTOR4 subdirectory on the floppy disk to the TUTOR4 subdirectory on your hard drive.

The floppy disk supplied with the book also contains a popular shareware text display utility, LIST.COM and a public domain font file, MONOSI.SHX. If you have already loaded these, you can skip ahead. If not, refer to page 92 in Chapter 3 for further instructions.

Start AutoCAD and open the A size drawing format, FORMAT_A.DWG. The drawing border, title block, and revision block will be displayed on the screen. Use the INSERT command to insert the file PCB2_LIB.DWG. You need to type in the full filename. This loads all the required PCB pad and part blocks. The insertion location is not important, since PCB2_LIB.DWG does not contain any drawing entities that will appear on the screen.

Next, use the SAVE AS command from the FILE menu and save the drawing as TUTOR4.DWG. Note that AutoCAD automatically assigns the .DWG suffix. This leaves your original drawing format file FORMAT_A.DWG unchanged. All subsequent editing is done with TUTOR4.DWG. At this point, the drawing file is set up and you are ready to start on the design.

Setting Up Layers

Open TUTOR4.DWG and then use the LAYER command to define any required layers. These layers are listed in Table 5-3. Most of these layers should already exist, since you started with the drawing format file FORMAT_A.DWG and then loaded the PCB2_LIB.DWG library.

Table 5-3   Required AutoCAD Layers

LAYER NAME	COLOR
SILK_COMP	WHITE
SILK_SOLDER	WHITE
TRACE_COMP	BLUE
TRACE_SOLDER	RED
PADS	YELLOW
PADS_COMP	CYAN
PADS_SOLDER	MAGENTA
VIAS	YELLOW
OUTLINE	WHITE
DRILL	WHITE
ASSEMBLY	WHITE
TITLEBLOCK	WHITE

Drawing the Board Outline

Use the LAYER command to set OUTLINE as the current layer. Set all layers to *on* except DRILL and ASSEMBLY. Use the ATTDISP command to set attribute display to normal. This inhibits display of invisible attributes, such as drill hole size. Use the GRID and SNAP commands to select a .1 inch grid and .025 inch snap.

Starting from a grid point, draw the board outline as shown in Figure 5-10 using the dimensions given in Figure 5-2. The outline consists of cut marks at each corner of the board. The length of the cut marks is not critical. General practice is to make the cut marks about .10 inch long.

Next, use the UCS and ORIGIN commands to set the origin point for the drawing to the lower left-hand corner of the board. This will facilitate subsequent component insertion and dimensioning.

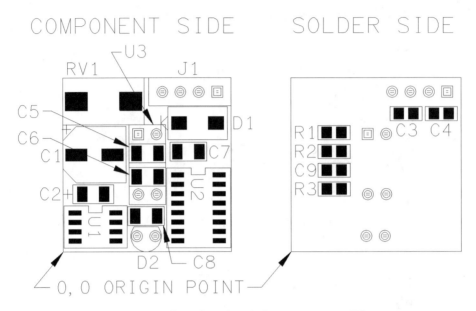

Figure 5-10   Board Outline and Component Placement

Placing Components

Set SILK_COMP as the current layer. First, place the top side components that have defined locations. Refer to Figures 5-1, 5-2, and 5-3. Use the dimensions given to insert U3, the slotted optical switch. U3 pin 1 is the insertion point for this part. Then place D2 and J1 as shown in Figure 5-2. Use the part block names listed on the bill of materials in Figure 5-3. Insert J1 so that its outline is superimposed on the corner of the board. At this point the precise location of D2 and other components is not critical. You can make slight adjustments later on.

Finish the top side component placement by placing the remaining components using Figure 5-10 as a guide. Many of the components will have to be rotated 90 or 270 degrees during insertion. The resistors and non-polarized capacitors can be rotated so that the reference designators are oriented as shown in the figure. This saves editing time later on. Polarized parts such as diodes and electrolytic capacitors must be inserted with the proper rotation. Note that C5 and C6 are nested within the outline of U3. Even though the part block for U3 is placed on the top side, U3 actually mounts to an aluminum base plate beneath the PCB. U3 leads pass up through the PCB and are hand soldered to pads on the top side.

After inserting all the top side components, use the ATTEDIT command to orient and locate the reference designator attributes as shown in Figure 5-10. You can also use ATTEDIT to correct or change the value of reference designators. In some cases, ATTEDIT may fail to catch an attribute in the selection set. Setting a smaller snap, such as .01 or .005 will help.

Standard practice is to move reference designators outside the component outline so that they will still be visible when the board is assembled. However, this is not always possible on SMT boards. Under no circumstances should reference designator legends be silkscreened underneath chip components. The thick ink can raise the chip components enough to cause serious soldering problems. For now, just leave the reference designators centered on the parts. Once the design is completed, they will be moved out of the way prior to generating artwork files.

After completing the top side component placement, your screen should resemble the left side of Figure 5-10. The next step is to place the solder side components, C3, C4, C9, R1, and R2. These are all 805 chip components. Use the LAYER command to turn off the SILK_COMP and PADS_COMP layers. The SILK_SOLDER, PADS, and PADS_SOLDER layers should be on. Insert the remaining components on the back side. Note that the modifier _SOLDER is used after the part block names to denote a back side part. Use CAP_805_SMD_SOLDER for the capacitors and R_805_SMD_SOLDER for the resistors. Insert the components in the approximate location as shown in Figure 5-10. Use the pads on J1 and U3 as a guide. Finish the back side component placement by moving the reference designators outside the component outlines.

Your screen should now resemble the right side of Figure 5-10. Save the drawing and then print a hardcopy of both the component (top) and solder (bottom) side using the LAYER command to select the required layers. You can use PLOT EXTENTS at 1:1 scale. The use of a laser or inkjet printer is recommended. Note that the pads of through hole parts do not appear filled on the screen or on paper hardcopy. At this point, the fill lines are not plotted with the correct width. The green outline represents the boundary of the pads. Later, when a Gerber format photoplotter data file is generated, the fill lines will have the correct width and the pads will appear filled. Since the SMT pads are created as polylines, they will display correctly if FILL mode is on.

This is also a good time to save a backup copy of the drawing to floppy disk. You should make a backup copy whenever a major stage in the design process has been completed.

Trace Routing

After the components have been placed, signal traces are routed on the both the TRACE_COMP and TRACE_SOLDER layers. Via pads are inserted on the VIAS layer where signals cross between layers. The PCB2_LIB parts library has two types of vias: a standard via with .055 inch diameter and .031 inch hole size and a micro via with .031 inch diameter and .018 inch hole size. Use micro vias for the tutorial design. The name of the micro via block in the library is MICROVIA.

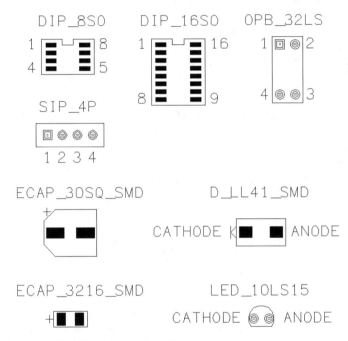

Figure 5-11   Typical Pin Assignments

Refer to Figure 5-11 and the general guidelines below for more information about pin assignments (all components are viewed from the top side):

- **SOICs**. Note that unlike through hole DIP ICs, pin 1 is not distinguished by the use of a special pad. If the orientation notch in the package is facing up, pin 1 is the upper left pin. Pin 1 is always counterclockwise from this notch. Pins are numbered in rows, with the last pin opposite pin 1.

- **Polarized capacitors**. The + symbol on the PCB layout is self explanatory.

- **Diodes**. The cathode is identified with a thick bar or diode symbol on the PCB layout.

- **LEDs**. There is no standard for assigning the cathode or anode pin to the flat side. Always check the particular manufacturer's data sheet.

- **Connectors**. Pin 1 is usually identified on the PCB layout with a square pad. Refer to the data sheet for details.

- **Slotted optical switch**. U3 pins are identified on Figure 5-11. Always refer to the manufacturer's data sheet for pin numbering on special parts.

Use the 16.7 mil grid and 8 mil trace design rule for the tutorial board. This design rule is explained in detail in Chapter 1 on page 27. The smallest trace used for signal connections is 8 mils. One 8 mil trace can run between SOIC pads located on .05 inch centers. Wider traces are used for power and ground distribution.

As explained in Chapter 3 on page 112, traces are photoplotted 1 mil oversize. You must compensate for this during the design phase. To obtain precise 8 mil traces on the final photoplots, you must draw the traces with a 7 mil polyline in AutoCAD.

Signal traces are initially drawn at 7 mil. Later, after all signal and power connections have been routed, many of these 7 mil traces can be changed to 12 mil. This improves reliability and manufacturing yield. Open areas near ground traces are then filled with solid ground plane patterns. These ground planes reduce noise susceptibility and electromagnetic interference.

The 16.7 mil grid size is a nominal value. The actual value is 50/3 mil. This gives three grid positions in between pads on 50 mil centers. Use the GRID command and enter the value .016667. Set the SNAP to one half the grid spacing. Use the value .008333. Start routing signal traces on the component side. Set the current layer to TRACE_COMP. When you insert micro vias, you do not need to change layers, since entities in the micro via pad block are automatically placed on the VIAS layer. Change to the TRACE_SOLDER layer for routing solder side traces.

Draw the traces using the suggested routing in Figures5-12 and 5-13. Use the POLYLINE command to draw traces. You must draw a continuous polyline from pad to pad. If you end a polyline at a corner and then draw another polyline, a chunk will appear to be missing at the corner as shown in Figure 3-10 in Chapter 3 on page 99. If this happens, you can use the PEDIT (polyline edit) command and JOIN option to join the polylines together again. As you progress with the trace routing, you may need to slightly adjust the location of some components.

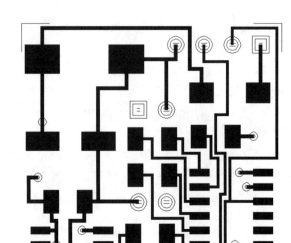

COMPONENT SIDE

Figure 5-12   Trace Routing on Component Side

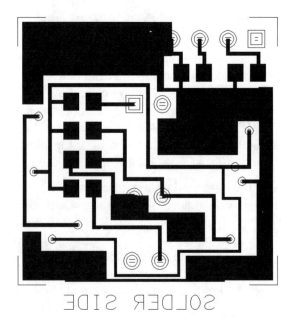

SOLDER SIDE

Figure 5-13   Trace Routing on Solder Side

After completing the signal trace routing, use wide polyline segments to create the ground plane areas on the solder side. Make sure the segments overlap at least one grid position. Then go back and where possible, use the PEDIT command to increase the trace width of signal connections to 12 mils. Make sure that you do not inadvertently create spacing violations, the minimum spacing must be 8 mil on the artwork. If the grid is 16.7 mil, traces drawn with 12 mil width must be separated at least 1-1/2 grid locations.

Next, add text legends to identify the component and solder sides of the board. These legends are placed on the TRACE_COMP and TRACE_SOLDER layers. Since no room exists within the board outline, place these text legends just outside the board as shown in Figures 5-12 and 5-13. Also add silkscreen text legends on the solder side to identify the board, revision level, designer's initials (use your own), and date as shown in Figure 5-15. Place these legends on the SILK_SOLDER layer. Use text style MONOSI with a height of .065 inch. Remember that you are viewing the design from the component side. You must mirror any text appearing on the solder side so that the text will appear right reading on the actual artwork. Use the MIRROR command to mirror text strings.

Save the drawing. If you have a color inkjet printer, you can print the component and solder sides together and use this as a check plot. If you are using a laser printer, print out each side separately. Check each trace against the schematic, red lining both the schematic and check plot as you proceed. Correct any errors, save the final drawing to your hard drive, and save a backup copy to floppy disk.

The PCB design is now complete,and the next task is to generate manufacturing documentation and artwork.

Using the AutoPADS Utilities

The AutoPADS utilities are used to convert AutoCAD data to Gerber format photoplotter data and Excellon format NC drill data, both of which are industry standards for PCB manufacturing. Information about photoplotting artwork and numerically controlled board drilling is given in Chapter 1 starting on page 17. For detailed information about Excellon and Gerber format, see Appendixes A and B.

The AutoPADS utility programs are included on the floppy disk supplied with the book. AutoPADS consists of the main AutoPADS (AutoCAD to Gerber) conversion utility, the AutoDRIL (AutoCAD to Excellon) conversion utility, and various support files.

Detailed instructions on loading AutoPADS, configuring AutoCAD, and using AutoPADS are given in Chapter 3 starting on page 99.

The same basic procedures, explained in Chapter 3 for a single sided board, are used for the SMT board in this tutorial exercise. The only significant differences are that several additional artwork layers are required and the manufacturing documentation is somewhat more complex.

Manufacturing Documentation

Manufacturing documentation consists of the Excellon format NC drill data, drill detail drawing, and board assembly drawing.

Extracting NC Drill Data and Running AutoDRIL

Follow the same procedure as explained in Chapter 3 on pages 99-104, except substitute the appropriate subdirectory and filenames for the current tutorial, TUTOR4. When you have completed extracting and converting the NC drill data, exit to DOS and use the LIST utility to examine the tool information header in the Excellon data file DRILL.CNC. Print out the screen listing by pressing the Alt+P keys. This will give you hardcopy of the tool information header, which gives the drill sizes and quantities. This information is required for the drill detail drawing.

Drill Detail and Assembly Drawings

Start AutoCAD and load the TUTOR4 drawing. Then follow the same procedure as explained in Chapter 3 on pages 105-107.

Use Figure 5-14 as a guide for the drill detail drawing. Use the text notes shown in this figure. Take a moment to examine these notes for a fine line double sided PTH PCB using SMOBC. Compare these notes with the notes for the double sided SMOBC board shown in Figure 4-17 on page 146. Save the drawing file and then print a hardcopy of the drill detail drawing.

Use Figure 5-15 as a guide for the PCB assembly drawing. Note that both the component side and solder side views appear in this drawing at a scale factor of 2:1. The larger scale factor enhances readability. Create this assembly drawing as follows. First save the PCB file TUTOR4 using another name, such as TUTOR4A. Work on the new TUTOR4A file to create the assembly drawing. Use the SCALE command to scale the board by a factor of two. Then use the COPY command to make a second copy of the board, which will become the solder side view. Move each view into position as shown in Figure 5-15. Use the LAYER command and the ERASE commands to selectively display and erase the entities that are not required on each view. To create the component side view, turn off all layers except SILK_SOLDER and then erase the entities on this layer.

REVISIONS			
REV	DESCRIPTION	DATE	APPROVED
1.0	PILOT PRODUCTION	12-15-96	

NOTES:
1. DRILL CHART GIVES FINISHED PLATED THRU HOLE SIZES
2. HOLE SIZE TOLERANCE: ±.003
3. HOLE LOCATION TOLERANCE: ±.003
4. MATERIAL: FR-4 GLASS FILLED EPOXY, .062 THICK
5. FOIL: DOUBLE SIDED MINIMUM 2 OZ COPPER
6. APPLY GREEN SOLDER MASK OVER BARE COPPER BOTH SIDES
7. SOLDER DIP AND HOT AIR LEVEL
8. APPLY WHITE LEGEND SILKSCREEN TO BOTH SIDES
9. MINIMUM TRACK WIDTH: .008 ±.002
10. MINIMUM SPACE: .008, MAXIMUM BOW AND TWIST: 1.5%

SIZE	QTY	SYM	TOOL
.018	10	⊕	1
.031		+	
.037	10	✕	2
.045		⊡	
.062		◇	
.145		⋈	

DO NOT SCALE	BUTTERWORTH-HEINEMANN
	80 MONTEVALE AVE., STONEHAM, MA 02180
UNLESS OTHERWISE NOTED DIMENSIONS ARE IN INCHES TOLERANCES .XX ±.02 .XXX ±.005	OPTICAL SENSOR FOR DISTRIBUTOR
DRAWN	DRILL DETAIL
APPROVED	

A SIZE	1X SCALE	1 OF 1 SHEET	4001 DRAWING NUMBER

Figure 5-14   Finished Drill Detail Drawing

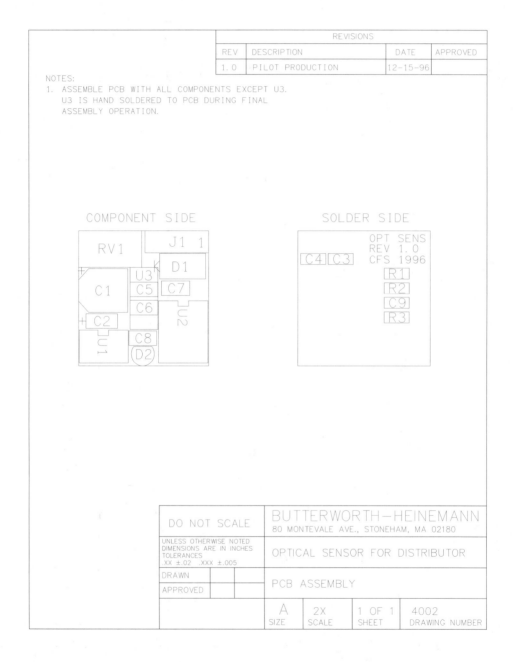

Figure 5-15   Finished PCB Assembly Drawing

To create the solder side view, turn off all layers except SILK_COMP and then erase the entities on this layer. Then turn both the SILK_COMP and SILK_SOLDER layers on again. Now only the desired entities are displayed on each view.

Add the text notes shown on Figure 5-15 to complete the PCB assembly drawing. Save the drawing file and then print a hardcopy of the drawing. This is also a good time to save another backup copy of all the files to floppy disk.

Board Artwork

The artwork required to manufacture the board includes the legend silkscreens for both sides of the board, component and solder side patterns, solder mask patterns for both sides of the board, and SMT solder paste patterns for both sides of the board. In all, eight separate artwork patterns are required. The SMT solder paste patterns are required for board assembly. The board assembly house applies solder paste to the board using stencils created from the SMT solder paste patterns.

As explained in Chapter 1, board manufacturers generally do not want artwork per se, but rather the Gerber photoplotter data for the various artwork layers. Your task will be to generate this Gerber data. The one exception is the SMT solder paste patterns. The board assembly house will require photoplotted artwork for these patterns. The board manufacturer can supply this artwork as part of the board manufacturing order.

Follow the same basic procedure as introduced in previous tutorials. First generate the binary ADI plot files for each required artwork pattern. Then use AutoPADS to convert the binary ADI plot files to Gerber format. For plotting and converting the various pieces of artwork, use the layer, color, pen, and Gerber D code assignments shown in Table 5-4. Detailed instructions appear on page 181.

Table 5-4   Layer Assignments for SMT PCB Artwork

ARTWORK	LAYER USAGE	COLOR	PEN/SIZE		D CODE/SIZE	
SILK_CMP	SILK_COMP	WHITE	2	.01	D12	.01
	OUTLINE	WHITE	2	.01	D12	.01
SILK_SOL	SILK_SOLDER	WHITE	2	.01	D12	.01
	OUTLINE	WHITE	2	.01	D12	.01
COMP	TRACE_COMP	BLUE	1	.002	D11	.003
	PADS	YELLOW	3	.02	D13	.02
		GREEN	127	.01	NOT PLOTTED	
	VIAS	YELLOW	3	.02	D13	.02
		GREEN	127	.01	NOT PLOTTED	
	PADS_COMP	CYAN	1	.002	D11	.003
	OUTLINE	WHITE	2	.01	D12	.01
SOLDER	TRACE_SOLDER	RED	1	.002	D11	.01
	PADS	YELLOW	3	.02	D13	.02
		GREEN	127	.01	NOT PLOTTED	
	VIAS	YELLOW	3	.02	D13	.02
		GREEN	127	.01	NOT PLOTTED	
	PADS_SOLDER	MAGENTA	1	.002	D11	.003
	OUTLINE	WHITE	2	.01	D12	.01
MASK_CMP	MASK_COMP	WHITE	2	.01	D12	.01
	PADS	YELLOW	4	.02	D14	.04
		GREEN	127	.01	NOT PLOTTED	
	PADS_COMP	CYAN	5	.002	D15	.012
	OUTLINE	WHITE	2	.01	D12	.01
MASK_SOL	MASK_SOLDER	WHITE	2	.01	D12	.01
	PADS	YELLOW	4	.02	D14	.03
		GREEN	127	.01	NOT PLOTTED	
	PADS_SOLDER	MAGENTA	5	.002	D15	.012
	OUTLINE	WHITE	2	.01	D12	.01
PAST_CMP	PADS_COMP	CYAN	1	.002	D11	.003
	OUTLINE	WHITE	2	.01	D12	.01
PAST_SOL	PADS_SOLDER	MAGENTA	1	.002	D11	.003
	OUTLINE	WHITE	2	.01	D12	.01

Silkscreen Artwork

The top side (component side) silkscreen artwork consists of two AutoCAD layers: SILK_COMP and OUTLINE. Use the LAYER command to turn these layers on. Turn off all the other layers in the drawing. Only the top side part outlines, silkscreen text including reference designators, and board cut marks should be displayed. All these entities should be white.

Next, you will plot this silkscreen layer. Make sure fill mode is turned on and you have done an AutoCAD regen. Click on the plot menu, select the 2000 DPI binary ADI plot driver and set up the required pen assignments. For each color, assign the appropriate pen number and size, as given in Table 5-4. Red, blue, cyan, and magenta are all pen 1 with size .002, white is pen 2 with size .010, yellow is pen 3 with size .020, and green is pen 127 (not converted by AutoPADS, but use size .010). Remember that pen 127 is used for colors that are for display only. Note that not all these pen assignments are immediately used. Make sure you select plot extents and adjust area fill on. Tell AutoCAD to write the plot data to a file. Use the filename SILK_CMP.

The back side (solder side) silkscreen artwork also consists of a two AutoCAD layers: SILK_SOLDER and OUTLINE. Use the LAYER command to turn on these layers. Turn off all the other layers in the drawing. Only the back side part outlines, silkscreen text including reference designators, and board cut marks should be displayed. All these entities should be white. Plot this silkscreen layer the same way as the top side, except use the filename SILK_SOL.

Component and Solder Side Artwork

The component side artwork consists of five AutoCAD layers: TRACE_COMP, PADS, VIAS, PADS_COMP, and OUTLINE. The TRACE_COMP layer contains all the copper traces. The PADS layer contains the through hole component pads. The VIAS layer contains all vias. The PADS_COMP layer contains top side SMT pads. Through hole pads and vias are drawn in two colors. Yellow is used for a fill pattern. This is what is photoplotted. Green is used as an outline of the pad for display purposes. The green color is assigned pen number 127 so that it will be ignored by AutoPADS. SMT pads are drawn in cyan. Use the LAYER command to turn on the TRACE_COMP, PADS, VIAS, PADS_COMP, and OUTLINE layers. Turn off all other layers in the drawing. Only the green/yellow through hole pads and vias, cyan top side SMT pads, blue component side traces, and white board cut marks should now be displayed. Plot the component side artwork. Keep the same pen assignments you previously set up.

Make sure that adjust area fill is turned on for all artwork plots. Tell AutoCAD to write the plot data to a file. Use the filename COMP.

The solder side artwork also consists of five AutoCAD layers: TRACE_SOLDER, PADS, VIAS, PADS_SOLDER, and OUTLINE. These layer assignments are analogous to those used for the component side, except that the copper traces and back side SMT pads are drawn in red and magenta, respectively. Use the LAYER command to turn on the TRACE_SOLDER, PADS, VIAS, PADS_SOLDER, and OUTLINE layers. Turn off all other layers in the drawing. Plot the solder side artwork using the filename SOLDER.

Solder Mask Artwork

Solder mask artwork is handled slightly differently. You want the solder mask pads to be .010 inch oversize and you do not want any vias to appear. Oversize pads are created with a .010 inch larger aperture to photoplot the pad fill pattern. Solder mask artwork sometimes contains ground planes (solid filled areas). These are also easily handled with the same technique.

The top side (component side) solder mask artwork consists of four AutoCAD layers: MASK_COMP, PADS, PADS_COMP, and OUTLINE. The MASK_COMP layer contains any solid areas or special patterns (not used in this tutorial). Use the LAYER command to turn on the PADS, PADS_COMP, and OUTLINE layers. Turn off all other layers in the drawing. Only the green/yellow through hole pads, cyan top side SMT pads, and white board cut marks should be displayed. Plot the top side solder mask artwork. You will need to change some pen assignments in the color table: assign yellow to pen 4 with size .020 and assign both cyan and magenta to pen 5 with size .002. Tell AutoCAD to write the plot data to a file. Use the filename MASK_CMP.

The back side (solder side) solder mask artwork also consists of four AutoCAD layers: MASK_SOLDER, PADS, PADS_SOLDER, and OUTLINE. The MASK_SOLDER layer is not used in this tutorial. Use the LAYER command to turn on the PADS, PADS_SOLDER, and OUTLINE layers. Turn off all other layers in the drawing. Plot the back side solder mask artwork using the filename MASK_SOL.

SMT Solder Paste Artwork

SMT solder paste artwork contains only the SMT pads plotted at the normal size, so you will use the original pen assignments again. The top side (component side) SMT solder paste artwork consists of two AutoCAD layers: PADS_COMP and OUTLINE. Use the LAYER command to turn on these two layers. Turn off all other layers in the drawing. Only the cyan top side SMT pads and white board cut marks should now be displayed. Plot the top side SMT solder paste artwork. You will need to change pen assignments for cyan and magenta back to pen 1. Tell AutoCAD to write the plot data to a file. Use the filename PAST_CMP.

The back side (solder side) SMT solder past artwork also consists of two AutoCAD layers, PADS_SOLDER and OUTLINE. Use the LAYER command to turn on these layers. Turn off all other layers in the drawing. Plot the back side SMT solder paste artwork using the filename PAST_SOL.

You have now generated binary ADI plot files for the eight required pieces of PCB artwork. The next step is to use AutoPADS to convert these files to Gerber format. When you are finished running AutoPADS, exit to DOS. Use the DOS DIR command to check the files in your TUTOR4 subdirectory. You should see the eight original .PLT files and eight new .GBR files. These are your Gerber artwork files.

Preparing Files for a Service Bureau

If you want to send the files for your completed SMT board to a photoplotting service bureau or board manufacturer, you can use the same procedures as explained in Chapter 3 on pages 117-120. A PCB manufacturer will require the files listed in Table 5-5.

Table 5-5   Files Required for PCB Manufacturing

FILENAME	DESCRIPTION
SILK_CMP.GBR SILK_SOL.GBR	Top and back side legend silkscreens
COMP.GBR SOLDER.GBR	Component and solder side artwork
MASK_CMP.GBR MASK_SOL.GBR	Top and back side solder mask artwork
PAST_CMP.GBR PAST_SOL.GBR	Top and back side SMT solder paste artwork (later used in PCB assembly)
DRILL.PLT or DRILL.GBR	Drill detail drawing
DRILL.CNC	Excellon drill data and tool header
README.DOC	Text file including information on apertures and the Gerber format

If you are having a service bureau plot the artwork, the drill detail drawing and Excellon drill data files can be omitted.

A sample README.DOC file suitable for a SMT board is in the TUTOR4 subdirectory on the floppy disk included with the book. The contents of the file are listed below. You can use this as a guideline for creating your own README.DOC file.

```
PCB ARTWORK DATA README FILE:
      PCB NAME:            OPTICAL SENSOR
      REV CODE:            1.0
      PART NUMBER:         7100-1130-010
      ZIP FILE:            TUTOR4.ZIP

SERVICES REQUIRED:
      FABRICATE 10 PROTOTYPE BOARDS WITH
      1 WEEK TURNAROUND. ALSO DELIVER PHOTOPLOTS
      OF SMT SOLDER PASTE MASKS. SHIP UPS RED.
      CALL FOR PURCHASE ORDER BEFORE
      PROCEEDING.

CONTACT:
      CHRIS SCHROEDER
      BUTTERWORTH-HEINEMANN
      80 MONTEVALE AVE.
      STONEHAM, MA 02180
      PH:  617-555-5555

DATA FILES:
      FILENAME                DESCRIPTION
      SILK_CMP.GBR            TOP SIDE SILKSCREEN ARTWORK
      SILK_SOL.GBR            BACK SIDE SILKSCREEN ARTWORK
      COMP.GBR                COMPONENT SIDE ARTWORK
      SOLDER.GBR              SOLDER SIDE ARTWORK
      MASK_CMP.GBR            TOP SIDE SOLDER MASK ARTWORK
      MASK_SOL.GBR            BACK SIDE SOLDER MASK ARTWORK
      PAST_CMP.GBR            TOP SIDE SMT SOLDER PASTE ARTWORK
      PAST_SOL.GBR            BACK SIDE SOLDER PASTE ARTWORK
      DRILL.PLT               DRILL DETAIL DRAWING (HPGL)
      DRILL.CNC               EXCELLON FORMAT N/C DRILL
                              DATA WITH TOOL SIZE HEADER

GERBER FORMAT NOTES:
      ENGLISH (INCH) UNITS
      ABSOLUTE COORDINATES
      XX.XXXX (2.4) DIGIT FORMAT
```

LEADING ZERO SUPPRESSION
* END OF BLOCK CHARACTER
M02* END OF PLOT

APERTURE LIST AND NOTES:
    POSITIONS ARE GERBER D-CODES. ALL
    APERTURES ARE ROUND WITH DIAMETERS
    IN MILS (I.E. 50 MILS = .05 INCH)

POSITION	SIZE
11	3
12	10
13	20
14	30
15	12

Conclusion

You have now learned the basic techniques for using AutoCAD to design a complex SMT board with components mounted on both sides.

In the next several chapters, the focus shifts to using AutoCAD as a tool to complete manufacturing documentation and check artwork for PCB designs created on other EDA/CAD systems. You will learn to import Gerber and HPGL (Hewlett-Packard Graphics Language) data into AutoCAD using special conversion programs.

6

Importing Gerber Files for Manufacturing Documentation

In the previous chapters, you learned how to draft schematics and design PCBs using AutoCAD. The next four chapters focus on using AutoCAD in a design environment alongside specialized electronic design automation (EDA) systems.

AutoCAD is intended as a general purpose drafting package and has limitations when it comes to the design of large, complex PCBs. Most companies find that specialized PCB EDA systems are a more cost-effective solution for the initial design phase. These systems include capabilities such as schematic capture, automatic placement and routing tools, and comprehensive design rules checking to eliminate possible errors. Some of these EDA systems lack general purpose drafting capabilities and cannot generate complete manufacturing documentation. Difficulties arise in meeting in-house documentation standards that may require special drawing details or a particular format for the titleblock and drawing notes. If design data can be imported from the EDA system, AutoCAD is a much more capable and flexible tool for preparing the manufacturing documentation. Required documentation typically includes the drill detail and board assembly drawings. Board outline and component location data also may be required in subsequent mechanical design tasks that involve housings and front panel layouts.

This chapter focuses on importing Gerber files into AutoCAD for the purpose of preparing manufacturing documentation. The AutoPADs utilities supplied on the disk accompanying this book include programs for converting Gerber files into AutoCAD DXB or DXF format. While the tutorial focuses on using AutoCAD, the same techniques can be used for importing Gerber data into other CAD systems. Most CAD software packages support AutoCAD DXF format. While most PCB EDA systems offer drivers for direct output of DXF data, this option usually costs hundreds or even thousands of dollars.

Obtaining Gerber Data

Since Gerber format is the industry standard used for photoplotting PCB artwork, all PCB EDA systems support Gerber format. Few photoplotters are directly interfaced on-line to EDA systems, so some means usually exists for generating Gerber files on magnetic tape or floppy disk. Most EDA systems run on networked PCs or workstations. If the EDA system is MS-DOS or Windows compatible, you can always write Gerber files out on floppy disk and use the floppy disk to transfer the files. You could also use the local area network for file transfer. If the EDA system is not PC compatible, a number of techniques can be used, including transfer by means of modem or conversion from magnetic tape to MS-DOS compatible floppy disk. Services bureaus that can do magnetic tape to MS-DOS floppy disk conversions exist in most major metropolitan areas. Occasionally, some experimentation and trial and error may be required.

Gerber data consists of ASCII text that can be examined with any text editor or the LIST utility (on the disk supplied with this book). Gerber data contains draws (traces on the PCB artwork or vectors representing graphics on documentation) and flashes (pads on the PCB artwork). Many possible Gerber format variations exist. Aspects of Gerber format include numerical format (number of digits in coordinates), absolute or incremental coordinates, English or metric units, zero suppression options, and end of block (data record) character. You must know this information in order to convert Gerber data. Appendix A includes a description of Gerber format and techniques for examining Gerber files to determine their format. Unless you are already familiar with Gerber format, spend a few minutes looking through this material.

AutoCAD DXB and DXF Format

DXB format utilizes binary data. AutoCAD can import and export DXB files. AutoCAD uses DXB format to transfer data to related programs such as AutoShade. The binary data format provides a compact means of representing graphics entities. DXB files load quickly; however not all AutoCAD entities are supported. DXB format does not support text strings or blocks. When exporting DXB files, AutoCAD explodes all blocks and strokes all text. DXB data resembles vector plotter files. In most cases, Gerber data for PCB documentation consists entirely of draws (line vectors). Conversion to DXB format offers the advantage of minimum file sizes and fast loading into AutoCAD.

DXF format utilizes ASCII data. AutoCAD and most other CAD systems support import and export of DXF data. DXF data has become the industry standard for CAD data interchange. Many desktop publishing and other types of graphics-oriented programs also provide DXF data interchange capability, making this a valuable tool across a wide spectrum of applications. DXF format supports all AutoCAD entities, including text strings and blocks. The only disadvantage is that DXF files are large and require a long time to load. Gerber files that contain flashes (pads or other special patterns such as fiducial marks) must be converted to DXF format. This is usually the case for PCB artwork. Chapter 8 covers the conversion of PCB artwork files for viewing in AutoCAD. Conversion of Gerber files containing manufacturing data into DXF format is primarily recommended for use with software other than AutoCAD Release 12 or 13. Note that conversion to DXF format is required if you are using AutoCAD LT, since this software does not support DXB format.

This chapter includes two tutorial exercises: one covering conversion of Gerber data into DXB format and the other covering conversion into DXF format. Both tutorials use the same sample Gerber files and show how to prepare basic manufacturing documentation. If you are using only AutoCAD Release 12 or 13 software, you can skip the DXF tutorial.

Starting the DXB Tutorial Exercise

This tutorial exercise shows you how to convert Gerber data into AutoCAD DXB format and then use AutoCAD to prepare basic manufacturing documentation for PCBs.

To complete the tutorial, you will require access to a PC running AutoCAD Release 12 or 13. Files and utility programs required for the tutorial exercise are included on the floppy disk supplied with this book. Design-related files are located in the subdirectory TUTOR5. FORMAT_A.DWG is an A size drawing format. PC_GBR5.EXE is a self-extracting ZIP file that contains Gerber data. The file conversion utility GBR2DXB.EXE required to convert Gerber data to DXB format is located in the AUTOPADS subdirectory.

Start the tutorial by creating the TUTOR5 subdirectory on your hard drive. Copy the files from the TUTOR5 subdirectory on the floppy disk to the TUTOR5 subdirectory on your hard drive. Extract the Gerber files by typing

CD\TUTOR5<ENTER>

PC_GBR5<ENTER>>

The extracted Gerber files are PC_DRIL5.GBR, which contains drill data, and PC_ASSY5.GBR, which contains assembly data.

The floppy disk supplied with this book also contains a popular shareware text display utility, LIST.COM, and a public domain font file, MONOSI.SHX. You can use the LIST.COM utility to examine Gerber files. Copy LIST.COM into your root or DOS directory or other directory included in your PC's PATH statement. Refer to Appendix D for more details, including shareware license and usage restrictions. MONOSI is a mono-spaced simplex font that gives highly legible results at the small text height settings required for PCB documentation. Copy MONOSI.SHX into your AutoCAD font subdirectory.

If you have completed the previous PCB design tutorials, you have already created an AutoPADS subdirectory that contains GBR2DXB.EXE on your hard drive.

If you have not done so already, create an AUTOPADS subdirectory on your hard drive. Copy all the files from the AUTOPADS subdirectory on the floppy disk to the AUTOPADS subdirectory on your hard drive.

Read through the following sections to learn how to use GBR2DXB before proceeding to convert the tutorial files.

Using the GBR2DXB Conversion Utility

The GBR2DXB program requires that all Gerber files have filenames with a .GBR extension. Once you have completed the tutorial and start using GBR2DXB to convert your own Gerber data, you may need to use the DOS REN command or Windows to rename your plot files. In accordance with AutoCAD naming conventions, DXB format files generated by the GBR2DXB program will have a .DXB extension. As the GBR2DXB program converts each Gerber file, it creates a new file with the original filename and a .DXB extension. The original Gerber file is not modified. The new DXB file is written to the same drive and subdirectory specified for the original Gerber file.

Load the GBR2DXB program by typing:

CD\AUTOPADS<ENTER>

GBR2DXB<ENTER>

The copyright notice screen appears and you can hit any key to continue and run the conversion program. The next screen is the Gerber format setup screen.

Throughout the GBR2DXB program, you can navigate the various menu options by pressing the Tab key to go forward or the Shift + Tab keys to go back to the previous choice. When you are prompted for a parameter value, layer name, or filename, enter the information and then press Enter. When you "tab" to menu options such as OK (means continue) or QUIT (stop program), the selected menu option will become highlighted. You can then execute the menu option by pressing the Enter key.

Gerber Format Setup

You should read Appendix A for a through discussion of Gerber data formats. You may have to change the default parameters depending on the format of your data. Most of the parameters are self-explanatory. The Gerber files used for the tutorial, PC_DRIL5.GBR, and PC_ASSY5.GBR are in the most common format: 2.4 decimal format, absolute coordinates, inch units, leading zero suppression, and * as the end of block character. Note that 2.4 decimal format means six total digits and four digits after the decimal point. This allows steps as small as .0001 inch. This is the default format for GBR2DXB.

AutoCAD Layer Setup

The AutoCAD layer entry screen prompts you for the layer name of the AutoCAD layer onto which all converted Gerber draws will be placed. You must enter a layer name. If you are unsure, use the layer name OBJECT. You can always use AutoCAD's editing commands later to change the layer assignment.

Layer Names by D Code Option

If you select the special layer name BYDCODE, the program will place Gerber draws onto layers named after the D codes used for the draws. For example, all draws made with D code D10 will be placed onto layer D10. Assigning layer names by D code is useful for preserving line width information. This feature is not used for the tutorial.

Gerber Filename Entry

The filename entry screen will prompt you for the name of the Gerber file that you are going to convert. You can specify a drive and path as part of the filename, just as you would with any other DOS command. But you must not include an extension. The program assumes the extension **.GBR** for the Gerber file and uses the same drive, path, and name with a .DXB extension for the output file that it creates.

If you select OK to continue, the conversion screen appears.

Conversion Process

Depending on the speed of your processor and the Gerber file size, the conversion process may require a minute or more. During the conversion process, you will see the disk access light on your PC blink as data is being read from and written to disk. When the conversion is completed, the number of lines and line extensions processed are displayed. At the end of the conversion process, you can select one of two options. You can CONTINUE to convert another file, or you can QUIT the program. If you select to continue, you will be given the option of changing the setup parameters.

Batch Conversion

GBR2DXB can automatically convert an entire batch of plot files without operator intervention. All of the plot files to be converted must reside in the same subdirectory. To start a batch conversion, simply enter the wildcard character * in place of a filename. Please note that you must still enter the proper drive and path before the wildcard character. For example, if your plot files reside in the PLOTS subdirectory on your C: drive, you would enter C:\PLOTS*.

The batch conversion option screen will appear. You can select whether plot files will be deleted or renamed after conversion. If your available disk space is limited, the DELETE option can help prevent running out of disk space. If you select the RENAME option, plot files will be renamed with a .SAV extension after conversion.

After you have selected the batch conversion option, the conversion process will start. A message window at the bottom of the screen will display the file number currently being converted and the total number of files in the batch.

As each file is converted, the filename and conversion results will be written to a log file. The log file, named GBR2DXB.LOG is automatically created at the start of each batch conversion in the same subdirectory specified for plot files. The contents of any prior log file will be erased. The log file is an ASCII text file that can be examined with any text editor or by use of the LIST utility.

Stopping the Program

During the conversion process, you can stop the program and return to the DOS prompt by pressing the Esc key. Any partially converted DXB file will be deleted. Please note that the Esc key works only while the conversion screen is displayed.

Error Messages

If an error occurs, GBR2DXB will display an appropriate error message. Most of the error messages are self-explanatory. The most common errors relate to entry of improper drive, path, or filenames. Remember that the path is relative to the subdirectory from which GBR2DXB is running. Thus if GBR2DXB is running from the C:\AUTOPADS subdirectory and the file that you want to convert, for example MYPLOT1.GBR, is loaded into the C:\PLOTS subdirectory, you must enter \PLOTS\MYPLOT1 as the path and filename on the filename entry screen.

Common Problems

GBR2DXB may not run correctly if memory-resident programs or print/plot spoolers are loaded. The program is not intended to be run from within AutoCAD either as a menu selection or by use of the SHELL command. You should quit AutoCAD (or any other program) before running GBR2DXB. GBR2DXB will run from a DOS window in Windows.

Scale Factor Problems

In most cases the scale factor will be correct and the converted drawing data will have the correct dimensions. If the converted drawing is 10X too large or too small, you probably used the wrong Gerber numeric format.

Correcting the Origin for Imported Data

The origin (the point in the drawing where X=0 and Y=0) of a converted drawing may not be in the expected location. You may have to use the AutoCAD MOVE command to move the entire drawing so that the drawing origin (or some other point) matches the AutoCAD origin.

Editing Text in Imported Data

All text in Gerber photoplotter files is stroked text. This text data now consists of individual lines. You cannot use the normal AutoCAD text editing commands such as CHANGE or CHGTEXT. If you need to edit text, you must erase the existing text first and then draw new text.

Neither of the standard AutoCAD text fonts, TXT or SIMPLEX, matches the fonts commonly used by most other systems. MONOSI (a mono-spaced simplex font) usually gives the best results.

Accuracy Limitations

One of the limitations that you may encounter when using drawing data converted from Gerber files involves the accuracy of the drawing database. Problems with the most common Gerber 2.4 format are infrequent since the resolution is .0001 inch. In the case of Gerber 2.3 format, the resolution is only .001 inch. Round-off errors can reduce the accuracy to a worst case value of ±.002 inch. If you use any of AutoCAD's automatic dimensioning features, double check all dimensions.

Completing the DXB Tutorial Exercise

Use the LIST utility to examine PC_DRIL5.GBR, one of the two Gerber files to be converted, and determine the format used. At the DOS prompt, type

CD\TUTOR5<ENTER>

LIST PC_DRIL5.GBR<ENTER>

This changes to the TUTOR5 subdirectory used for this exercise and runs LIST.COM. The resulting screen display is shown in Figure 6-1.

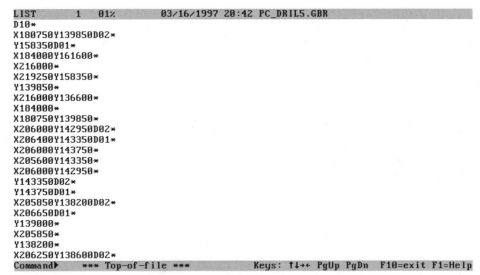

Figure 6-1   PC_DRIL5.GBR Gerber File Format

The Gerber format shown in Figure 6-1 is 2.4 numerical format, absolute coordinates, English units, leading zero suppression, and * end of block character. Refer to Appendix A for more information on Gerber data and interpreting Gerber format. Note that you cannot entirely determine the format of Gerber data by just looking at it. You can make a good guess for Gerber files that represent manufacturing documentation. If your guess is wrong, the most likely consequence is an incorrectly scaled drawing. You can correct this type of error in AutoCAD by rescaling the drawing to a reasonable size.

Use GBR2DXB to convert PC_DRIL5.GBR. You can accept the default values on the Gerber format setup screen. Enter the layer name DRILL on the AutoCAD layer setup screen.

After the conversion is completed, select the CONTINUE option. Then select CHANGE SETUP OPTIONS. You can again accept the default Gerber format values, but use the AutoCAD layer name ASSEMBLY to convert the second Gerber file, PC_ASSY5.GBR. After the second conversion is complete, select QUIT to return to DOS. Your TUTOR5 subdirectory should now contain two new files, PC_DRIL5.DXB and PC_ASSY5.DXB.

If you use the LIST utility to examine one of these DXB files, you will find the text string "AutoCAD DXB 1.0" on the first line. The rest of the file appears as unintelligible binary data.

Preparing the Drill Detail Drawing from DXB Data

Start AutoCAD and open the A size drawing format, FORMAT_A.DWG. The drawing border, title block, and revision block will be displayed on the screen. Use the STYLE command to set MONOSI with a height of .075 inch as the current text style.

Use the DXBIN command to load the PC_DRIL5.DXB file. Use the ZOOM EXTENTS command to display all the entities. The PCB outline, drill symbols, and drill chart appear near the top right corner of the display area. Converted graphics entities loaded into AutoCAD usually appear at some strange location. In this case, the Gerber driver in the original EDA system had centered the PCB on a 36×24 inch plot area. Consequently the board appears shifted about 18×12 inch from the AutoCAD origin. Use the MOVE command to center the PCB outline and position the drill chart as shown in Figure 6-2. In some cases the graphics entities loaded from a DXB file may overlap existing drawing entities. If this occurs, use the LAYER command to selectively display and edit the various entities.

Next, do another ZOOM EXTENTS and then use the SAVE AS command from the FILE menu and save the drawing as TUTOR5.DWG. Note that AutoCAD automatically assigns the .DWG suffix. This leaves your original drawing format file FORMAT_A.DWG unchanged. All subsequent editing is done with TUTOR5.DWG.

Set the UCS origin at the lower left corner of the PCB outline. Since the board has cutout corners, you must align the cursor crosshairs with the left and bottom edges of the PCB. The suggested technique is to zoom in tight, set the snap to .005, align the crosshairs, and then set the new UCS origin.

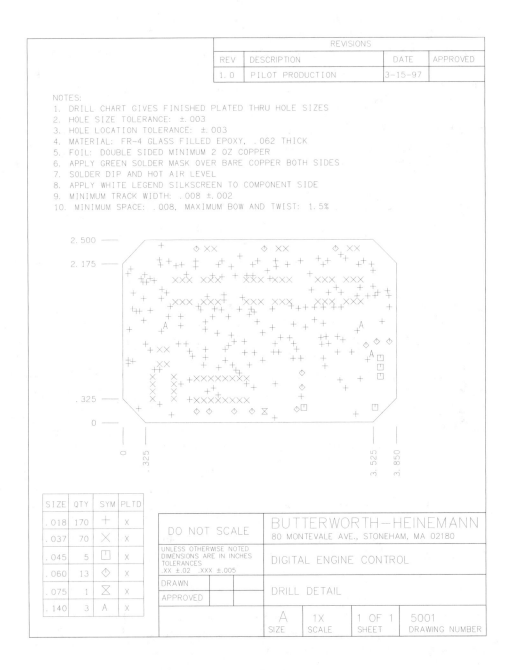

Figure 6-2   Finished Drill Detail Drawing

Set ortho mode on, set snap to .025 and then use ordinate dimensioning to dimension the board outline as shown in Figure 6-2. Note that ordinate dimensioning is preferred for PCBs, since all features are NC drilled and NC routed on the basis of an origin point. Ordinate dimensioning also produces less drawing clutter than conventional dimensioning. If you are not familiar with ordinate dimensioning in AutoCAD, refer to your AutoCAD documentation.

Next, edit the drill table. Note that the drill sizes appear in mils. For example, 18 is .018 inches. You want the drill sizes to appear in inch units. Print a hardcopy of your drawing for reference or jot down the drill sizes and quantities on a note pad. You cannot directly edit converted text, since the text consists of stroked lines. To edit text, you must erase it and then redraw the new text. Erase all the text in the drill chart, but do not erase the drill symbols. Then use the DTEXT command to enter the drill sizes in inch units and the quantities as shown in Figure 6-2. You now have a clean, professional-looking drill chart.

Use the DTEXT command to add the drill notes as shown in the top left corner of Figure 6-2. The drill notes appearing in the figure are generic notes for manufacturing a double sided PCB using SMOBC.

The last step is to add the required text information to the revision block and title block. This includes the drawing title, scale factor, sheet number, drawing number, revision code, description, and date. Use Figure 6-2 as a guide.

The drill detail drawing is now complete. Save the drawing and print a hardcopy.

Preparing the Assembly Drawing from DXB Data

Use the same basic steps as for the drill detail drawing you just completed. Start AutoCAD and open the A size drawing format, FORMAT_A.DWG. The drawing border, title block, and revision block will be displayed on the screen. Use the STYLE command to set MONOSI with a height of .075 inch as the current text style.

Use the DXBIN command to load the PC_ASSY5.DXB file. Use the ZOOM EXTENTS command to display all the entities. The PCB outline, components, and reference designators appear near the top right corner of the display area. Use the MOVE command to center the PCB outline as shown in Figure 6-3.

Next, do another ZOOM EXTENTS and then use the SAVE AS command from the FILE menu and save the drawing as TUTOR5A.DWG. All subsequent editing is done with TUTOR5A.DWG.

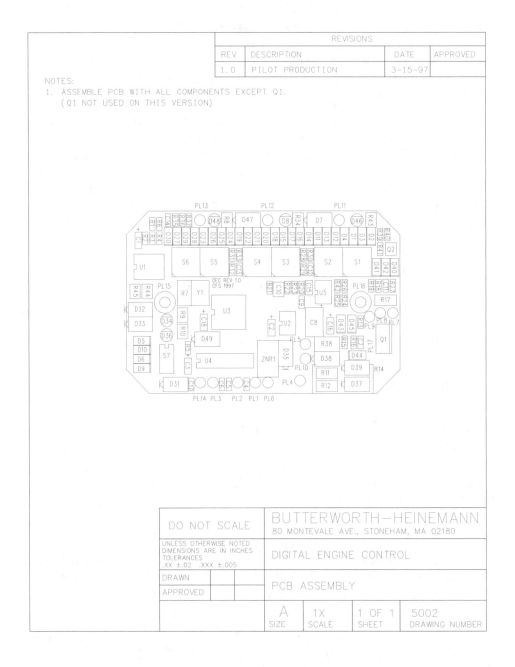

Figure 6-3   Finished PCB Assembly Drawing

Set snap to .025 and then use the DTEXT command to add the text notes shown in Figure 6-3 near the top of the drawing. The last step is to add the required text information to the revision block and title block. This includes the drawing title, scale factor, sheet number, drawing number, revision code, description, and date.

The PCB assembly drawing is now complete. Save the drawing and then print a hardcopy.

You have now completed the DXB tutorial exercise.

Starting the DXF Tutorial Exercise

This tutorial exercise shows you how to convert Gerber data into AutoCAD DXF format and then use AutoCAD to prepare basic manufacturing documentation for PCBs.

To complete the tutorial, you will require access to a PC running AutoCAD Release 12 or 13 or AutoCAD LT. Files and utility programs required for the tutorial exercise are included on the floppy disk supplied with this book. The file conversion utility GBR2DXF.EXE required to convert Gerber data to DXF format is located in the AUTOPADS subdirectory.

Design-related files are located in the subdirectory TUTOR5. FORMAT_A.DWG is an A size drawing format. PC_GBR5.EXE is a self-extracting ZIP file that contains Gerber data. PC_DOC5.APE contains Gerber aperture size information required by the GBR2DXF conversion utility.

Start the tutorial by creating the TUTOR5 subdirectory on your hard drive. Copy the files from the TUTOR5 subdirectory on the floppy disk to the TUTOR5 subdirectory on your hard drive. Extract the Gerber files by typing

CD\TUTOR5<ENTER>

PC_GBR5<ENTER>

The extracted Gerber files are PC_DRIL5.GBR, which contains drill data, and PC_ASSY5.GBR, which contains assembly data.

The floppy disk supplied with this book also contains a popular shareware text display utility, LIST.COM, and a public domain font file, MONOSI.SHX. You can use the LIST.COM utility to examine Gerber files. Copy LIST.COM into your root or DOS directory or other directory included in your PC's PATH statement. Refer to Appendix D for more details, including shareware license and usage restrictions. MONOSI is a mono-spaced simplex font that gives highly legible results at the small text height settings required for PCB documentation. Copy MONOSI.SHX into your AutoCAD font subdirectory.

If you have completed the previous PCB design tutorials, you have already created an AutoPADS subdirectory that contains GBR2DXF.EXE on your hard drive.

If you have not done so already, create an AUTOPADS subdirectory on your hard drive. Copy all the files from the AUTOPADS subdirectory on the floppy disk to the AUTOPADS subdirectory on your hard drive.

Read through the following sections to learn how to use GBR2DXF before proceeding to convert the tutorial files.

Using the GBR2DXF Conversion Utility

The GBR2DXF program requires that all Gerber files have filenames with a .GBR extension. Once you have completed the tutorial and started using GBR2DXF to convert your own Gerber data, you may need to use the DOS REN command or Windows to rename your plot files. In accordance with AutoCAD naming conventions, DXF format files generated by the GBR2DXF program have a .DXF extension. As the GBR2DXF program converts each Gerber file, it creates a new file with the original filename and a .DXF extension. The original Gerber file is not modified. The new DXF file is written to the same drive and subdirectory specified for the original Gerber file.

Load the GBR2DXF program by typing

      CD\AUTOPADS<ENTER>

      GBR2DXF<ENTER>

The copyright notice screen appears, and you can hit any key to continue and run the conversion program.

Throughout the GBR2DXF program, you can navigate the various menu options by pressing the Tab key to go forward or the Shift + Tab keys to go back to the previous choice. When you are prompted for a parameter value, layer name, or filename, enter the information and then press Enter. When you "tab" to menu options such as OK (means continue) or QUIT (stop program), the selected menu option will become highlighted. You can then execute the menu option by pressing the Enter key.

Aperture Assignments

If you are not familiar with the concept of photoplotter apertures, please read the material about Gerber format in Appendix A.

The next screen is the aperture filename entry screen. Aperture assignments are stored in files with the extension .APE. You can specify a drive and path as part of the filename, just as you would with any other DOS command. But you must not include any extension. The program assumes the extension .APE for the aperture file. Once you have entered a filename, you can select one of four options displayed at the bottom of the screen. You can CONTINUE with the conversion process. You can EDIT the aperture file. You can LIST the aperture file to a printer, or you can QUIT the program.

Creating a New Aperture File

If you want to create a new aperture file, just enter a new filename. A warning screen will appear to inform you that no file was found with this new name. You are then given the option of redoing the filename or creating a new file. If you create a new aperture file, the program will automatically continue to the aperture file edit screen.

Editing an Aperture File

The aperture file edit screen shown in Figure 6-4 displays a list of aperture numbers and sizes. The aperture number refers to the Gerber D code. Valid Gerber D codes range from D10 to D255. The aperture size is always specified in inches. Valid sizes range from .001 to 1 inch. For a given application, all of the apertures may not be used. In fact, if you define an aperture as having zero size, any Gerber draw or flash commands for that aperture will be ignored. You can use this feature selectively to enable and disable conversion of certain apertures.

Below the aperture list area is an entry box for aperture size. You can use the Tab keys to navigate between the various screen areas. When you are within the aperture list area, you can use the cursor keys (arrows) on your keyboard to highlight a particular aperture. If you then press the Enter key, you will navigate to the aperture size entry box, and you can enter a new size for the aperture you just selected.

When you have completed your editing, you can select one of four options displayed at the bottom of the screen. You can CONTINUE with the conversion process. You can SAVE the changes you have made to the aperture file. You can LIST the aperture file to a printer, or you can QUIT the program.

If you select SAVE, you can either keep the existing filename or save your changes to a new filename. Changes you have made to the aperture assignments will remain in effect as long as GBR2DXF is running, regardless of whether you elect to save the changes. If you elect to continue, the next screen is the Gerber format setup screen.

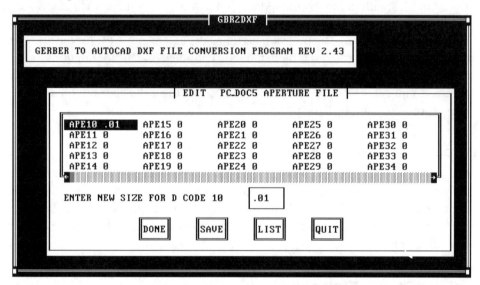

Figure 6-4   GBR2DXF Aperture File Edit Screen

Gerber Format Setup

You should read Appendix A for a through discussion of Gerber data formats. You may have to change the default parameters depending on the format of your data. Most of the parameters are self-explanatory. The Gerber files used for the tutorial, PC_DRIL5.GBR, and PC_ASSY5.GBR are in the most common format: 2.4 decimal format, absolute coordinates, inch units, leading zero suppression, and * as the end of block character. Note that 2.4 decimal format means six total digits and four digits after the decimal point. This allows steps as small as .0001 inch. This is the default format for GBR2DXF.

Gerber Filename Entry

The filename entry screen will prompt you for the name of the Gerber file that you are going to convert. You can specify a drive and path as part of the filename, just as you would with any other DOS command. But you must not include an extension. The program assumes the extension .GBR for the Gerber file and uses the same drive, path, and filename with a .DXF extension for the output file it creates.

AutoCAD Layer Setup

The AutoCAD layer entry screen prompts you for the layer name of the AutoCAD layer onto which all converted Gerber draws will be placed. You must enter a layer name. If you are unsure, use the layer name OBJECT. You can always use AutoCAD's editing commands later to change the layer assignment. If you select OK to continue, the first conversion option screen appears.

Conversion Options

The first screen allows you to select one of three conversion options for Gerber draws. You can select conversion to LINES, POLYLINES, or NONE. If you select NONE, all Gerber draws will be ignored. The second screen allows you to select one of two conversion options for Gerber flashes. You can select conversion to BLOCKS or NONE. If you select conversion to NONE, all Gerber flashes will be ignored.

For conversion of PCB documentation, select the LINES option for Gerber draws and the NONE option for Gerber flashes. After you have made the conversion option selections, the conversion process will start.

Conversion Process

Depending on the speed of your processor and the Gerber file size, the conversion process may require a minute or more. During the conversion process, you will see the disk access light on your PC blink as data is being read from and written to disk. When the conversion is completed, the number of blocks, lines, and polylines processed is displayed. At the end of the conversion process, you can select one of three options. You can LIST the conversion results to a printer. You can CONTINUE to convert another file, or you can QUIT the program. If you elect to continue, you will be given the option of changing the setup parameters.

Stopping the Program

During the conversion process, you can stop the program and return to the DOS prompt by pressing the Esc key. Any partially converted DXF file will be deleted. Please note that the Esc key works only while the conversion screen is displayed.

Error Messages

If an error occurs, GBR2DXF will display an appropriate error message. Most of the error messages are self-explanatory. The most common errors relate to entry of improper drive, path, or filenames, or printer off-line. Remember that the path is relative to the subdirectory from which GBR2DXF is running. Thus if GBR2DXF is running from the C:\AUTOPADS subdirectory and the file that you want to convert, for example MYPLOT1.GBR, is loaded into the C:\PLOTS subdirectory, you must enter \PLOTS\MYPLOT1 as the path and filename on the filename entry screen.

Common Problems

GBR2DXF may not run correctly if memory-resident programs or print/plot spoolers are loaded. The program is not intended to be run from within AutoCAD either as a menu selection or by use of the SHELL command. You should quit AutoCAD (or any other program) before running GBR2DXF. GBR2DXF will run from a DOS window in Windows.

As explained earlier, GBR2DXF can convert Gerber flashes to AutoCAD blocks. The AutoCAD block will be given the same name as the Gerber D code assigned to the aperture used for the flash. All of the block names used in a particular file are listed in the conversion results printout. Before you load the DXF file, you must define every aperture block listed in the conversion results within AutoCAD. GBR2DXF does not create the block definitions in the DXF file. Only the block name and insertion point are included. If you do not define the required aperture blocks within the AutoCAD drawing before importing the converted DXF file, you will get an error message, and AutoCAD will abort the import process.

Conversion of PCB artwork files that contain Gerber flashes and techniques for creating the required AutoCAD aperture blocks are discussed in the Chapter 7. PCB drill and assembly drawing documentation files do not normally include Gerber flashes. You should not select the option to convert flashes when converting these types of files.

Scale Factor Problems

In most cases the scale factor will be correct, and the converted drawing data will have the correct dimensions. If the converted drawing is 10X too large or too small, you probably used the wrong Gerber numeric format.

Correcting the Origin for Imported Data

The origin (the point in the drawing where X=0 and Y=0) of a converted drawing may not be in the expected location. You may have to use the AutoCAD MOVE command to move the entire drawing so that the drawing origin (or some other point) matches the AutoCAD origin.

Editing Text in Imported Data

All text in Gerber photoplotter files is stroked text. This text data now consists of individual lines. You cannot use the normal text editing commands such as CHANGE or CHGTEXT. If you need to edit text, you must erase the existing text first.

Neither of the standard AutoCAD text fonts, TXT or SIMPLEX, matches the fonts commonly used by most other systems. MONOSI (a mono-spaced simplex font) usually gives the best results.

Accuracy Limitations

One of the limitations that you may encounter when using drawing data converted from Gerber files involves the accuracy of the drawing database. Problems with the most common Gerber 2.4 format are infrequent since the resolution is .0001 inch. In the case of Gerber 2.3 format, the resolution is only .001 inch. Round-off errors can reduce the accuracy to a worst case value of ±.002 inch. If you use any of AutoCAD's automatic dimensioning features, double check all dimensions.

Completing the DXF Tutorial Exercise

Use the LIST utility to examine PC_DRIL5.GBR, one of the two Gerber files to be converted, and determine the format used. At the DOS prompt, type

CD\TUTOR5<ENTER>

LIST PC_DRIL5.GBR<ENTER>

This changes to the TUTOR5 subdirectory used for this exercise and runs LIST.COM. The resulting screen display is shown in Figure 6-1.

The Gerber format shown in Figure 6-1 is 2.4 numerical format, absolute coordinates, English units, leading zero suppression, and * end of block character. Refer to Appendix A for more information on Gerber data and interpreting Gerber format. Note that you cannot entirely determine the format of Gerber data by just looking at it. You can make a good guess for Gerber files that represent manufacturing documentation. If your guess is wrong, the most likely consequence is an incorrectly scaled drawing. You can correct this type of error in AutoCAD by rescaling the drawing to a reasonable size.

Use GBR2DXF to convert PC_DRIL5.GBR. Use the aperture file PC_DOC5.APE. This file was loaded into the TUTOR5 subdirectory and contains information on the size of the apertures in the two sample Gerber files used for the tutorial exercise. When you enter the aperture filename, you must include the path but not the extension, for example C:\TUTOR5\PC_DOC5. Select the EDIT aperture file option. The screen shown in Figure 6-4 appears. You can examine the aperture assignments. The apertures used in the two sample Gerber files are as follows:

D Code	Size (inch)
D10	.01
D40	.008

Note that when you start to use GBR2DXF to convert your own Gerber files, you must first define appropriate aperture files. EDA system managers generally establish one or more standard aperture lists that are always used for particular types of designs, so this should not be too difficult.

GBR2DXF uses the aperture file information for two purposes:

1. **Selective conversion**. If you assign zero size to a D code (aperture), the program ignores any Gerber draws or flashes with that D code.

2. **Polyline conversion**. When Gerber draws are converted to polylines, the size associated with the D code is used as the polyline width.

Examine the PC_DOC5 aperture file on the edit screen and then select CONTINUE to proceed. The Gerber format setup screen will appear. You can accept the default values on the Gerber format setup screen.

The next screen allows you to select the conversion options. For PCB manufacturing documentation, always convert Gerber draws to AutoCAD lines. Select LINES for the draw conversion option. Gerber flashes do not appear in manufacturing documentation, so select NONE for the Gerber flash conversion option.

On the next screen, enter the name of the Gerber file to be converted. When you enter the filename, you must include the path but not the extension, for example C:\TUTOR5\PC_DRIL5.

Enter the layer name DRILL on the AutoCAD layer setup screen. After the conversion is completed, select the CONTINUE option. You do not need to change the setup. Use the AutoCAD layer name ASSEMBLY to convert the second Gerber file, PC_ASSY5.GBR. After the second conversion is complete, select QUIT to return to DOS. Your TUTOR5 subdirectory should now contain two new files, PC_DRIL5.DXF and PC_ASSY5.DXF.

To familiarize yourself with DXF format, use the LIST utility to examine PC_DRIL5.DXF. The resulting screen display is shown in Figure 6-5. DXF files consist of ASCII text. You can find more information about DXF format in your AutoCAD documentation.

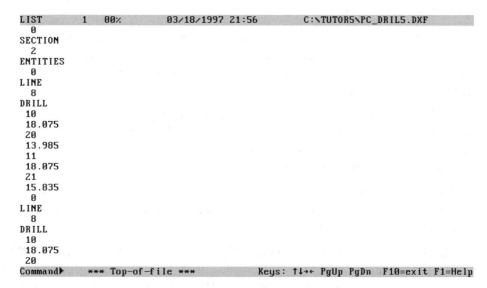

Figure 6-5   PC_DRIL5.DXF File Format

Preparing the Drill Detail Drawing from DXF Data

Start AutoCAD and open the A size drawing format, FORMAT_A.DWG. The drawing border, title block, and revision block will be displayed on the screen. Use the STYLE command to set MONOSI with a height of .075 inch as the current text style.

Use the DXFIN command to load the PC_DRIL5.DXF file. Use the ZOOM EXTENTS command to display all the entities. The PCB outline, drill symbols, and drill chart appear near the top right corner of the display area. Converted graphics entities loaded into AutoCAD usually appear at some strange location. In this case, the Gerber driver in the original EDA system had centered the PCB on a 36 × 24 inch plot area. Consequently the board appears shifted about 18 × 12 inch from the AutoCAD origin. Use the MOVE command to center the PCB outline and position the drill chart as shown in Figure 6-2. In some cases the graphics entities loaded from a DXF file may overlap existing drawing entities. If this occurs, use the LAYER command to selectively display and edit the various entities.

Next, do another ZOOM EXTENTS and then use the SAVE AS command from the FILE menu and save the drawing as TUTOR5.DWG. Note that AutoCAD automatically assigns the .DWG suffix. This leaves your original drawing format file FORMAT_A.DWG unchanged. All subsequent editing is done with TUTOR5.DWG.

Set the UCS origin at the lower left corner of the PCB outline. Since the board has cutout corners, you must align the cursor crosshairs with the left and bottom edges of the PCB. The suggested technique is to zoom in tight, set the snap to .005, align the crosshairs, and then set the new UCS origin.

Set ortho mode on, set snap to .025, and then use ordinate dimensioning to dimension the board outline as shown in Figure 6-2. Note that ordinate dimensioning is preferred for PCBs, since all features are NC drilled and NC routed on the basis of an origin point.

Ordinate dimensioning also produces less drawing clutter than conventional dimensioning. If you are not familiar with ordinate dimensioning in AutoCAD, refer to your AutoCAD documentation.

Next, edit the drill table. Note that the drill sizes appear in mils. For example, 18 is .018 inches. You want the drill sizes to appear in inch units. Print a hardcopy of your drawing for reference or jot down the drill sizes and quantities on a note pad. You cannot directly edit converted text, since the text consists of stroked lines. To edit text, you must erase it and then redraw the new text. Erase all the text in the drill chart, but do not erase the drill symbols. Then use the DTEXT command to enter the drill sizes in inch units and the quantities shown in Figure 6-2. You now have a clean, professional-looking drill chart.

Use the DTEXT command to add the drill notes as shown in the top left corner of Figure 6-2. The drill notes appearing in the figure are generic notes for manufacturing a double sided PCB using SMOBC.

The last step is to add the required text information to the revision block and title block. This includes the drawing title, scale factor, sheet number, drawing number, revision code, description, and date. Use Figure 6-2 as a guide.

The drill detail drawing is now complete. Save the drawing and print a hardcopy.

Preparing the Assembly Drawing from DXF Data

Use the same basic steps as for the drill detail drawing you just completed. Start AutoCAD and open the A size drawing format, FORMAT_A.DWG. The drawing border, title block, and revision block will be displayed on the screen. Use the STYLE command to set MONOSI with a height of .075 inch as the current text style.

Use the DXFIN command to load the PC_ASSY5.DXF file. Use the ZOOM EXTENTS command to display all the entities. The PCB outline, components, and reference designators appear near the top right corner of the display area. Use the MOVE command to center the PCB outline as shown in Figure 6-3.

Next, do another ZOOM EXTENTS and then use the SAVE AS command from the FILE menu and save the drawing as TUTOR5A.DWG. All subsequent editing is done with TUTOR5A.DWG.

Set snap to .025 and then use the DTEXT command to add the text notes shown in Figure 6-3 near the top of the drawing. The last step is to add the required text information to the revision block and title block. This includes the drawing title, scale factor, sheet number, drawing number, revision code, description, and date.

The PCB assembly drawing is now complete. Save the drawing and print a hardcopy.

You have now completed the DXF tutorial exercise.

Conclusion

You have now learned the basic techniques for converting Gerber data and importing this data into AutoCAD for the purpose of preparing manufacturing documentation. The techniques for converting and importing DXF data are applicable not only to AutoCAD but to most other CAD and desktop publishing systems that support DXF format.

In the next chapter, you will learn about an alternative approach using HPGL.

7

Importing HPGL Files for Manufacturing Documentation

In the last chapter, you learned techniques for importing Gerber files containing PCB manufacturing data from EDA systems into AutoCAD. You then used AutoCAD's powerful drafting and editing capabilities to prepare PCB manufacturing documentation from the imported Gerber data.

This chapter focuses on an alternative technique involving import of HPGL plotter data files. EDA systems universally support HPGL format data output, in no small part because of the great popularity of Hewlett-Packard plotters. In some cases, HPGL files may be more readily accessible than Gerber files. The AutoPADS utilities supplied on the disk accompanying this book include programs for converting HPGL files into AutoCAD DXB or DXF format. While the tutorial focuses on using AutoCAD, the same techniques can be used for importing Gerber data into other CAD systems that support DXF format.

Obtaining HPGL Data

Most EDA systems run on networked PCs or workstations. Hewlett-Packard plotters are typically a shared resource attached to a plot server or directly attached to the network. In either case, you can usually direct plot data to a MS-DOS compatible file on disk. Older EDA systems may have on-line plotters with a RS-232 serial interface. In this case, you can capture data to a file by using a PC to eavesdrop on the RS-232 link. The PC requires a serial communications port, a special Y-type eavesdropping cable, and communications software. Refer to the section at the end of this chapter for a detailed discussion of plotter eavesdropping techniques.

Note that HPGL/2 format is not the same as HPGL. HPGL/2 includes additional commands and support for devices such as laser and inkjet printers. The conversion utilities discussed in this chapter require HPGL. EDA/CAD system drivers used to output HPGL data for conversion should be configured for an HP7580 or HP7586 series plotter.

Overview of HPGL Data Format

HPGL format is a command language originated by Hewlett-Packard for controlling pen plotters. HPGL format consists of individual instructions composed of ASCII characters. You can examine an HPGL file using a text editor or the LIST utility (on the disk supplied with this book).

All HPGL commands share a common syntax, a two character instruction mnemonic, followed by a parameter field, and a terminator. The parameter field is omitted with some instructions. If more than one parameter is used, the parameters are separated by a comma or space. The terminator is generally a semicolon. For example

> PA2000,3000;

This instruction moves the pen to the absolute position X=2000 and Y=3000. Appendix C provides detailed information on HPGL data format. While you may find that some familiarity with HPGL is useful, you will not require detailed knowledge to use the conversion programs successfully.

AutoCAD DXB and DXF Format

DXB format utilizes binary data. AutoCAD can import and export DXB files. AutoCAD uses DXB format to transfer data to related programs such as AutoShade. The binary data format provides a compact means of representing graphics entities. DXB files load quickly; however, not all AutoCAD entities are supported. DXB format does not support text strings or blocks. When exporting DXB files, AutoCAD explodes all blocks and strokes all text. DXB data resembles vector plotter files. In most cases HPGL data for PCB documentation consists entirely of lines (straight vectors). Conversion to DXB format offers the advantage of minimum file sizes and fast loading into AutoCAD.

DXF format utilizes ASCII data. AutoCAD and most other CAD systems support import and export of DXF data. DXF data has become the industry standard for CAD data interchange. Many desktop publishing and other types of graphics-oriented programs also provide DXF data interchange capability, making this a valuable tool across a wide spectrum of applications. DXF format supports all AutoCAD entities, including text strings and blocks. The only disadvantage is that DXF files are large and require a long time to load. On rare occasions, you may encounter HPGL plot files that contain text strings. To avoid loss of the text information, you must convert these files into DXF. Otherwise, conversion of HPGL into DXF format is primarily recommended for use with software other than AutoCAD Release 12 or 13. Note that conversion to DXF format is required if you are using AutoCAD LT, since this software does not support DXB format.

This chapter includes two tutorial exercises: one covering conversion of HPGL data into DXB format and the other covering conversion into DXF format. Both tutorials use the same sample HPGL plot files and show how to prepare basic manufacturing documentation. If you are using only AutoCAD Release 12 or 13 software, you can skip the DXF tutorial.

Starting the DXB Tutorial Exercise

This tutorial exercise shows you how to convert HPGL data into AutoCAD DXB format and then use AutoCAD to prepare basic manufacturing documentation for PCBs.

To complete the tutorial, you will require access to a PC running AutoCAD Release 12 or 13. Files and utility programs required for the tutorial exercise are included on the floppy disk supplied with this book. Design related files are located in the subdirectory TUTOR6. FORMAT_A.DWG is an A size drawing format. PC_HPGL6.EXE is a self-extracting ZIP file that contains HPGL plot data. The file conversion utility HPGL2DXB.EXE required to convert HPGL data to DXB format is located in the AUTOPADS subdirectory.

Start the tutorial by creating the TUTOR6 subdirectory on your hard drive. Copy the files from the TUTOR6 subdirectory on the floppy disk to the TUTOR6 subdirectory on your hard drive. Extract the HPGL files by typing

CD\TUTOR6<ENTER>

PC_HPGL6<ENTER>

The extracted HPGL files are PC_DRIL6.PLT, which contains drill data, and PC_ASSY6.PLT, which contains assembly data.

The floppy disk supplied with this book also contains a popular shareware text display utility, LIST.COM, and a public domain font file, MONOSI.SHX. You can use the LIST.COM utility to examine HPGL files. Copy LIST.COM into your root or DOS directory or other directory included in your PC's PATH statement. Refer to Appendix D for more details, including shareware license and usage restrictions. MONOSI is a mono-spaced simplex font that gives highly legible results at the small text height settings required for PCB documentation. Copy MONOSI.SHX into your AutoCAD font subdirectory.

If you have completed the previous PCB design tutorials, you have already created an AutoPADS subdirectory that contains HPGL2DXB.EXE on your hard drive.

If you have not done so already, create an AUTOPADS subdirectory on your hard drive. Copy all the files from the AUTOPADS subdirectory on the floppy disk to the AUTOPADS subdirectory on your hard drive.

Read through the following sections to learn how to use HPGL2DXB before proceeding to convert the tutorial files.

Using the HPGL2DXB Conversion Utility

The HPGL2DXB program requires that all HPGL files have filenames with a .PLT extension. Once you have completed the tutorial and started using HPGL2DXB to convert your own HPGL data, you may need to use the DOS REN command or Windows to rename your plot files. In accordance with AutoCAD naming conventions, DXB format files generated by the HPGL2DXB program will have a .DXB extension. As the HPGL2DXB program converts each HPGL file, it creates a new file with the original filename and a .DXB extension. The original HPGL file is not modified. The new DXB file is written to the same drive and subdirectory specified for the original HPGL file.

Load the HPGL2DXB program by typing

> **CD\AUTOPADS<ENTER>**

> **HPGL2DXB<ENTER>**

The copyright notice screen appears and you can hit any key to continue and run the conversion program.

Throughout the HPGL2DXB program, you can navigate the various menu options by pressing the Tab key to go forward or the Shift + Tab keys to go back to the previous choice. When you are prompted for a parameter value, layer name, or filename, enter the information and then press Enter. When you "tab" to menu options such as OK (means continue) or QUIT (stop program), the selected menu option will become highlighted. You can then execute the menu option by pressing the Enter key.

The next screen is the linetype conversion option screen.

Linetype Conversion Options

Some CAD systems use the HPGL linetype entity to draw dashed lines. If you select YES for the linetype conversion option, each HPGL linetype will be placed on a separate AutoCAD layer. In most cases you will want to select YES for the linetype conversion option.

HPGL Filename Entry

The filename entry screen will prompt you for the name of the HPGL plot file that you are going to convert. You can specify a drive and path as part of the filename, just as you would with any other DOS command. But you must not include an extension. The program assumes the extension .PLT for the HPGL plot file and uses the same drive, path, and filename with a .DXB extension for the output file it creates. Next, you can select CONTINUE or QUIT.

If you elect to continue, the conversion screen appears.

Conversion Process

Depending on the speed of your processor and the HPGL file size, the conversion process may require a minute or more. During the conversion process, you will see the disk access light on your PC blink as data is being read from and written to disk. When the conversion is completed, the number of lines, arcs, and circles processed is displayed. If HPGL text entities are found, the number of text strings found and a warning message will be displayed. HPGL2DXB ignores HPGL text entities. At the end of the conversion process, you can select CONTINUE or QUIT. If you want to convert more files, select CONTINUE. You will return to the linetype conversion option screen.

Batch Conversion

HPGL2DXB can automatically convert an entire batch of plot files without operator intervention. All of the plot files to be converted must reside in the same subdirectory. To start a batch conversion, simply enter the wildcard character * in place of a filename. Please note that you must still enter the proper drive and path before the wildcard character. For example, if your plot files reside in the PLOTS subdirectory on your C: drive, you would enter C:\PLOTS*.

The batch conversion option screen will appear. You can select whether plot files will be deleted or renamed after conversion. If your available disk space is limited, the DELETE option can help prevent running out of disk space. If you select the RENAME option, plot files will be renamed with a .SAV extension after conversion.

After you have selected the batch conversion option, the conversion process will start. A message window at the bottom of the screen will display the file number currently being converted and the total number of files in the batch.

As each file is converted, the filename and conversion results will be written to a log file. The log file, named HPGL2DXB.LOG is automatically created at the start of each batch conversion in the same subdirectory specified for plot files. The contents of any prior log file will be erased. The log file is an ASCII text file that can be examined with any text editor or by use of the LIST utility.

Stopping the Program

During the conversion process, you can stop the program and return to the DOS prompt by pressing the Esc key. Any partially converted DXB file will be deleted. Please note that the Esc key works only while the conversion screen is displayed.

Error Messages

If an error occurs, HPGL2DXB will display an appropriate error message. Most of the error messages are self-explanatory. The most common errors relate to entry of improper drive, path, or filenames. Remember that the path is relative to the subdirectory from which HPGL2DXB is running. Thus if HPGL2DXB is running from the C:\AUTOPADS subdirectory and the file that you want to convert, for example MYPLOT1.PLT, is loaded into the C:\PLOTS subdirectory, you must enter \PLOTS\MYPLOT1 as the path and filename on the filename entry screen.

Common Problems

HPGL2DXB may not run correctly if memory-resident programs or print/plot spoolers are loaded. The program is not intended to be run from within AutoCAD either as a menu selection or by use of the SHELL command. You should quit AutoCAD (or any other program) before running HPGL2DXB. HPGL2DXB will run from a DOS window in Windows.

Scale Factor Problems

In most cases the scale factor will be correct and the converted drawing data will have the correct dimensions. If you are converting between metric and English units, you must correct the scaling of the data you have converted by using the AutoCAD SCALE command after the DXB file has been imported:

Metric (centimeters) to English (inch) use scale factor = .254

English (inch) to metric (centimeters) use scale factor = 3.937

Correcting the Origin for Imported Data

The origin (the point in the drawing where X=0 and Y=0) of a converted drawing may not be in the expected location. Two factors affect the origin. First, most Hewlett-Packard plotters locate the origin at the center of the plotting area. Second, plots may be offset to make better use of the plotter media and to create borders. You may have to use the AutoCAD MOVE command to move the entire drawing so that the drawing origin (or some other point) matches the AutoCAD origin.

Editing Text in Imported Data

HPGL2DXB only converts stroked text. This text data now consists of individual lines. You cannot use the normal AutoCAD text editing commands such as CHANGE or CHGTEXT. If you need to edit text, you must erase the existing text first and then draw new text..

Neither of the standard AutoCAD text fonts, TXT or SIMPLEX, matches the fonts commonly used by most other systems. MONOSI (a mono-spaced simplex font) usually gives the best results.

Accuracy Limitations

HPGL normally uses 1016 plotter units per inch, which is equivalent to a resolution of about .001 inch. Round-off errors can reduce the accuracy to a worst case value of ±.002 inch. If you use any of AutoCAD's automatic dimensioning features, double check all dimensions.

Completing the DXB Tutorial Exercise

Use the LIST utility to examine PC_DRIL6.PLT (one of the plot files to be converted) so you will gain familiarity with the appearance of HPGL data. At the DOS prompt, type

     CD\TUTOR6<ENTER>

     LIST PC_DRIL6.PLT<ENTER>

This changes to the TUTOR6 subdirectory used for this exercise and runs LIST.COM. The resulting screen display is shown in Figure 7-1.

```
LIST        1   02%          03/19/1997 21:58 PC_DRIL6.PLT
←.01024;3:DF;CT1;PA;PU-16256,-10668;PR;
SP1;
PU 14300,8621;PD 0,1879;
PD 330,331;
PD 3252,0;
PD 330,-331;
PD 0,-1879;
PD -330,-330;
PD -3252,0;
PD -330,330;
PU 508,-330;PD -178,0;
PD -330,330;
PD 0,178;
PU 0,1524;PD 0,177;
PD 330,331;
PD 178,0;
PU 2845,0;PD 229,0;
PD 330,-331;
PD 0,-177;
PU 0,-1524;PD 0,-178;
PD -330,-330;
PD -229,0;
PU -787,645;PD 40,40;
Command▶   *** Top-of-file ***      Keys: ↑↓→← PgUp PgDn  F10=exit F1=Help
```

Figure 7-1   PC_DRIL6.PLT HPGL File Format

The first line of HPGL data shown in Figure 7-1 sends setup commands to the plotter. The command SP1 on the second line causes the plotter to select pen 1. Subsequent commands are PU (pen up move) or PD (pen down move) followed by X,Y coordinates.

Use HPGL2DXB to convert PC_DRIL6.PLT. On the AutoCAD layer screen, you can accept the default option to convert HPGL line types to AutoCAD layers. After the conversion is completed, select the CONTINUE option and convert the second HPGL file, PC_ASSY6.PLT. After the second conversion is complete, select QUIT to return to DOS. Your TUTOR6 subdirectory should now contain two new files, PC_DRIL6.DXB and PC_ASSY6.DXB.

If you use the LIST utility to examine one of these DXB files, you will find the text string "AutoCAD DXB 1.0" on the first line. The rest of the file appears as unintelligible binary data.

Preparing the Drill Detail Drawing from DXB Data

Start AutoCAD and open the A size drawing format, FORMAT_A.DWG. The drawing border, title block, and revision block will be displayed on the screen. Use the STYLE command to set MONOSI with a height of .075 inch as the current text style.

Use the DXBIN command to load the PC_DRIL6.DXB file. Use the ZOOM EXTENTS command to display all the entities. The PCB outline, drill symbols, and drill chart appear near the lower left corner of the display area. Use the MOVE command to center the PCB outline and position the drill chart as shown in Figure 7-2. In some cases the graphics entities loaded from a DXB file may overlap existing drawing entities. If this occurs, use the LAYER command to selectively display and edit the various entities.

Once the imported entities are in position, use the CHANGE command to change their layer assignment to the DRILL layer.

Next, do another ZOOM EXTENTS and then use the SAVE AS command from the FILE menu and save the drawing as TUTOR6.DWG. Note that AutoCAD automatically assigns the .DWG suffix. This leaves your original drawing format file FORMAT_A.DWG unchanged. All subsequent editing is done with TUTOR6.DWG.

Set the UCS origin at the lower left corner of the PCB outline. Since the board has cutout corners, you must align the cursor crosshairs with the left and bottom edges of the PCB. The suggested technique is to zoom in tight, set the snap to .005, align the crosshairs, and then set the new UCS origin.

Set ortho mode on, set snap to .025, and then use ordinate dimensioning to dimension the board outline as shown in Figure 7-2. Note that ordinate dimensioning is preferred for PCBs, since all features are NC drilled and NC routed on the basis of an origin point. Ordinate dimensioning also produces less drawing clutter than conventional dimensioning. If you are not familiar with ordinate dimensioning in AutoCAD, refer to your AutoCAD documentation.

Next, edit the drill table. Note that the drill sizes appear in mils. For example, 18 is .018 inches. You want the drill sizes to appear in inch units. Print a hardcopy of your drawing for reference or jot down the drill sizes and quantities on a note pad. You cannot directly edit converted text, since the text consists of stroked lines. To edit text, you must erase it and then redraw the new text. Erase all the text in the drill chart, but do not erase the drill symbols. Then use the DTEXT command to enter the drill sizes in inch units and the quantities as shown in Figure 7-2. You now have a clean, professional-looking drill chart.

Use the DTEXT command to add the drill notes as shown in the top left corner of Figure 7-2. The drill notes appearing in the figure are generic notes for manufacturing a double sided PCB using SMOBC.

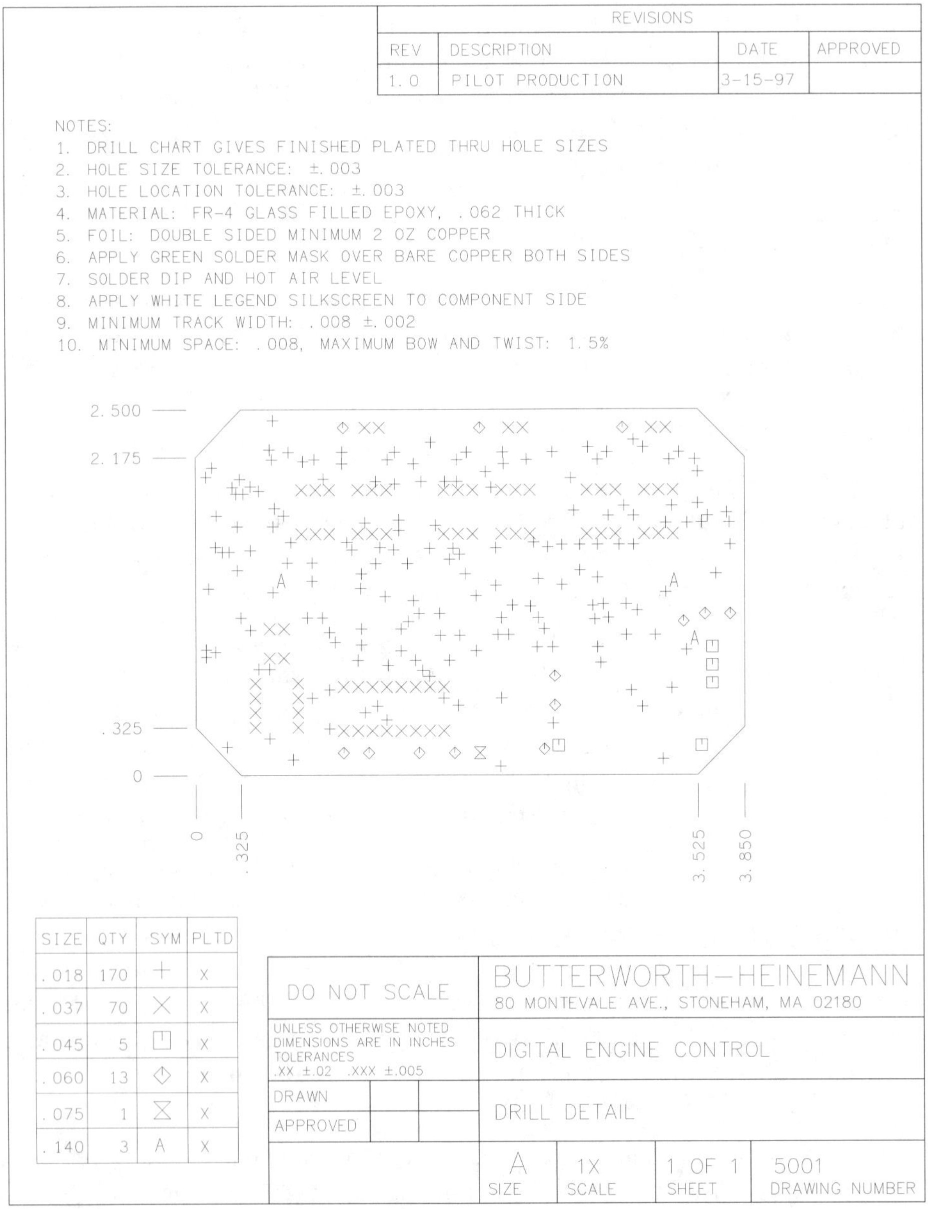

Figure 7-2   Finished Drill Detail Drawing

The last step is to add the required text information to the revision block and title block. This includes the drawing title, scale factor, sheet number, drawing number, revision code, description, and date. Use Figure 7-2 as a guide.

The drill detail drawing is now complete. Save the drawing and then print a hardcopy.

Preparing the Assembly Drawing from DXB Data

Use the same basic steps as for the drill detail drawing you just completed. Start AutoCAD and open the A size drawing format, FORMAT_A.DWG. The drawing border, title block, and revision block will be displayed on the screen. Use the STYLE command to set MONOSI with a height of .075 inch as the current text style.

Use the DXBIN command to load the PC_ASSY6.DXB file. Use the ZOOM EXTENTS command to display all the entities. The PCB outline, components, and reference designators appear near the lower left corner of the display area. Use the MOVE command to center the PCB outline as shown in Figure 7-3.

Once the imported entities are in position, use the CHANGE command to change their layer assignment to the ASSEMBLY layer.

Next, do another ZOOM EXTENTS and then use the SAVE AS command from the FILE menu and save the drawing as TUTOR6A.DWG. All subsequent editing is done using TUTOR6A.DWG.

Set snap to .025 and then use the DTEXT command to add the text notes shown in Figure 7-3 near the top of the drawing. The last step is to add the required text information to the revision block and title block. This includes the drawing title, scale factor, sheet number, drawing number, revision code, description, and date.

The PCB assembly drawing is now complete. Save the drawing and print a hardcopy.

You have now completed the DXB tutorial exercise.

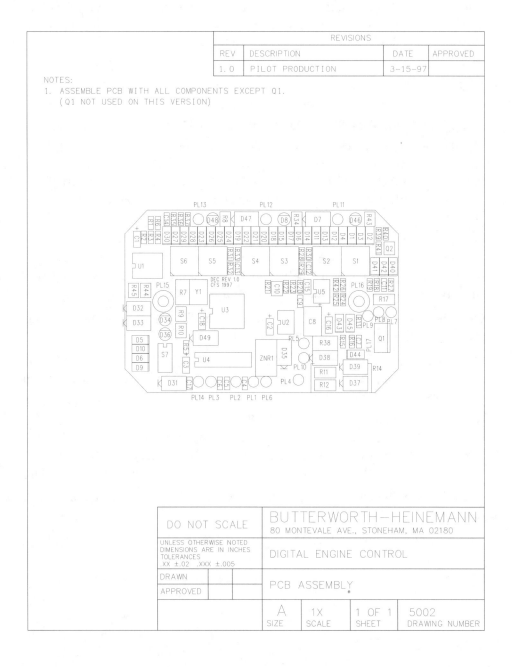

Figure 7-3   Finished PCB Assembly Drawing

Starting the DXF Tutorial Exercise

This tutorial exercise shows you how to convert HPGL data into AutoCAD DXF format and then use AutoCAD to prepare basic manufacturing documentation for PCBs.

To complete the tutorial, you will require access to a PC running AutoCAD Release 12 or 13 or AutoCAD LT. Files and utility programs required for the tutorial exercise are included on the floppy disk supplied with this book. The file conversion utility HPGL2DXF.EXE required to convert HPGL data to DXF format is located in the AUTOPADS subdirectory. Design-related files are located in the subdirectory TUTOR6. FORMAT_A.DWG is an A size drawing format. PC_HPGL6.EXE is a self-extracting ZIP file that contains HPGL plot data.

Start the tutorial by creating the TUTOR6 subdirectory on your hard drive. Copy the files from the TUTOR6 subdirectory on the floppy disk to the TUTOR6 subdirectory on your hard drive. Extract the HPGL files by typing

CD\TUTOR6<ENTER>

PC_HPGL6<ENTER>

The extracted HPGL files are PC_DRIL6.PLT, which contains drill data, and PC_ASSY6.PLT, which contains assembly data.

The floppy disk supplied with this book also contains a popular shareware text display utility, LIST.COM, and a public domain font file, MONOSI.SHX. You can use the LIST.COM utility to examine Gerber files. Copy LIST.COM into your root or DOS directory or other directory included in your PC's PATH statement. Refer to Appendix D for more details, including shareware license and usage restrictions. MONOSI is a mono-spaced simplex font that gives highly legible results at the small text height settings required for PCB documentation. Copy MONOSI.SHX into your AutoCAD font subdirectory.

If you have completed the previous PCB design tutorials, you have already created an AutoPADS subdirectory that contains HPLG2DXF.EXE on your hard drive.

If you have not done so already, create an AUTOPADS subdirectory on your hard drive. Copy all the files from the AUTOPADS subdirectory on the floppy disk to the AUTOPADS subdirectory on your hard drive.

Read through the following sections to learn how to use HPGL2DXF before proceeding to convert the tutorial files.

Using the HPGL2DXF Conversion Utility

The HPGL2DXF program requires that all HPGL files have filenames with a .PLT extension. Once you have completed the tutorial and started using HPGL2DXF to convert your own HPGL data, you may need to use the DOS REN command or Windows to rename your plot files. In accordance with AutoCAD naming conventions, DXF format files generated by the HPGL2DXF program will have a .DXF extension. As the HPGL2DXF program converts each HPGL file, it creates a new file with the original filename and a .DXF extension. The original HPGL file is not modified. The new DXF file is written to the same drive and subdirectory specified for the original HPGL file.

Load the HPGL2DXF program by typing

CD\AUTOPADS<ENTER>

HPGL2DXF<ENTER>>

The copyright notice screen appears and you can hit any key to continue and run the conversion program.

Throughout the HPGL2DXF program, you can navigate the various menu options by pressing the Tab key to go forward or the Shift + Tab keys to go back to the previous choice. When you are prompted for a filename or other text or numeric data, enter the data and then press Enter. When you "tab" to menu options such as OK (means continue) or QUIT (stop program), the selected menu option will become highlighted. You can then execute the menu option by pressing the Enter key.

Text Conversion Parameters

The next program screen is the default text conversion parameters screen shown in Figure 7-4. HPGL provides for three classes of text fonts: fixed space vector, variable space arc, and fixed space arc fonts. For each class of HPGL text font, there is a corresponding AutoCAD text style and width factor that most closely matches it. Unless you have previously encountered problems that you are trying to correct, you should accept the defaults. Note that SIMPLEX is a standard AutoCAD style.

If you select the EDIT menu option, three successive screens with edit windows will appear. In each of these screens you can accept or change the AutoCAD style and width factor for the corresponding HPGL font. After the last of the edit screens, the program will return to the main screen that lists the text conversion parameters. When you are satisfied with the text conversion parameters, select the ACCEPT menu option to continue.

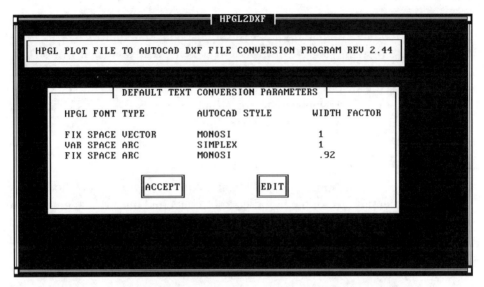

Figure 7-4   HPGL2DXF Text Conversion Parameters

Linetype Conversion Options

The next screen is the line type conversion option screen. Some CAD systems use the HPGL linetype entity to draw dashed lines. If you select YES for the linetype conversion option, each HPGL linetype will be placed on a separate AutoCAD layer. Unless you have encountered problems, you should select YES for the linetype conversion option.

HPGL Filename Entry

The filename entry screen will prompt you for the name of the HPGL plot file that you are going to convert. You can specify a drive and path as part of the filename, just as you would with any other DOS command. But you must not include an file extension. The program assumes the extension .PLT for the HPGL plot file and uses the same drive, path, and name with a .DXF extension for the output file it creates. Next, you can select CONTINUE or QUIT.

If you elect to continue, the conversion process will start.

Conversion Process

Depending on the speed of your processor and the HPGL file size, the conversion process may require a minute or more. During the conversion process, you will see the disk access light on your PC blink as data is being read from and written to disk. When the conversion is completed, the number of lines, arcs, circles, and text strings processed is displayed. At the end of the conversion process, you can select CONTINUE or QUIT. If you want to convert more files, select CONTINUE. You will return to the text conversion parameter screen.

Batch Conversion

HPGL2DXF can automatically convert an entire batch of plot files without operator intervention. All of the plot files to be converted must reside in the same subdirectory. To start a batch conversion, simply enter the wildcard character * in place of a filename. Please note that you must still enter the proper drive and path before the wildcard character. For example, if your plot files reside in the PLOTS subdirectory on your C: drive, you would enter C:\PLOTS*.

The batch conversion option screen will appear. You can select whether plot files will be deleted or renamed after conversion. If your available disk space is limited, the DELETE option can help prevent running out of disk space. If you select the RENAME option, plot files will be renamed with a .SAV extension after conversion.

After you have selected the batch conversion option, the conversion process will start. A message window at the bottom of the screen will display the file number currently being converted and the total number of files in the batch.

As each file is converted, the filename and conversion results will be written to a log file. The log file, named HPGL2DXF.LOG, is automatically created at the start of each batch conversion in the same subdirectory specified for plot files. The contents of any prior log file will be erased. The log file is an ASCII text file that can be examined with any text editor or by use of the LIST utility.

Stopping the Program

During the conversion process, you can stop the program and return to the DOS prompt by pressing the Esc key. Any partially converted DXF file will be deleted. Please note that the Esc key works only while the conversion screen is displayed.

Error Messages

If an error occurs, HPGL2DXF will display an appropriate error message. Most of the error messages are self-explanatory. The most common errors relate to entry of improper drive, path, or filenames. Remember that the path is relative to the subdirectory from which HPGL2DXF is running. Thus if HPGL2DXF is running from the C:\AUTOPADS subdirectory and the file that you want to convert, for example MYPLOT1.PLT, is loaded into the C:\PLOTS subdirectory, you must enter \PLOTS\MYPLOT1 as the path and filename on the filename entry screen.

Common Problems

HPGL2DXF may not run correctly if memory-resident programs or print/plot spoolers are loaded. The program is not intended to be run from within AutoCAD either as a menu selection or by use of the SHELL command. You should quit AutoCAD (or any other program) before running HPGL2DXF. HPGL2DXF will run from a DOS window in Windows.

Setting Up AutoCAD Text Styles

Most EDA/CAD systems generate text consisting of stroked lines, not HPGL text strings. AutoCAD text styles are irrelevant with stroked text. However, if HPGL text strings are reported at the end of the conversion process, you must set up the required AutoCAD text styles before importing the DXF data. AutoCAD will generate an error message if unsupported text styles are encountered.

Use the AutoCAD STYLE command to set up text styles to match those that you selected during the conversion process. In most cases you will require the SIMPLEX and MONOSI text styles. The SIMPLEX text style is supplied with AutoCAD. MONOSI is supplied on the disk with this book. You can accept the default parameters during the STYLE command dialogue.

Scale Factor Problems

In most cases the scale factor will be correct and the converted drawing data will have the correct dimensions. If you are converting from metric to English units, you must correct the scaling of the data you have converted by using the AutoCAD SCALE command after the DXF file has been imported:

Metric (centimeters) to English (inch) use scale factor = .254

English (inch) to metric (centimeters) use scale factor = 3.937

Correcting the Origin for Imported Data

The origin (the point in the drawing where X=0 and Y=0) of a converted drawing may not be in the expected location. Two factors affect the origin. First, most Hewlett-Packard plotters locate the origin at the center of the plotting area. Second, users offset plots to make better use of the plotter media and to create borders. You may have to use the AutoCAD MOVE command to move the entire drawing so that the drawing origin (or some other point) matches the AutoCAD origin.

Editing Text in Imported Data

HPGL2DXF converts both stroked text and HPGL text strings. In some cases, both may appear. Stroked text consists of individual lines. You cannot use the normal AutoCAD text editing commands such as CHANGE or CHGTEXT to edit stroked text. If you need to edit stroked text, you must erase the existing text first and then draw new text.

Neither of the standard AutoCAD text fonts, TXT or SIMPLEX, matches the stroked fonts commonly used in most other systems. MONOSI (a mono-spaced simplex font) usually gives the best results.

You can use AutoCAD text editing commands to edit converted HPGL text strings. Some EDA/CAD systems generate HPGL text consisting of individual characters rather than entire strings (lines). You must edit this text one character at a time unless you choose to erase it and then redraw it.

Accuracy Limitations

HPGL normally uses 1016 plotter units per inch, which is equivalent to a resolution of about .001 inch. Round-off errors can reduce the accuracy to a worst case value of ±.002 inch. If you use any of AutoCAD's automatic dimensioning features, double check all dimensions.

Completing the DXF Tutorial Exercise

Use the LIST utility to examine PC_DRIL6.PLT (one of the plot files to be converted) and to gain familiarity with the appearance of HPGL data. At the DOS prompt, type

CD\TUTOR6<ENTER>

LIST PC_DRIL6.PLT<ENTER>

This changes to the TUTOR6 subdirectory used for this exercise and runs LIST.COM. The resulting screen display is shown in Figure 7-1.

The first line of HPGL data shown in Figure 7-1 sends setup commands to the plotter. The command SP1 on the second line causes the plotter to select pen 1. Subsequent commands are PU or PD followed by X,Y coordinates.

Use HPGL2DXF to convert PC_DRIL6.PLT. You can accept the default text conversion parameters. On the AutoCAD layer screen, you can accept the default option to convert HPGL line types to AutoCAD layers. After the conversion is completed, select the CONTINUE option and convert the second HPGL file, PC_ASSY6.PLT. After the second conversion is complete, select QUIT to return to DOS. Your TUTOR6 subdirectory should now contain two new files, PC_DRIL6.DXF and PC_ASSY6.DXF.

To familiarize yourself with DXF format, use the LIST utility to examine PC_DRIL6.DXF. The resulting screen display is shown in Figure 7-5. DXF files consist of ASCII text. You can find more information about DXF format in your AutoCAD documentation.

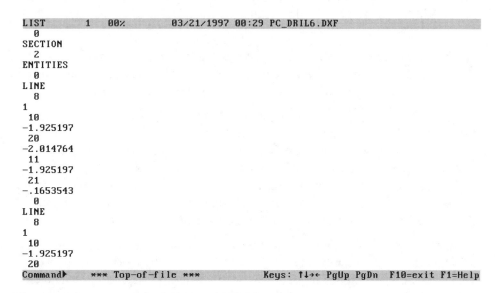

Figure 7-5   PC_DRIL6.DXF File Format

Preparing the Drill Detail Drawing from DXF Data

Start AutoCAD and open the A size drawing format, FORMAT_A.DWG. The drawing border, title block, and revision block will be displayed on the screen. Use the STYLE command to set MONOSI with a height of .075 inch as the current text style.

Use the DXFIN command to load the PC_DRIL6.DXF file. Use the ZOOM EXTENTS command to display all the entities. The PCB outline, drill symbols, and drill chart appear near the lower left corner of the display area. Use the MOVE command to center the PCB outline and position the drill chart as shown in Figure 7-2. In some cases the graphics entities loaded from a DXF file may overlap existing drawing entities. If this occurs, use the LAYER command to selectively display and edit the various entities.

Once the imported entities are in position, use the CHANGE command to change their layer assignment to the DRILL layer.

Next, do another ZOOM EXTENTS and then use the SAVE AS command from the FILE menu and save the drawing as TUTOR6.DWG. Note that AutoCAD automatically assigns the .DWG suffix. This leaves your original drawing format file FORMAT_A.DWG unchanged. All subsequent editing is done with TUTOR6.DWG.

Set the UCS origin at the lower left corner of the PCB outline. Since the board has cutout corners, you must align the cursor crosshairs with the left and bottom edges of the PCB. The suggested technique is to zoom in tight, set the snap to .005, align the crosshairs, and then set the new UCS origin.

Set ortho mode on, set snap to .025, and then use ordinate dimensioning to dimension the board outline as shown in Figure 7-2. Note that ordinate dimensioning is preferred for PCBs, since all features are NC drilled and NC routed based on an origin point. Ordinate dimensioning also produces less drawing clutter than conventional dimensioning. If you are not familiar with ordinate dimensioning in AutoCAD, refer to your AutoCAD documentation.

Next, edit the drill table. Note that the drill sizes appear in mils. For example, 18 is .018 inches. You want the drill sizes to appear in inch units. Print a hardcopy of your drawing for reference or jot down the drill sizes and quantities on a note pad. You cannot directly edit converted text, since the text consists of stroked lines. To edit text, you must erase it and then redraw the new text. Erase all the text in the drill chart, but do not erase the drill symbols. Then use the DTEXT command to enter the drill sizes in inch units and the quantities as shown in Figure 7-2. You now have a clean, professional-looking drill chart.

Use the DTEXT command to add the drill notes as shown in the top left corner of Figure 7-2. The drill notes in the figure are generic notes for manufacturing a double sided PCB using SMOBC.

The last step is to add the required text information to the revision block and title block. This includes the drawing title, scale factor, sheet number, drawing number, revision code, description, and date. Use Figure 7-2 as a guide.

The drill detail drawing is now complete. Save the drawing and print a hardcopy.

Preparing the Assembly Drawing from DXF Data

Use the same basic steps as for the drill detail drawing you just completed. Start AutoCAD and open the A size drawing format, FORMAT_A.DWG. The drawing border, title block, and revision block will be displayed on the screen. Use the STYLE command to set MONOSI with a height of .075 inch as the current text style.

Use the DXFIN command to load the PC_ASSY6.DXF file. Use the ZOOM EXTENTS command to display all the entities. The PCB outline, components, and reference designators appear near the lower left corner of the display area. Use the MOVE command to center the PCB outline as shown in Figure 7-3.

Once the imported entities are in position, use the CHANGE command to change their layer assignment to the ASSEMBLY layer.

Next, do another ZOOM EXTENTS and then use the SAVE AS command from the FILE menu and save the drawing as TUTOR6A.DWG. All subsequent editing is done with TUTOR6A.DWG.

Set snap to .025 and then use the DTEXT command to add the text notes shown in Figure 7-3 near the top of the drawing. The last step is to add the required text information to the revision block and title block. This includes the drawing title, scale factor, sheet number, drawing number, revision code, description, and date.

The PCB assembly drawing is now complete. Save the drawing and print a hardcopy.

You have now completed the DXF tutorial exercise.

HPGL Data Capture via Plotter Eavesdropping

Many older EDA systems have Hewlett-Packard or other HPGL compatible plotters that are directly interfaced (on-line) with an RS-232 serial link. HPGL commands are sent over the RS-232 link during the plotting process. If you cannot obtain HPGL data via redirection of plotter output to a disk file, you can capture data by using a PC to eavesdrop on the plotter's RS-232 link. The PC that you use will require a serial communications port. Most laptop computers include a serial port and are very handy for this purpose. You will need to fabricate the RS-232 Y-type eavesdropping cable shown in Figure 7-6. And you will require a communications program with file capture (also called *downloading*) capability such as PROCOMM PLUS (by Quarterdeck Corporation, 13160 Mindanao Way, Marina del Rey, California 90292, Phone: 310-309-3700). Various DOS and Windows versions are available.

Fabricating the RS-232 Eavesdropping Cable

Refer to Figure 7-6 for the wiring diagram. Use a 6 inch length of multi-conductor cable between PL1 and PL2. Use a two conductor cable for the connection to PL3. Make this cable just long enough to reach your PC to minimize the chance of picking up noise. The total length of RS-232 connections should remain less than 50 feet. You can obtain the required parts at your local Radio Shack store.

Eavesdropping with PROCOMM PLUS

You will need to determine the baud rate, number of data and stop bits, and parity used by the RS-232 link to the plotter. Refer to your plotter manual and to the setup switches that are found on the back of the plotter. Write down these communication parameters for reference.

Carefully read the user's manual and familiarize yourself with the operation of PROCOMM PLUS. You will use the ASCII download capability to capture HPGL files. The plotter must be operating while the CAD system is sending data, as there is a fairly complex handshaking sequence that occurs at the beginning of the plotting process.

Install the Y-type cable, load PROCOMM PLUS, and set up the communications parameters. You can use all the default values for ASCII file transfer. You should be able to see data being sent to the plotter on your screen. Refer to the PROCOMM PLUS manual for details on initiating download of ASCII data.

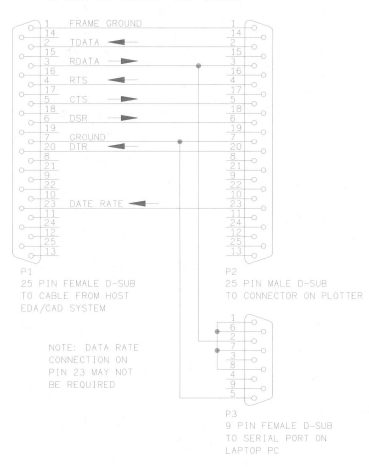

Figure 7-6   RS-232 Eavesdropping Cable

Conclusion

You have now learned the basic techniques for converting HPGL data and importing this data into AutoCAD for the purpose of preparing manufacturing documentation. The techniques for converting and importing DXF data are applicable not only to AutoCAD but also to most other CAD and desktop publishing systems that support DXF format.

In the next chapter, you will learn how to convert Gerber files containing PCB artwork data and how to import this data into AutoCAD for viewing.

8

Importing Gerber Artwork Files for Viewing

In the two previous chapters, you learned how to import PCB documentation data in Gerber and HPGL format into AutoCAD and then prepare manufacturing drawings. This chapter focuses on importing PCB artwork data in Gerber format into AutoCAD for viewing and checking. Most low cost PCB EDA systems do not have a provision for importing and viewing Gerber files. Without any means of checking Gerber files, a minor error such as an incorrect aperture assignment could cause a significant loss of time and money. If you do not have access to a specialized Gerber viewing program, you can use the techniques shown in this chapter to use AutoCAD for this purpose.

The AutoPADs utilities supplied on the disk that accompanies this book include a program for converting Gerber files into AutoCAD DXF format. While the tutorial focuses on using AutoCAD, the same techniques can be used for importing Gerber data into other CAD systems. Most CAD software packages support AutoCAD DXF format.

Obtaining Gerber Data

Since Gerber format is the industry standard for photoplotting PCB artwork, all PCB EDA systems support Gerber format. Few photoplotters are directly interfaced on-line to EDA systems, so some means usually exist for generating Gerber files on magnetic tape or floppy disk. Most EDA systems run on networked PCs or workstations. If the EDA system is MS-DOS or Windows compatible, you can always write Gerber files out on floppy disk and use the floppy disk to transfer the files. You could also use the local area network for file transfer. If the EDA system is not PC compatible, a number of techniques can be used, including transfer by means of modem or conversion from magnetic tape to MS-DOS compatible floppy disk. Services bureaus that can do magnetic tape to MS-DOS floppy disk conversions exist in most major metropolitan areas. Occasionally, some experimentation and trial and error may be required.

Gerber data consists of ASCII text that can be examined with any text editor or the LIST utility (on the disk supplied with this book). Gerber data contains draws (traces on the PCB artwork) and flashes (pads on the PCB artwork). Many possible Gerber format variations exist. Aspects of Gerber format include numerical format (number of digits in coordinates), absolute or incremental coordinates, English or metric units, zero suppression options, and end of block (data record) character. You must know this information in order to convert Gerber data. Appendix A includes information on Gerber data and techniques for examining Gerber files to determine their format. Unless you are already familiar with Gerber format, spend a few minutes looking through this material.

AutoCAD DXF Format

DXF format utilizes ASCII data. AutoCAD and most other CAD systems support import and export of DXF data. DXF data has become the industry standard for CAD data interchange. Many desktop publishing and other types of graphics-oriented programs also provide DXF data interchange capability, making this a valuable tool across a wide spectrum of applications. DXF format supports all AutoCAD entities including blocks. The only disadvantage is that DXF files are large and require a long time to load.

Starting the Tutorial Exercise

This tutorial exercise shows you how to convert Gerber artwork data into AutoCAD DXF format and then use AutoCAD to view the artwork for checking purposes.

To complete the tutorial, you will require access to a PC running AutoCAD Release 12 or 13 or AutoCAD LT.

Files and utility programs required for the tutorial exercise are included on the floppy disk supplied with this book. The file conversion utility GBR2DXF.EXE required to convert Gerber data to DXF format is located in the AUTOPADS subdirectory.

The TUTOR7 subdirectory contains design-related files. PC_ART7.DWG is an AutoCAD prototype drawing that contains certain blocks required when importing the converted Gerber files. PC_ART7.APE contains Gerber aperture size information required by the GBR2DXF conversion utility. The TUTOR7 subdirectory also contains Gerber artwork data files for a double sided board. The Gerber artwork data files and corresponding layer assignments are listed in Table 8-1 on the next page.

Start the tutorial by creating the TUTOR7 subdirectory on your hard drive. Copy the files from the TUTOR7 subdirectory on the floppy disk to the TUTOR7 subdirectory on your hard drive.

Table 8-1   Layer Assignments for Extracted Gerber Files

FILENAME	USAGE	AUTOCAD LAYER	COLOR
SILK_CMP.GBR	LEGEND SILKSCREEN	SILK_COMP	WHITE
COMP.GBR	COMPONENT SIDE ARTWORK	ART_COMP	BLUE
SOLDER.GBR	SOLDER SIDE ARTWORK	ART_SOLDER	RED
MASK_SOL.GBR	SOLDER MASK ARTWORK	MASK_SOLDER	YELLOW

The floppy disk supplied with this book also contains a popular shareware text display utility, LIST.COM. You can use the LIST.COM utility to examine Gerber files. Copy LIST.COM into your root or DOS directory or other directory included in your PC's PATH statement. Refer to Appendix D for more details, including shareware license and usage restrictions.

If you have completed the previous PCB design tutorials, you have already created an AutoPADS subdirectory that contains GBR2DXF.EXE on your hard drive.

If you have not done so already, create an AUTOPADS subdirectory on your hard drive. Copy all the files from the AUTOPADS subdirectory on the floppy disk to the AUTOPADS subdirectory on your hard drive.

Read through the following sections to learn how to use GBR2DXF before proceeding to convert the tutorial files.

Using the GBR2DXF Conversion Utility

The GBR2DXF program requires that all Gerber files have filenames with a .GBR extension. Once you have completed the tutorial and started using GBR2DXF to convert your own Gerber data, you may need to use the DOS REN command or Windows to rename your plot files. In accordance with AutoCAD naming conventions, DXF format files generated by the GBR2DXF program will have a .DXF extension. As the GBR2DXF program converts each Gerber file, it creates a new file with the original filename and a .DXF extension. The original Gerber file is not modified.

The new DXF file is written to the same drive and subdirectory specified for the original Gerber file.

Load the GBR2DXF program by typing

> **CD\AUTOPADS<ENTER>**
>
> **GBR2DXF<ENTER>**

The copyright notice screen appears, and you can hit any key to continue and run the conversion program.

Throughout the GBR2DXF program, you can navigate the various menu options by pressing the Tab key to go forward or the Shift + Tab keys to go back to the previous choice. When you are prompted for a parameter value, layer name, or filename, enter the information and then press Enter. When you "tab" to menu options such as OK (means continue) or QUIT (stop program), the selected menu option will become highlighted. You can then execute the menu option by pressing the Enter key.

Aperture Assignments

If you are not familiar with the concept of photoplotter apertures, please read the material about Gerber format in Appendix A.

The next screen is the aperture filename entry screen. Aperture assignments are stored in files with the extension .APE. You can specify a drive and path as part of the filename, just as you would with any other DOS command. But you must not include an extension. The program assumes the extension .APE for the aperture file. Once you have entered a filename, you can select one of four options displayed at the bottom of the screen. You can CONTINUE with the conversion process. You can EDIT the aperture file. You can LIST the aperture file to a printer, or you can QUIT the program.

Creating a New Aperture File

If you want to create a new aperture file, just enter a new filename. A warning screen will appear to inform you that no file was found with this new name. You are then given the option of redoing the filename or creating a new file. If you create a new aperture file, the program will automatically continue to the aperture file edit screen.

Editing an Aperture File

The aperture file edit screen shown in Figure 8-1 displays a list of aperture numbers and sizes. The aperture number refers to the Gerber D code. Valid Gerber D codes range from D10 to D255. The aperture size is always specified in inches. Valid sizes range from .001 to 1 inch. For a given application, all of the apertures may not be used. In fact, if you define an aperture as having zero size, any Gerber draw or flash commands for that aperture will be ignored. You can use this feature to selectively enable and disable conversion of certain apertures.

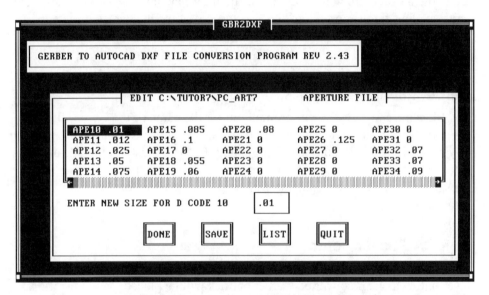

Figure 8-1   GBR2DXF Aperture File Edit Screen

Below the aperture list area is an entry box for aperture size. You can use the normal Tab commands to navigate between the various screen areas. When you are within the aperture list area, you can use the cursor keys (arrows) on your keyboard to highlight a particular aperture. If you then press the ENTER key, you will navigate to the aperture size entry box and you can enter a new size for the aperture you just selected.

When you have completed your editing, you can select one of four options displayed at the bottom of the screen. You can CONTINUE with the conversion process. You can SAVE the changes you have made to the aperture file. You can LIST the aperture file to a printer, or you can QUIT the program. If you select SAVE, you can either keep the existing filename or save your changes to a new filename. Changes you have made to the aperture assignments will remain in effect as long as GBR2DXF is running, regardless of whether you select to save the changes. If you select to continue, the next screen is the Gerber format setup screen.

Gerber Format Setup

You should read Appendix A for a through discussion of Gerber data formats. You may have to change the default parameters depending on the format of your data. Most of the parameters are self-explanatory. The Gerber files used for the tutorial are in the most common format: 2.4 decimal format, absolute coordinates, inch units, leading zero suppression, and * as the end of block character. Note that 2.4 decimal format means six total digits and four digits after the decimal point. This allows steps as small as .0001 inch. This is the default format for GBR2DXF.

Gerber Filename Entry

The filename entry screen will prompt you for the name of the Gerber file that you are going to convert. You can specify a drive and path as part of the filename, just as you would with any other DOS command. But you must not include an extension. The program assumes the extension .GBR for the Gerber file and uses the same drive, path, and filename with a .DXF extension for the output file it creates.

AutoCAD Layer Setup

The AutoCAD layer entry screen prompts you for the layer name of the AutoCAD layer onto which all converted Gerber entities will be placed. You must use a different layer name for each artwork layer, for example the suggested layer names in Table 8-1. If you are unsure, use layer names such as TEMP1, TEMP2, and so on. You can always use AutoCAD's editing commands later to change the layer assignments. If you select OK to continue, the first conversion option screen appears.

Conversion Options

The first screen allows you to select one of three conversion options for Gerber draws. You can select conversion to LINES, POLYLINES, or NONE. If you select NONE, all Gerber draws will be ignored. The second screen allows you to select one of two conversion options for Gerber flashes. You can select conversion to BLOCKS or NONE. If you select conversion to NONE, all Gerber flashes will be ignored.

For conversion of PCB artwork, always select the POLYLINES option for Gerber draws and the BLOCKS option for Gerber flashes. After you have made the conversion option selections, the conversion process will start.

Conversion Process

Depending on the speed of your processor and the Gerber file size, the conversion process may require a minute or more. During the conversion process, you will see the disk access light on your PC blink as data is being read from and written to disk. When the conversion is completed, the number of blocks, lines, and polylines processed is displayed. At the end of the conversion process, you can select one of three options. You can LIST the conversion results to a printer. You can CONTINUE to convert another file, or you can QUIT the program. If you elect to continue, you will be given the option of changing the setup parameters.

Stopping the Program

During the conversion process, you can stop the program and return to the DOS prompt by pressing the Esc key. Any partially converted DXF file will be deleted. Please note that the Esc key works only while the conversion screen is displayed.

Error Messages

If an error occurs, GBR2DXF will display an appropriate error message. Most of the error messages are self-explanatory. The most common errors relate to entry of improper drive, path, or filenames, or printer off-line. Remember that the path is relative to the subdirectory from which GBR2DXF is running. Thus if GBR2DXF is running from the C:\AUTOPADS subdirectory and the file that you want to convert, for example MYPLOT1.GBR, is loaded into the C:\PLOTS subdirectory, you must enter \PLOTS\MYPLOT1 as the path and filename on the filename entry screen.

Common Problems

GBR2DXF may not run correctly if memory-resident programs or print/plot spoolers are loaded. The program is not intended to be run from within AutoCAD either as a menu selection or by use of the SHELL command. You should quit AutoCAD (or any other program) before running GBR2DXF. GBR2DXF will run from a DOS window in Windows.

As explained earlier, GBR2DXF converts Gerber flashes to AutoCAD blocks. The AutoCAD block will be given the same name as the Gerber D code assigned to the aperture used for the flash. All of the block names used in a particular file are listed in the conversion results printout. Before you load the DXF file, you must define every aperture block listed in the conversion results within AutoCAD. Generally a prototype drawing that contains aperture block definitions is used for this purpose. Note that GBR2DXF does not create the block definitions in the DXF file. Only the block name and insertion point are included. If you do not define the required aperture blocks within the AutoCAD drawing before importing the converted DXF file, you will get an error message, and AutoCAD will abort the import process.

Scale Factor Problems

In most cases the scale factor will be correct and the converted artwork will have the correct dimensions. If the converted artwork is 10X too large or too small, you probably used the wrong Gerber numeric format.

Correcting the Origin for Imported Data

The origin (the point where X=0 and Y=0) of converted artwork may not be in the expected location. You may have to use the AutoCAD MOVE command to move the artwork entities to match the AutoCAD origin.

Editing Text in Imported Data

All text in Gerber photoplotter files is stroked text. This text data now consists of individual lines. You cannot use the normal text editing commands such as CHANGE or CHGTEXT. If you need to edit text, you must erase the existing text first.

Neither of the standard AutoCAD text fonts, TXT or SIMPLEX, matches the fonts commonly used by most other systems. MONOSI (a mono-spaced simplex font), usually gives the best results.

Accuracy Limitations

One of the limitations that you may encounter when using artwork data converted from Gerber files involves the accuracy of the drawing database. Problems with the most common Gerber 2.4 format are infrequent since the resolution is .0001 inch. In the case of Gerber 2.3 format, the resolution is only .001 inch. Round-off errors can reduce the accuracy to a worst case value of ±.002 inch.

Completing the Tutorial Exercise

Use the LIST utility to examine one of the Gerber files to be converted. Examine the legend silkscreen file SILK_CMP.GBR. At the DOS prompt type

CD\TUTOR7<ENTER>

LIST SILK_CMP.GBR<ENTER>

This changes to the TUTOR7 subdirectory used for this exercise and runs LIST.COM. The resulting screen display is shown in Figure 8-2.

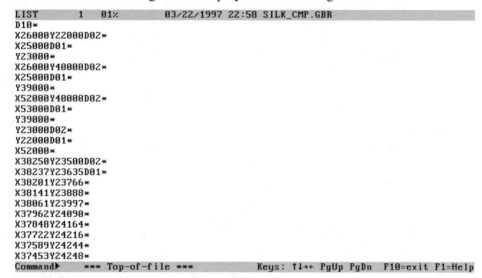

Figure 8-2   SILK_CMP.GBR Gerber File Format

The Gerber format shown in Figure 8-2 is 2.4 numerical format, absolute coordinates, English units, leading zero suppression, and * end of block character. Refer to Appendix A for more information on Gerber data and interpreting Gerber format. Note that you cannot entirely determine the format of Gerber data by simply looking at it. You can make a good guess for Gerber files that represent manufacturing documentation. If you guess incorrectly, the most likely consequence is an incorrectly scaled drawing. You can correct this type of error in AutoCAD by rescaling the drawing to a reasonable size.

Use GBR2DXF to convert SILK_CMP.GBR. Use the aperture file PC_ART7.APE. This file was loaded into the TUTOR7 subdirectory and contains information on the size of the apertures in the Gerber files used for the tutorial exercise. When you enter the aperture filename, you must include the path but not the extension, for example C:\TUTOR7\PC_ART7. Select the EDIT aperture file option. The screen shown in Figure 8-1 appears. You can examine the aperture assignments. The following apertures are used in the sample Gerber files:

D Code	Size (inch)	Shape
D10	.01	Round
D11	.012	Round
D12	.025	Round
D13	.05	Round
D14	.075	Round
D15	.085	Round
D16	.10	Round
D18	.055	Round
D19	.06	Round
D20	.08	Round
D26	.125	Round
D32	.07	Round
D33	.07	Square
D34	.09	Round
D57	.11	Round
D58	.135	Round
D70	.06	Square

Note that when you start to use GBR2DXF to convert your own Gerber files, you must first define appropriate aperture files. EDA system managers generally establish one or more standard aperture lists that are always used for particular types of designs, so this should not be too difficult.

GBR2DXF uses the aperture file information for two purposes:

1. **Selective conversion**. If you assign zero size to a D code (aperture), the program ignores any Gerber draws or flashes with that D code. Other than ignoring zero-size apertures, aperture size information is not used in the process of converting Gerber flashes to AutoCAD blocks. AutoCAD blocks are named the same as the D codes used for the Gerber flashes. The blocks do not contain any size information from the GBR2DXF aperture file.

2. **Polyline conversion**. When Gerber draws are converted to polylines, the size associated with the D code is used as the polyline width.

Examine the PC_ART7 aperture file on the edit screen and then select CONTINUE to proceed. The Gerber format setup screen will appear. You can accept the default values on the Gerber format setup screen.

The next screen allows you to select the conversion options. For PCB artwork, always convert Gerber draws to AutoCAD polylines. Select POLYLINES for the draw conversion option. Select BLOCKS for the Gerber flash conversion option.

On the next screen, enter the name of the Gerber file to be converted. When you enter the filename, you must include the path but not the extension, for example C:\TUTOR7\SILK_CMP.

Enter the corresponding AutoCAD layer name from Table 8-1 on the AutoCAD layer setup screen. After the conversion is completed, select the CONTINUE option. You do not need to change the setup. Convert the remaining Gerber files using the AutoCAD layer names from Table 8-1. After you have completed the conversions, select QUIT to return to DOS. Your TUTOR7 subdirectory should now contain four DXF files.

To familiarize yourself with DXF format, use the LIST utility to examine SILK_COMP.DXF. The resulting screen display is shown in Figure 8-3. DXF files consist of ASCII text. You can find more information about DXF format in your AutoCAD documentation.

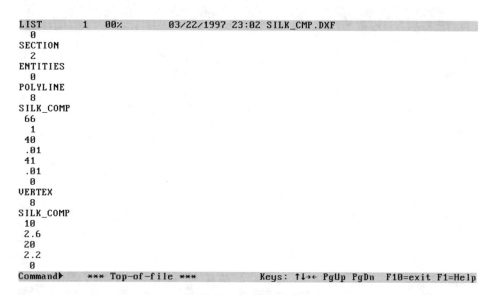

Figure 8-3   SILK_COMP.DXF File Format

Viewing Converted Artwork Files in AutoCAD

Start AutoCAD and open the prototype drawing, PC_ART7.DWG. This drawing contains the aperture block definitions required for importing the DXF files.

The prototype drawing PC_ART7.DWG can be used only with this tutorial exercise. Before you can import any of your own converted DXF files, you must first define appropriate prototype drawings with the required aperture block definitions. You can use the same size information that you use for creating the aperture files required by GBR2DXF. Techniques for defining aperture blocks are discussed at the end of this chapter.

Use the DXFIN command to load the four DXF files listed in Table 8-1. Use the FILL command to set fill mode on. Then use the ZOOM EXTENTS command to display all the entities. The PCB outline, components, pads, and traces all should appear superimposed on top of one another. Use the SAVE AS command from the FILE menu and save the drawing as TUTOR7.DWG. Note that AutoCAD automatically assigns the .DWG suffix. This leaves your original prototype drawing file PC_ART7.DWG unchanged. All subsequent work is done with TUTOR7.DWG.

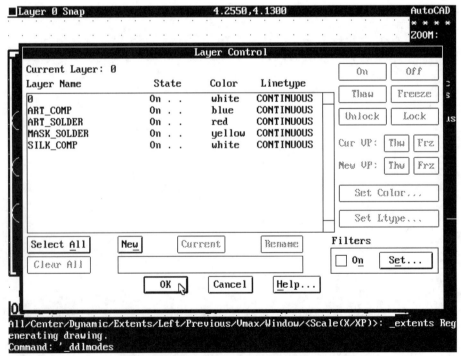

Figure 8-4   AutoCAD Layers For PCB Artwork

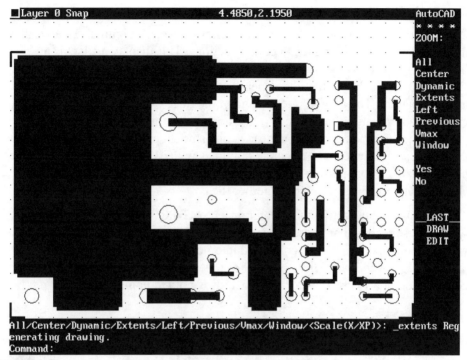

Figure 8-5   ART_SOLDER Layer Display

Use the LAYER command to set up layer colors as shown in Figure 8-4. The color assignments are based on Table 8-1. Note that the layer name information was imported with the DXF files.

Use the LAYER command to examine one artwork layer at a time. Figure 8-5 shows the screen display when the ART_SOLDER layer is turned on.

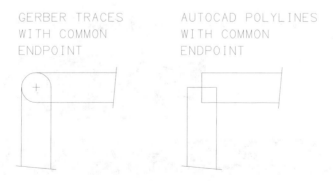

Figure 8-6   Polyline Display Artifact

Artwork Display Limitations

Close examination of the solder side artwork displayed in Figure 8-5 shows that traces appear to be missing small corner sections. This display artifact is a limitation of the conversion process from Gerber traces to AutoCAD polylines. Figure 8-6 shows the artifact more clearly. Gerber traces are drawn with a round aperture pattern. The photoplotted image of the trace extends beyond the actual endpoint coordinates by the radius of the aperture. Separate traces that join together at a common endpoint appear as one smooth entity. AutoCAD polylines are drawn with square ends. Separate polylines with a common endpoint appear to have a small section missing. You must take this artifact into account when checking artwork from converted Gerber files.

The polyline display artifact also can impact SMT PCB artwork. SMT devices typically use rectangular pads. These pads are often photoplotted as a Gerber trace with a square aperture. When converted into polylines, the traces that represent these SMT pads will appear too short. For this reason, the use of GBR2DXF to convert Gerber artwork files for SMT boards is not recommended.

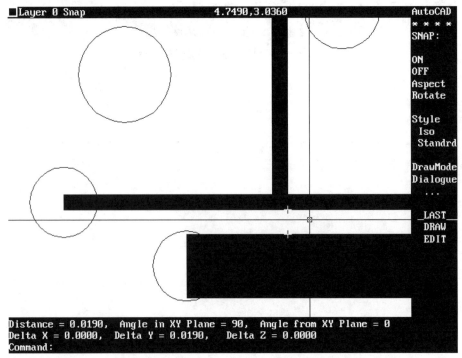

Figure 8-7   Trace-to-Trace Clearance Measurement

Measuring Clearances Between Artwork Features

You can use AutoCAD to check clearances between PCB artwork features.
Possible clearance violations include trace-to-trace, trace-to-pad, and pad-to-pad.
Other design rule violations might include improper solder mask-to-pad clearance
or spacing violations between traces and ground plane areas. Start by displaying a
particular layer. Scan for obvious violations. Zoom into possible problem areas.
Set snap to a small value such as .001 or .0005 inch. Then use the DISTANCE
command and click the cursor onto any two points between which you want to
measure the distance. Figures 8-7 and 8-8 show examples of trace-to-trace and
trace-to-pad clearance measurements. The two small sets of crosshairs near the
cursor indicate the measurement points.

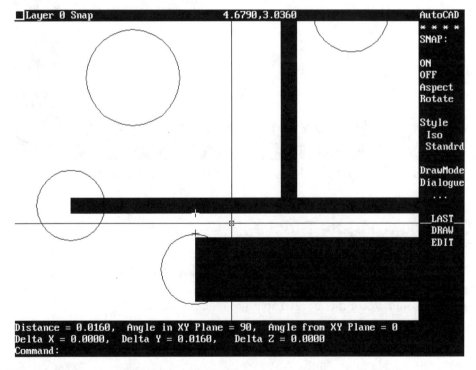

Figure 8-8   Trace-to-Pad Clearance Measurement

You can use a similar technique to measure solder mask-to-pad clearance. Turn on
the solder mask and solder side artwork layers. The solder mask clearance area is
displayed as a larger yellow pad surrounding the red solder side pad. Then use the
distance command to measure the clearance between the two pads as shown in
Figure 8-9. Most design rules are based on a .005 inch clearance, which
corresponds to a .01 inch oversize solder mask pad.

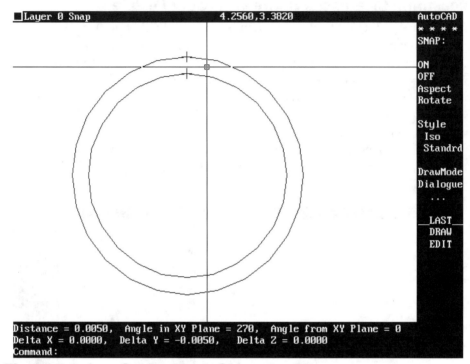

Figure 8-9   Solder Mask Clearance Measurement

Creating Aperture Blocks

Before you can import a DXF file, you must define the required aperture blocks. The conversion results listing shows the required aperture blocks. The tutorial exercise includes a prototype drawing with the required aperture blocks. Some suggestions on creating your own aperture blocks follow.

Most aperture blocks are either round or square patterns. You can use a simple circle or line to represent the outline of the aperture. This will reduce screen regeneration and redraw times. Aperture blocks are given the same name as the Gerber D code, for example a Gerber D20 flash becomes an AutoCAD block named D20. The entities used to create aperture blocks must be created on layer 0 (zero) with color and linetype BYBLOCK or BYLAYER. Use the center of the pattern as the insertion base point.

Conclusion

With this chapter you have learned how to convert Gerber data for PCB artwork into DXF files and how to import and view these files in AutoCAD. The imported artwork data can be used for checking clearances and verifying that the Gerber files are complete and correct before expensive photoplots are run.

The next chapter covers techniques for importing Excellon format NC drill files into AutoCAD.

9

Importing Excellon Format NC Drill Data

The previous chapter covered techniques for importing PCB artwork data in Gerber format into AutoCAD. In this chapter, you will learn how to import Excellon format NC drill data into AutoCAD. Excellon format is the industry standard for PCB NC drill data. All PCB EDA systems can generate Excellon format NC drill files. Situations may arise in which you must import NC drill data into AutoCAD. You can use AutoCAD to check the NC drill files by comparing the imported data to the PCB drill detail drawing. Serious errors, such as incorrect tool assignments, missing tools, or incorrect scaling would immediately become apparent. If you are using AutoCAD to design a housing for a PCB, you can use the imported NC drill data to determine precise mounting hole locations for front panel components such as switches and LEDs.

The AutoPADs utilities supplied on the disk that accompanies this book include a program for converting Excellon files into AutoCAD DXF format. While the tutorial focuses on using AutoCAD, the same techniques can be used for importing Excellon data into other CAD systems. Most CAD software packages support AutoCAD DXF format.

Obtaining Excellon Data

Since Excellon format is the industry standard for NC drilling, all PCB EDA systems support Gerber format. Since the Excellon data must be transferred to the board manufacturer, some means exist for writing out files on a transferable medium. Older EDA systems used punched paper tape for Excellon data transfer, but you are not likely to encounter this today. Most EDA systems now run on networked PCs or workstations. If the EDA system is MS-DOS or Windows compatible, you can easily write the Excellon data onto floppy disk and then use the floppy disk to transfer the files. You could also use the local area network for file transfer. If the EDA system is not PC compatible, a number of techniques can be used, including transfer by means of modem or conversion from magnetic tape to MS-DOS compatible floppy disk. Services bureaus that can do magnetic tape to

253

MS-DOS floppy disk conversions exist in most major metropolitan areas. Occasionally, some experimentation and trial and error may be required.

Excellon data consists of ASCII text that can be examined with any text editor or the LIST utility (on the disk supplied with this book). Excellon data contains tool selection commands and X,Y coordinate positioning commands. Standard Excellon data has a preset 2.3 numerical format (two digits before and three digits after the decimal point), absolute coordinates, English inch units, trailing zero suppression, and an ASCII carriage return as the end of block (data record) character. Appendix B includes information on Excellon data format.

AutoCAD DXF Format

DXF format utilizes ASCII data. AutoCAD and most other CAD systems support import and export of DXF data. DXF data has become the industry standard for CAD data interchange. Many desktop publishing and other types of graphics-oriented programs also provide DXF data interchange capability, making this a valuable tool across a wide spectrum of applications. DXF format supports all AutoCAD entities, including blocks. The only disadvantage is that DXF files are large and require a long time to load.

Starting the Tutorial Exercise

This tutorial exercise shows you how to convert Excellon NC drill data into AutoCAD DXF format and then use AutoCAD to check the data and determine coordinates.

To complete the tutorial, you will require access to a PC running AutoCAD Release 12 or 13 or AutoCAD LT. Files and utility programs required for the tutorial exercise are included on the floppy disk supplied with this book. The file conversion utility CNC2DXF.EXE required to convert Excellon data to DXF format is located in the AUTOPADS subdirectory.

Design-related files are located in the subdirectory TUTOR8. The file TUTOR8.DWG is an AutoCAD prototype drawing that contains certain blocks required to import the converted Excellon file. TUTOR8.CNC contains the Excellon NC drill data for a double sided board with a mix of through hole and surface mount devices. This is the same board used for the tutorials in Chapters 7 and 8.

Start the tutorial by creating the TUTOR8 subdirectory on your hard drive. Copy the files from the TUTOR8 subdirectory on the floppy disk to the TUTOR8 subdirectory on your hard drive.

The floppy disk supplied with this book also contains a popular shareware text display utility, LIST.COM. You can use the LIST.COM utility to examine Excellon files. Copy LIST.COM into your root or DOS directory, or other directory included in your PC's PATH statement. Refer to Appendix D for more details, including shareware license and usage restrictions.

If you have completed the previous PCB design tutorials, you have already created an AutoPADS subdirectory that contains CNC2DXF.EXE on your hard drive.

If you have not done so already, create an AUTOPADS subdirectory on your hard drive. Copy all the files from the AUTOPADS subdirectory on the floppy disk to the AUTOPADS subdirectory on your hard drive.

Read through the following sections to learn how to use CNC2DXF before proceeding to convert the tutorial files.

Using the CNC2DXF Conversion Utility

The CNC2DXF program requires that all Excellon files have filenames with a .CNC extension. Once you have completed the tutorial and started using CNC2DXF to convert your own Gerber data, you may need to use the DOS REN command or Windows to rename your plot files. In accordance with AutoCAD naming conventions, DXF format files generated by the CNC2DXF program will have a .DXF extension. As the CNC2DXF program converts each Excellon file, it creates a new file with the original filename and a .DXF extension. The original Excellon file is not modified. The new DXF file is written to the same drive and subdirectory specified for the original Excellon file.

Load the CNC2DXF program by typing

CD\AUTOPADS<ENTER>

CNC2DXF<ENTER>

The copyright notice screen appears, and you can hit any key to continue and run the conversion program. The next screen that appears is the Excellon format setup screen.

Throughout the CNC2DXF program, you can navigate the various menu options by pressing the Tab key to go forward or the Shift + Tab keys to go back to the previous choice. When you are prompted for a parameter value, layer name, or filename, enter the information and then press Enter. When you "tab" to menu options such as OK (means continue) or QUIT (stop program), the selected menu option will become highlighted. You can then execute the menu option by pressing the Enter key.

Excellon Format Setup

You should read the material in Appendix B about Excellon data format. The default values on the setup menu will usually be correct. Most of the parameters are self-explanatory.

Excellon Filename Entry

The filename entry screen will prompt you for the name of the Excellon file that you are going to convert. You can specify a drive and path as part of the filename, just as you would with any other DOS command. But you must not include an extension. The program assumes the extension .CNC for the Excellon file and uses the same drive, path, and filename with a .DXF extension for the output file it creates.

Conversion Process

CNC2DXF converts Excellon NC drill hole commands into AutoCAD blocks. All blocks are placed on the DRILL layer. The block name is the same as the Excellon tool select code. For example, all holes drilled with T1 (tool 1) will be converted into blocks named T1.

Unless you have a very slow processor, the conversion process should not take more than a few seconds. During the conversion process, you will see the disk access light on your PC blink as data is being read from and written to disk. When the conversion is completed, the program displays the number of drill holes processed. At the end of the conversion process, you can select one of two options. You can CONTINUE to convert another file, or you can QUIT the program. If you elect to continue, you will be given the option of changing the setup parameters.

Stopping the Program

During the conversion process, you can stop the program and return to the DOS prompt by pressing the Esc key. Any partially converted DXF file will be deleted. Please note that the Esc key works only while the conversion screen is displayed.

Error Messages

If an error occurs, CNC2DXF will display an appropriate error message. Most of the error messages are self-explanatory. The most common errors relate to entry of improper drive, path, or filenames or printer off-line. Remember that the path is relative to the subdirectory from which CNC2DXF is running. Thus if CNC2DXF is running from the C:\AUTOPADS subdirectory and the file that you want to convert, for example MYPCB1.CNC, is loaded into the C:\BOARDS subdirectory, you must enter \BOARDS\MYPCB1 as the path and filename on the filename entry screen.

Common Problems

CNC2DXF may not run correctly if memory-resident programs or print/plot spoolers are loaded. The program is not intended to be run from within AutoCAD either as a menu selection or by use of the SHELL command. You should quit AutoCAD (or any other program) before running CNC2DXF. CNC2DXF will run from a DOS window in Windows.

As explained earlier, CNC2DXF converts Excellon NC drill hole commands to AutoCAD blocks. The AutoCAD block will be given the same name as the Excellon T code assigned to the tool used for the particular drill hole. Before you load the DXF file, you must define blocks with tool symbols for all the T codes used in the Excellon file. Generally a prototype drawing that contains standard tool block definitions is used for this purpose. Note that CNC2DXF does not create the tool block definitions in the DXF file. Only the tool block name and insertion point are included. If you do not define the required tool blocks within the AutoCAD drawing before importing the converted DXF file, you will get an error message, and AutoCAD will abort the import process.

Scale Factor Problems

In most cases the scale factor will be correct and the converted artwork will have the correct dimensions. If the converted artwork is 10X too large or too small, you probably used the wrong Excellon numeric format.

Correcting the Origin for Imported Data

The origin (the point where X=0 and Y=0) of converted data may not be in the expected location. You may have to use the AutoCAD MOVE command to move the data to match the AutoCAD origin.

Accuracy Limitations

Standard Excellon data with a 2.3 numeric format has a resolution of .001 inch. Round-off errors can reduce the accuracy to a worst case value of ±.002 inch.

Completing the Tutorial Exercise

Use the LIST utility to examine the Excellon file, TUTOR8.CNC. At the DOS prompt type

CD\TUTOR8<ENTER>

LIST TUTOR8.CNC<ENTER>

This changes to the TUTOR8 subdirectory used for this exercise and runs LIST.COM. The resulting screen display is shown in Figure 9-1.

```
LIST        1    08%        03/23/1997 18:18 TUTOR8.CNC
%
T1F0S0
X00225Y00191
X00075Y00808
X00141Y00841
X00075Y00858
X00091Y01275
X003Y014
X00241Y01525
X00191Y01525
X00141Y01558
X003Y017
X0015Y01775
X00291Y01925
X00265Y0197
X00317Y02025
X00075Y0204
X00116Y02104
X0055Y02425
X00525Y02225
X00541Y02158
X00391Y01975
X0045Y01945
Command▶    *** Top-of-file ***        Keys: ↑↓→← PgUp PgDn  F10=exit F1=Help
```

Figure 9-1   TUTOR8.CNC Excellon File Format

The standard Excellon format shown in Figure 9-1 is 2.3 numerical format, absolute coordinates, English units, and trailing zero suppression. Carriage returns are used as the end of block character. Refer to Appendix B for more information on Excellon data.

You should always examine Excellon NC drill data files with a text editor or the LIST utility before conversion. In some cases, EDA/CAD systems may generate a header with drill size and other information that is not Excellon format data. PCB manufacturers usually look for this information, print it, and then delete it from the file before using the NC data. CNC2DXF ignores most header information, but it is possible that certain types of headers may cause strange results. If this appears to be the case, you must delete the header before converting the file.

Use CNC2DXF to convert TUTOR8.CNC using the default Excellon format parameters. The TUTOR8.CNC file contains NC drill information for the PCB shown in Figure 6-2 on page 196. The following tool codes and sizes are used:

T Code	Size (inch)
T1	.018
T2	.037
T3	.045
T4	.060
T5	.075
T6	.140

Note that when you start to use CNC2DXF to convert your own Excellon files, you must know what tools codes are used. This information is generally supplied in written form with the PCB manufacturing documentation or as a header in the Excellon file. By convention, tools are generally numbered starting with T1 for the smallest hole size.

After you have completed the conversion, select QUIT to return to DOS. Your TUTOR8 subdirectory should now contain a TUTOR8.DXF file with the converted NC drill data. You may want to examine this DXF file with a text editor or the LIST utility. You can find more information about DXF format in your AutoCAD documentation.

Importing the Converted NC Drill Data into AutoCAD

Start AutoCAD and open the prototype drawing, TUTOR8.DWG. This drawing contains the tool block definitions required for importing the DXF file. The drawing also contains the board outline dimensions and mounting hole locations.

TUTOR8.DWG contains tool block definitions for T1 through T5. The tool codes and corresponding hole sizes are listed in a table near the top left corner of the drawing. The tool blocks consist of drill symbols that appear the same as those shown in Figure 6-2. Later, when you import your own converted DXF files, you can use TUTOR8.DWG as a basis for creating your own prototype drawing with tool blocks. Just add any additional required tools blocks or edit the existing definitions.

Use the DXFIN command to import the converted DXF file, TUTOR8.DXF. Then use the ZOOM EXTENTS command to display all the entities. The drill symbols that correspond to the imported NC drill hole data should appear at the left of the display area outside the board outline.

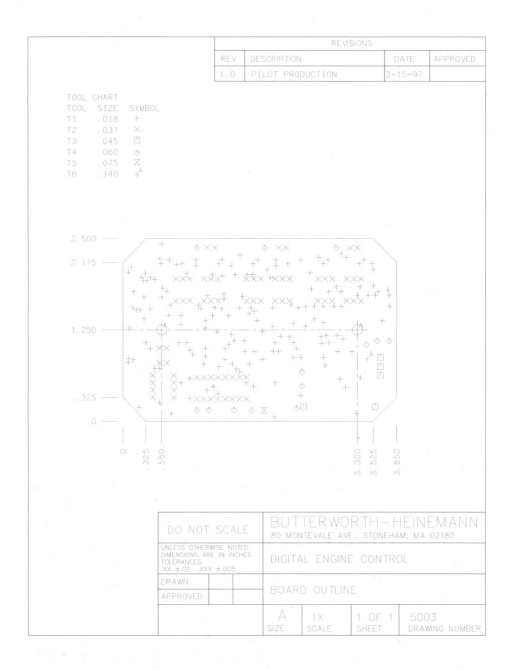

Figure 9-2   Finished Drawing with Imported NC Drill Data

Next, use the MOVE command to superimpose the drill symbols correctly within the board outline. You can use the center of the left mounting hole (A hole) as a reference point. Remember that you can use the ZOOM DYNAMIC command within MOVE to zoom into selected areas and various object snap modes to select points precisely. Select all the drill symbol entities to be moved. Use the insert of the left A hole symbol as the base point. Use the center of the left mounting hole (shown within the board outline) as the second point. The drawing should now look like Figure 9-2.

Measuring Distances Between Features

Set the UCS origin at the lower left corner of the board outline. Now you can use the AutoCAD DISTANCE command and click the cursor onto any two points between which you want to measure the distance. You can use this technique to measure the distance between a reference feature such as a mounting or tooling hole and a hole for a component the location of which is in question.

Note that all the tool blocks consist of symmetric symbols with a feature such as an intersection or endpoint clearly identifying the center location. The center location is also the insert point of the block. You can easily object snap onto the center location.

Creating Tool Blocks

Tool blocks are given the same name as the Excellon T code. For example, an Excellon T2 drill hole command becomes an AutoCAD block named T2. The entities used to create tool blocks must be created on layer 0 (zero) with color and linetype BYBLOCK or BYLAYER. Tool blocks consisting of drill symbols are a logical choice, since this facilitates checking against the PCB drill drawing. Good practice dictates using symmetrical symbols with a center feature. Use the center feature as the insertion base point.

Conclusion

In this chapter you have learned how to import Excellon NC drill data into AutoCAD. The imported NC data can be used for checking hole locations and verifying that the Excellon file is complete and correct before committing to board manufacturing.

The final tutorial exercise in the next chapter covers techniques for converting HPGL data into Gerber format for specialized applications.

10

Converting HPGL to Gerber Format

In previous chapters, you learned how to design PCBs using AutoCAD. Gerber artwork files were generated by means of conversion of AutoCAD binary ADI data into Gerber format. While this is an very efficient technique, some versions of AutoCAD such as AutoCAD LT lack the plot driver required for output of binary ADI data. This chapter introduces an alternative technique that involves conversion of HPGL into Gerber format. The HPGL2GBR conversion program is used for this purpose. You can also use the HPGL2GBR program to generate Gerber output from a wide range of other vendors' CAD systems, since the great popularity of Hewlett-Packard plotters assures universal support for HPGL output.

Introduction to the Tutorial

The tutorial exercise shows you how to generate HPGL files for a small double sided PCB and then convert these files to Gerber format.

To complete the tutorial, you will require access to a PC running AutoCAD Release 12 or 13 or AutoCAD LT for Windows 95. Earlier versions of AutoCAD LT have problems when directing HPGL plot data to a file and may not function correctly.

The PCB design from Chapter 4 is used as a basis for this tutorial. While the PCB design techniques introduced in Chapters 3 and 4 are summarized in this chapter, you should work through the exercises in Chapters 3 and 4 to gain a complete understanding of the subject. If you are using AutoCAD LT, you can complete the exercises in Chapter 3 and 4 up to the point of generating artwork.

Files and utility programs required for the tutorial exercise are included on the floppy disk supplied with this book. Design-related files are located in the subdirectory TUTOR9. The file TUTOR9.DWG contains the completed PCB design from Chapter 4. The file conversion utility HPGL2GBR required to convert HPGL data to Gerber format is located in the AUTOPADS subdirectory.

Start the tutorial by creating the TUTOR9 subdirectory on your hard drive. Copy the drawing file from the TUTOR9 subdirectory on the floppy disk to the TUTOR9 subdirectory on your hard drive.

The floppy disk supplied with this book also contains a popular shareware text display utility, LIST.COM and a public domain font file, MONOSI.SHX. You can use the LIST.COM utility to examine template files and bill of materials files. Copy LIST.COM into your root or DOS directory or other directory included in your PC's PATH statement. Refer to appendix D for more details, including shareware license and usage restrictions. MONOSI is a mono-spaced simplex font that gives highly legible results at the small text height settings required for schematics and PCBs. All the part symbols in the PCB library are defined with the MONOSI font. Copy MONOSI.SHX into your AutoCAD font subdirectory.

If you have completed the previous PCB design tutorials, you have already created an AutoPADS subdirectory that contains HPGL2GBR.EXE on your hard drive.

If you have not done so already, create an AUTOPADS subdirectory on your hard drive. Copy all the files from the AutoPADS subdirectory on the floppy disk to the AUTOPADS subdirectory on your hard drive.

Structured Design Approach

Achieving professional PCB design results with AutoCAD requires a structured design approach. This design approach includes the use of AutoCAD layers, blocks, and attributes and conversion of AutoCAD data into the Gerber and Excellon data required by board manufacturers.

Before continuing, you might spend some time reviewing layer, block, and attribute concepts in your AutoCAD documentation. The layer assignments used for PCB design are shown in Table 10-1. These layer assignments are appropriate for double sided PTH boards utilizing conventional through hole components.

Table 10-1   AutoCAD Layers for PCB Design

LAYER NAME	COLOR	PEN	SIZE	NOTES
SILK_COMP	WHITE	2	.01	
TRACE_COMP	BLUE	1	.005	
TRACE_SOLDER	RED	1	.005	

Table 10-1 (Cont.) AutoCAD Layers for PCB Design

LAYER NAME	COLOR	PEN	SIZE	NOTES
PADS	GREEN	8	N/A	DISPLAY ONLY
	YELLOW	3	.02	FILL PATTERN
VIAS	GREEN	8	N/A	DISPLAY ONLY
	YELLOW	3	.02	FILL PATTERN
MASK_COMP	WHITE	2	.01	
MASK_SOLDER	WHITE	2	.01	
OUTLINE	WHITE	2	.01	
DRILL	WHITE	2	.01	
ASSEMBLY	WHITE	2	.01	
TITLEBLOCK	WHITE	2	.01	

Each layer has an associated color, pen number, and pen width. With the exception of polylines, AutoCAD does not allow direct association of a line width parameter with graphic entities. The technique used to control and specify different line widths is the use of color. Different line widths are represented by colors. A particular pen is then assigned to each color for plotting. In turn, each pen has a defined pen width.

Let's examine the layer assignments in Table 10-1 in more detail. Please note that these layer assignments are the same as those introduced in Chapter 3 on pages 83-85 with the exception of the pen number used for green. The terminology can be somewhat confusing: for example the term *solder mask* refers to the artwork used for screening green solder resist on the PCB surface. Boards can have both a solder side and component side solder mask. Also note that artwork is created by means of plotting a composite of multiple layers. For example, the solder side artwork consists of the OUTLINE, PADS, and TRACE_SOLDER layers.

- **SILK_COMP**. This layer contains component outlines and legends (reference designators) that are silkscreened with white ink on the top side of the PCB. The silkscreen outlines and legends are displayed in white and plotted with pen 2, which is assigned a width of .01 inch. This is an industry standard width that gives good results with the silkscreening process.

- **TRACE_COMP**. This layer contains all circuit traces and other copper patterns on the component side of the PCB. The component side is displayed in blue and plotted with pen 1, which is assigned a width of .005 inch. Circuit traces and solid copper areas are drawn as polylines. The AutoCAD plot driver strokes the pen back and forth to fill in polylines. Using a fine pen width such as .005 inch allows narrow polylines down to about .012 inch.

- **TRACE_SOLDER**. This layer contains all circuit traces and other copper patterns on the solder side of the PCB. For a single sided board, all circuit traces are on the solder side. The solder side is displayed in red and plotted with pen 1, which is assigned a width of .005 inch. The same plotting considerations as noted for the component side apply to the solder side.

- **PADS**. This layer contains pads for through hole components. In all the tutorial exercises, pads for through hole parts are identical on both the component and solder sides of the PCB. Two colors are used for pads. Green is used to display the outline of the pad for design and checking purposes. Note that the conversion program HPGL2GBR ignores any plot data for pen number 8. Pen number 8 is assigned to green to prevent this color from plotting. Yellow is used for the fill pattern. This yellow fill pattern is plotted with pen 3, which is assigned a width of .02 inch.

- **VIAS**. This layer contains pads for vias. In all other respects, this layer is treated the same as the PADS layer. The use of a separate VIAS layer allows a solder mask artwork to be generated without clearance areas for vias.

- **MASK_COMP.** This layer contains any special solder mask patterns required for the top (component) side of the board. The tutorial exercises in this book do not require special solder mask patterns. When the solder mask artwork is plotted, oversize component pads are plotted along with any special patterns on this layer. The oversize pads are created by means of changing the pen number of the yellow fill pattern on the PADS layer to pen 4 which is then plotted with a width of .03 inch. The resulting pads are .01 inch oversize as customary for solder mask artwork.

- **MASK_SOLDER**. This layer contains any special solder mask patterns required for the back (solder) side of the board.

- **OUTLINE.** This layer contains cut marks, scribe lines, and other features that define the board outline. These features are displayed in white and plotted with pen 2, which is assigned a width of .01 inch. The board manufacturer uses the outline features to depanelize individual boards by means of shearing or NC routing operations.

- **DRILL**. This layer contains drill size symbols and attributes associated with the pads of through hole components and vias. The DRILL layer also contains manufacturing notes. Drill size attributes are extracted and converted to

Excellon format NC drill data. The drill size symbols and manufacturing notes appear in the drill detail drawing, which is part of the documentation required for PCB manufacturing.

- **ASSEMBLY**. This layer contains notes and details that will appear in the PCB assembly drawing.

- **TITLEBLOCK**. This layer contains the drawing border, title block, and revision block used for manufacturing documentation.

At first glance, the number of required layers may seem overwhelming and confusing. In fact, the use of a structured approach with artwork defined by multiple layers greatly simplifies the design process.

Pad Blocks

AutoCAD blocks are used for all pads on the PCB. Pad blocks are in turn nested within part blocks that represent the components on the PCB. Individual pads can also appear by themselves. Examples include vias, the connections between layers on double sided boards, and mounting holes.

Figure 10-1 shows a typical round pad block. The pad block consists of entities on two layers: PADS and DRILL. The insertion base point is the center of the pad. For conventional single and double sided boards using through hole components, only a single pads layer is required since identical pads are used on both sides of the board.

Entities on the PADS layer consist of a green display outline and a yellow fill pattern. The green display outline is used during the design process and for printing check plots on a laser printer. It represents the outer boundary of the pad and allows a quick visual determination of clearances to adjacent pads and traces. For final artwork, plotting of the green outline is suppressed by means of assigning the color green to a nonexistent pen number.

The yellow fill pattern must be drawn so that the pad has the correct outline on the final artwork plot. Enough overlap must exist between adjacent fill lines to assure that the interior of the pad is plotted as a solid area without clear streaks. A .02 inch pen width is used for plotting the pads as they appear on the component and solder side of the PCB. The outline of the fill pattern must be offset by half the pen width. Thus the yellow outline must be created with a radius .01 inch less than the actual radius of the pad. Internal fill lines are spaced .015 inch apart, resulting in an overlap of .005 inch. The internal fill lines extend to within about .01 inch of the yellow outline.

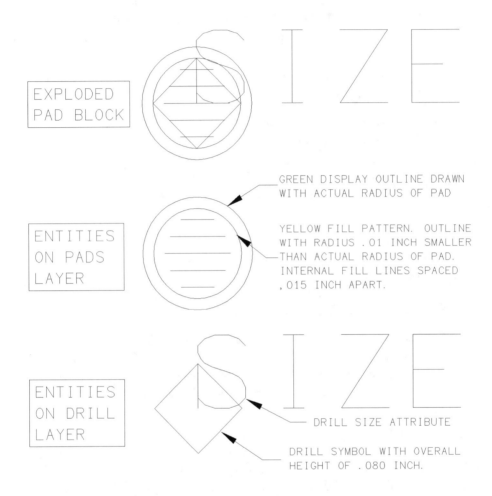

Figure 10-1   Detail of a Pad Block

Entities on the DRILL layer consist of a drill size symbol and attribute. Drill symbols appear on the PCB manufacturing drawing (also referred to as the *drill detail drawing*). A unique symbol is used for each drill size. Thus both round and square pads with a .037 inch drill hole would use the same drill symbol. The following industry standards exist for drill symbols:

- **Size**. Since the most common hole spacing is on .1 inch centers, drill symbols are usually drawn so that they will fit into a .08 × .08 inch box. This assures that adjacent symbols do not overlap. In some cases holes are closer together and some overlap will occur, but the .08 × .08 drill symbol size is a good compromise. Smaller symbols would reduce legibility.

- **Symbol**. The most common drill symbol is a cross (+). Drill symbols should clearly identify the center of the pad and be symmetric about the pad centerline. Note that the drill symbol in Figure 10-1 has a line drawn from the top of the box to the center of the pad.

AutoCAD attributes are used to associate drill size information with the pad block. The drill size attribute along with the X and Y coordinates for each pad on the board can then by extracted with the ATTEXT command and written to a file. The information in this file can in turn be converted into Excellon format NC drill data for the board manufacturer.

Drill size is a preset, invisible attribute with prompt and tag set to SIZE. The attribute value is preset to the required drill hole size. Since the drill size attribute is defined as an invisible attribute, it is not displayed unless the ATTDISP parameter is set to on. The drill size attribute does not normally need to be displayed during PCB design operations or plotted. It is only used to extract information in the creation of the Excellon NC drill data. Note that the tag SIZE, not the preset value is shown in Figure 10-1 since the pad block in the figure has been exploded. When attributes are created, they are drawn in the current text style. The font and height of an invisible attribute are not critical. A convenient insertion point for the drill size attribute is the center of the pad. The choice of this location is arbitrary; it does not affect the NC drill data. The X and Y coordinates extracted for NC drill data refer to the insertion point of the pad block itself.

Part Blocks

AutoCAD blocks are used for all parts (components) on the PCB. Figure 10-2 shows a typical part block. Pads blocks are nested within the part block definition. The part block consists of entities on three layers. These layers include the two layers used for the pads (PADS and DRILL) and the SILK_COMP layer. The center of the upper left pad is generally used as the insertion point. For front panel components such as switches and potentiometers, the center of the mounting hole is a more logical insertion point.

All entities on the SILK_COMP layer are drawn in white. These entities consist of the part outline and the reference designator. The part outline is generally drawn to correspond to the dimensions of the part body and may include orientation and polarity symbols (for example a diode symbol or + symbol for an electrolytic capacitor).

AutoCAD attributes are used to associate a reference designator with the pad block. One could simply use plain text, but an attribute has certain advantages. Attributes in blocks can easily be edited, including the attribute text location and angle. This editing capability is important for PCB design. The reference designator attribute is a preset, visible attribute with prompt and tag set to REF. The attribute value is preset to a generic value, such as C? for a capacitor or R? for a resistor. When the part block is inserted, AutoCAD displays this generic preset value and prompts for the actual value to be used on the board.

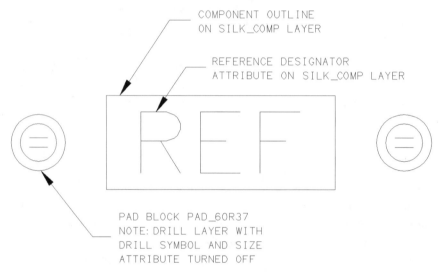

COMPONENT OUTLINE
ON SILK_COMP LAYER

REFERENCE DESIGNATOR
ATTRIBUTE ON SILK_COMP LAYER

PAD BLOCK PAD_60R37
NOTE: DRILL LAYER WITH
DRILL SYMBOL AND SIZE
ATTRIBUTE TURNED OFF

Figure 10-2   Detail of a Part Block

Note that the tag REF, not the preset value is shown in Figure 10-2 since the part block in the figure has been exploded. When attributes are created, they are drawn in the current text style. The MONOSI font, a monospaced sans serif font, is recommended for optimum legibility. The recommended height is .065 inch. The insertion point for the reference designator attribute is the center of the part.

Trace Width Considerations

As explained in Chapter 3 on page 112, traces are photoplotted 1 mil oversize. This is not a major factor with 25 mil or wider traces on generous grid spacings, but you must compensate for anything smaller. The tutorial design uses a 25 mil grid and 13 mil trace design rule; 12 mil polylines are used to draw all signal traces intended to be photoplotted at 13 mil on the final artwork.

Completing the Tutorial Exercise

Your task will be to plot out HPGL files for the tutorial PCB design and then convert these files into Gerber format using the HPGL2GBR conversion program.

Start AutoCAD and open the tutorial PCB design file, TUTOR9.DWG. Use the LAYER command to examine the layers present in the design and compare these layers to those in Table 10-1. Note that that MASK_COMP and MASK_SOLDER layers are not present, since this design does not require any special solder mask patterns other than oversized pads.

Manufacturing Documentation

Manufacturing documentation consists of the Excellon format NC drill data, drill detail drawing, and board assembly drawing. The TUTOR9.DWG file already contains all manufacturing documentation-related items on the appropriate layers. Preparation of the manufacturing documentation, including extraction of NC drill data, is independent of the technique used to generate Gerber artwork files. Refer to the material in Chapter 3 starting on page 99 for details. While this material is specific to AutoCAD and AutoCAD LT, similar techniques can be used with other CAD systems.

Board Artwork

The artwork required to manufacture the board includes the component legend silkscreen, component side pattern, solder side pattern, and solder mask pattern. As explained in Chapter 1, board manufacturers generally do not want artwork per se, but rather the Gerber photoplotter data for the various artwork layers. Your task will be to generate this data.

AutoCAD HPGL Plot Driver Configuration

The HPGL2GBR utility converts HPGL plot data files into Gerber format photoplotter files. Before you can output HPGL from AutoCAD, you must configure the plot driver. The following instructions apply to AutoCAD LT for Windows 95:

1. At the File menu, select (click on) Print.

2. Select the Plot Configuration submenu.

3. Select Print/Plot Setup and Default Selection.

4. Select Hewlett-Packard (HPGL).

5. Select the Print/Plot submenu.

6. Select Model 7580. Accept COM1 as the output port for now. Later, when you are ready to plot, you will select the Plot To File option on the main Plot Configuration menu.

7. Back at the main Plot Configuration menu, select Adjust Area Fill. You do not need to change the default paper size and orientation values (MAX size and zero values for rotation and X,Y origin). Make sure the scale factor remains set to 1=1 for plotted inches versus drawing units.

AutoCAD Limitations

The AutoCAD HPGL plot driver has certain limitations. The resolution is fixed at 1016 steps per inch. Plotter steps mean the same thing as DPI on a laser photoplotter using Gerber data. However, laser photoplotters generally have resolutions of 1000, 2000, or 4000 DPI. Round-off errors during conversion from HPGL to Gerber format can result in a worst case accuracy (error) of ±.002 inch.

AutoCAD also is somewhat unique among CAD programs in that it does not directly associate widths with lines in the drawing. Polylines do have a defined width, but they are plotted by stroking (moving the pen back and forth). When you define a pen width (e.g., .005 inch) for plotting, AutoCAD uses the information to calculate the amount of stroking required to fill polylines and other solid areas. If you make the selection to adjust area fill boundaries for pen width during the configuration process, the pen is offset by half its width while stroking polylines and solids.

Please note that the pen widths on the plot menu in AutoCAD determine only how AutoCAD will fill wide polylines. These pen widths **do not** directly control the width of lines. **The pen number is what determines the line width in the actual plotting device.** It is very important to clearly understand this distinction.

AutoCAD HPGL Plotting Considerations

Before you proceed, you may want to review the material on plotting in your AutoCAD reference manual. To generate an HPGL plot file from AutoCAD, use the PRINT menu. Next, set up your pen assignments. A color table will be displayed and you will have the option of selecting pen numbers for each color. Pen 8 is used for colors that you don't want to plot (e.g., the green pad display outline). You should always select line type 0 (continuous line). Pen speed is ignored.

After you have completed the pen assignments, you can set up the area you want to plot. In most cases you will want to select the plot Extents option. Make sure you always select the Adjust Area Fill option; otherwise all polyline widths will be incorrect. After you have selected the area of the drawing that you want to plot, you can enter the filename for the plot file. The filename must include the drive and path to the subdirectory that you have created for your plot data.

Once you have properly configured AutoCAD, you can keep current plotting values, such as pen assignments, for subsequent plots. Be careful not to change the adjust area fill setting (yes) or plot scale (always 1=1).

Plot origin causes confusion with HPGL data. Hewlett-Packard established the center of the plot area (this is the paper size dimension on the plot configuration menu) as the X=0, Y=0 point for the HPGL data. The AutoCAD plot driver starts drawing at the lower left hand corner of the plot. You can see this by using the preview function. Consequently, most small boards are plotted with data containing negative coordinates. The HPGL2GBR program allows entry of X,Y offsets to prevent the occurrence of negative coordinates in the Gerber data, since this can cause problems with some photoplotting systems.

In general, you should create all your designs with the drawing origin (X=0 and Y=0) at the lower left hand corner. No entities should be placed at negative X or Y coordinates. The plot origin should also be X=0 and Y=0, which is the default. When running HPGL2GBR, enter X,Y offsets equal to half the maximum paper dimension. This will prevent negative X and Y coordinates from appearing in the Gerber data.

Gerber Output from HPGL2GBR

You should read Appendix A for a discussion of Gerber data format and an overview of photoplotting technology. You will usually be sending the converted Gerber data files to a service bureau or board manufacturer for photoplotting. HPGL2GBR has a Gerber format setup screen. The default Gerber format is that which is most commonly used in the industry: 2.4 decimal format, absolute coordinates, inch units, leading zero suppression, and * as the end of block character. Note that 2.4 format means six total digits and four digits after the decimal point. This allows steps as small as .0001 inch and helps minimize round-off errors. Use the Gerber 2.4 format unless you have a specific reason not to.

Aperture Assignments

HPGL2GBR automatically assigns a Gerber aperture D code for each AutoCAD pen number. AutoCAD pen numbers 1 to 7 are converted to Gerber D codes 11 to 17 (Gerber D codes start at number 10). Pen number 8 is ignored. This is useful for data that you do not want to convert, such as pad display outlines.

Plotting and Conversion Considerations

Traces on the PCB are drawn with AutoCAD polylines with some defined width. Assign pen 1 to all colors used for polylines. Assign a size of .005 inch to pen 1. HPGL2GBR converts pen 1 to aperture D11 in the Gerber file. D11 could then be assigned the same size of .005 inch in photoplotting of the Gerber file. However, slight clear streaks may appear on the photoplotted artwork because of insufficient overlap of lines in filled areas and wide traces. For this reason, you should assign a .006 inch size for aperture D11. This will result in some overlap and should eliminate any clear streaks in the photoplotted artwork. The photoplotted traces will be .001 inch wider than the AutoCAD polylines. If greater accuracy is required for specialized applications, you can compensate by reducing the width of the polylines .001 inch. For example, if you want precise .013 inch wide photoplotted traces (a common design rule for double sided PCBs), use .012 inch wide polylines. Note that fill mode must be turned on and adjust area fill selected for plotting any polylines or other filled objects.

Solid areas (also called *fills* or *ground planes*) with an irregular shape are often required. The AutoCAD SOLID command is quite versatile for this purpose. The same considerations that apply to polylines apply to solids. They should be drawn in the same color as the polylines on a given layer.

Photoplotted lines include component outlines, cut marks, and text on the PCB. These types of lines are usually photoplotted at .010 inch width. This width gives good results for graphics that are to be silkscreened on the PCB with an epoxy ink. AutoCAD line entities are used for these types of lines. Use the color white for lines. Then assign pen 2 to the color white. HPGL2GBR converts pen 2 to aperture D12. Assign a .010 inch size to aperture D12 for photoplotting.

Pads are created as AutoCAD blocks consisting of a green display outline and yellow fill pattern. The green display outline shows the actual outer dimension of the pad. This green outline is assigned pen 8, which is ignored by HPGL2GBR.

Only the yellow pad fill pattern is photoplotted. The dimensions of the fill pattern are adjusted to compensate for the aperture width so that the pad is photoplotted at the correct size. Pen 3 is assigned to the yellow pad fill pattern. HPGL2GBR converts pen 3 to aperture D13. For a normal pad on the component or solder side artwork layers, assign a size of .020 inch to aperture D13.

Photoplotting oversized solder mask pads is very easy. Change the pen assignment for the yellow pad fill pattern to pen 4. HPGL2GBR converts pen 4 to aperture D14. By means of assigning a larger size to aperture D14, the pads can be photoplotted oversize. For .010 inch oversize pads, use a size of .030 inch for aperture D14. If you require any special solder mask clearance areas, you can create solid patterns on the MASK_SOLDER layer.

Generating the HPGL Plot Files

Make sure that you have properly configured AutoCAD for the HPGL plot driver as explained on page 271. Then start AutoCAD and open the TUTOR9 drawing file. For plotting and converting the pieces of artwork, use the layer, color, pen, and Gerber D code assignments shown in Table 10-2. The layer combinations will make more sense as you read further.

Table 10-2   Layer Assignments for Double Sided PCB Artwork

ARTWORK	LAYER USAGE	COLOR	PEN/SIZE		D CODE/SIZE	
SILK_CMP	SILK_COMP	WHITE	2	.01	D12	.01
	OUTLINE	WHITE	2	.01	D12	.01
ART_CMP	TRACE_COMP	BLUE	1	.005	D11	.006
	PADS	YELLOW	3	.02	D13	.02
		GREEN	8	.01	NOT PLOTTED	
	VIAS	YELLOW	3	.02	D13	.02
		GREEN	8	.01	NOT PLOTTED	
	OUTLINE	WHITE	2	.01	D12	.01
ART_SOL	TRACE_SOLDER	RED	1	.005	D11	.006
	PADS	YELLOW	3	.02	D13	.02
		GREEN	8	.01	NOT PLOTTED	
	VIAS	YELLOW	3	.02	D13	.02
		GREEN	8	.01	NOT PLOTTED	
	OUTLINE	WHITE	2	.01	D12	.01
MASK_SOL	MASK_SOLDER	WHITE	2	.01	D12	.01
	PADS	YELLOW	4	.02	D14	.03
		GREEN	8	.01	NOT PLOTTED	
	OUTLINE	WHITE	2	.01	D12	.01

Silkscreen Artwork

The silkscreen artwork consists of two AutoCAD layers: SILK_COMP and OUTLINE. Use the LAYER command to turn on these layers. Turn off all the other layers in the drawing. The component outlines, silkscreen text including reference designators, and board cut marks should be displayed as shown in Figure 10-3. All these entities should be white.

Next, you will plot this silkscreen layer. Make sure fill mode is turned on and you have done a AutoCAD regen. Click on the print menu, select the HPGL plot driver, and set up the required pen assignments. For each color, assign the appropriate pen number and size, as given in Table 10-2. Red and blue are both pen 1 with size .005, white is pen 2 with size .010, yellow is pen 3 with size .020, and green is pen 8 (not converted by HPGL2GBR, but use size .010). Remember that pen 8 is used for colors that are for display only. Note that not all these pen assignments are used immediately. Make sure you select plot extents and adjust area fill on. Tell AutoCAD to write the plot data to a file. Use the filename SILK_CMP.

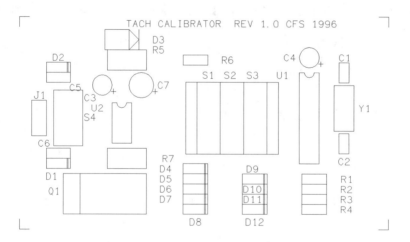

Figure 10-3   Silkscreen Artwork Display

Component Side Artwork

The component side artwork consists of four AutoCAD layers: TRACE_COMP, PADS, VIAS, and OUTLINE. The TRACE_COMP layer contains all the copper traces on the component side. The PADS and VIAS layers contains the pads and vias. Pads and vias are drawn in two colors. Yellow is used for a fill pattern. This is what is photoplotted. Green is used as an outline of the pad (or via) for display purposes. The color green is assigned pen number 8 so that it will be ignored by HPGL2GBR. Use the LAYER command to turn on the TRACE_COMP, PADS, VIAS, and OUTLINE layers. Turn off all other layers in the drawing. The green/yellow pads and vias, blue component side traces, and white board cut marks should now be displayed as shown in Figure 10-4. Plot the component side artwork. Keep the same pen assignments you previously set up. Make sure that Adjust Area Fill is turned on for all artwork plots. Tell AutoCAD to write the plot data to a file. Use the filename ART_CMP.

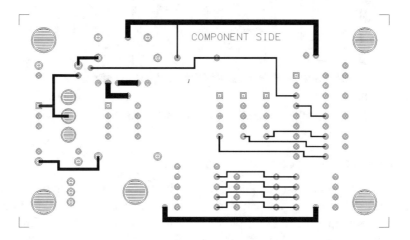

Figure 10-4   Component Side Artwork Display

Solder Side Artwork

The solder side artwork also consists of four AutoCAD layers: TRACE_SOLDER, PADS, VIAS, and OUTLINE. The TRACE_SOLDER layer contains all the copper traces on the solder side. All other layer and plotting considerations are the same as for the component side artwork discussed earlier. Use the LAYER command to turn on the TRACE_SOLDER, PADS, VIAS, and OUTLINE layers. Turn off all other layers in the drawing. Only the green/yellow pads and vias, red solder side traces, and white board cut marks should now be displayed. Plot the solder side artwork. Keep the same pen assignments you previously set up. Make sure that adjust area fill is turned on for all artwork plots. Tell AutoCAD to write the plot data to a file. Use the filename ART_SOL.

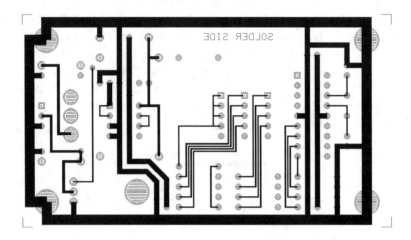

Figure 10-5   Solder Side Artwork Display

Solder Mask Artwork

The solder mask artwork is handled slightly differently. You want the solder mask pads to be .010 inch oversize. This can easily be done with a .010 inch larger aperture to photoplot the pad fill pattern. Solder mask artwork sometimes contains ground planes (solid filled areas). These are also easily handled with the same technique.

The solder mask artwork consists of three AutoCAD layers: MASK_SOL, PADS, and OUTLINE. The MASK_SOL layer contains any solid areas or special patterns (not used in this tutorial). Use the LAYER command to turn on the PADS, and OUTLINE layers. Turn off all other layers in the drawing. The green/yellow pads and white board cut marks should now be displayed as shown in Figure 10-6. Plot the solder mask artwork. You will need to change one pen assignment in the color table: assign yellow to pen 4 with size .020. Later, the solder mask pads will be photoplotted oversize. Tell AutoCAD to write the plot data to a file. Use the filename MASK_SOL.

You have now generated HPGL plot files for the four pieces of board artwork. The next step is to use HPGL2GBR to convert these files to Gerber format.

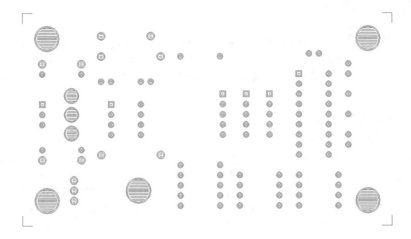

Figure 10-6   Solder Mask Artwork Display

Running HPGL2GBR to Generate Gerber Data

AutoCAD will automatically assign a .PLT extension to any HPGL plot files that you create. When you run HPGL2GBR, it will assign a .GBR extension to the converted Gerber file. The path and filename are retained. The original AutoCAD plot file will remain unchanged. The new files are written to the same drive and subdirectory.

To run the HPGL2GBR program, exit to DOS and type

CD\AUTOPADS<ENTER>

HPGL2GBR<ENTER>

The copyright notice screen appears, and you can hit any key to continue and run the conversion program.

Throughout the HPGL2GBR program, you can navigate the various menu options by pressing the Tab key to go forward or the Shift + Tab keys to go back to the previous choice. When you are prompted for a parameter value or filename, enter the information and then press the Enter key. When you "tab" to menu options such as OK (means continue) or QUIT (stop program), the selected menu option will become highlighted. You can then execute the menu option by pressing the Enter key.

X and Y Offset Entry

To prevent negative X and Y coordinates from appearing in the Gerber data, the HPGL2GBR program allows entering offsets. Entering X and Y offsets equal to half the maximum plot size (X offset of 22 inches and Y offset of 12 inches for an HP7580 plotter) will usually eliminate problems with negative coordinates.

Plot Filename Entry

The filename entry screen will prompt you for the name of the HPGL plot file that you are going to convert. You can specify a drive and path as part of the filename, just as you would with any other DOS command. But you must not include an extension. The program assumes the extension .PLT for the HPGL file and uses the same drive, path, and filename with a .GBR extension for the Gerber output file it creates.

Please note that HPGL2GBR does not support long filenames when running from a DOS window in Windows 95.

After you have entered the filename, the conversion process will start.

Conversion Process

Depending on the speed of your processor and the file size, the conversion process could require a minute or more for a very large file. During the conversion process, you will see the disk access light on your PC blink as data is being read from and written to disk. When the conversion is completed, the number of Gerber draws that were processed is displayed. After the conversion is completed, you can select one of two options. You can CONTINUE to convert another file or you can QUIT the program.

HPGL2GBR uses only Gerber draw commands since these are the only kind of data output from the AutoCAD HPGL plot driver. Solid patterns such as PCB pads and targets are not converted into Gerber flash commands as is done with most PCB design software. AutoCAD will automatically fill these solid areas with many stroked lines (these become Gerber draws).

Any HPGL arc, circle, and text entities are reported but not converted. These types of entities would not normally be encountered.

Stopping the Program

During the conversion process, you can stop the program and return to the DOS prompt by pressing the Esc key. Any partially converted GBR file will be deleted. Please note that the Esc key works only while the conversion screen is displayed.

Error Messages

If an error occurs, HPGL2GBR will display an appropriate error message. Most of the error messages are self-explanatory. The most common errors relate to entry of improper drive, path, or filenames or printer off-line. Remember that the path is relative to the subdirectory from which HPGL2GBR is running. Thus if HPGL2GBR is running from the C:\AUTOPADS subdirectory and the file that you want to convert, for example MYPLOT1.PLT, is loaded into the C:\PLOTS subdirectory, you must enter \PLOTS\MYPLOT1 as the path and filename on the filename entry screen.

Common Problems

HPGL2GBR may not run correctly if memory resident programs or print/plot spoolers are loaded. The program is not intended to be run from within CAD systems as a menu selection or by use of the SHELL command. You should quit AutoCAD (or any other program) before running HPGL2GBR. HPGL2GBR will run from a DOS window in Windows.

Converting the Plot Files

Run HPGL2GBR and convert the four HPGL plot files that you created (SILK_CMP.PLT, ART_CMP.PLT, ART_SOL.PLT, and MASK_SOL.PLT). Use the default Gerber format setup parameters. When you are finished, exit HPGL2GBR and use the DOS DIR command to check the files in your TUTOR9 subdirectory. You should see the four original .PLT files and four new .GBR files. These are your artwork files.

You can use the information presented in Chapter 4 on pages 149 and 150 for sending Gerber files to a service bureau or board manufacturer.

Conclusion

Congratulations! You have completed the last of the tutorial exercises. At this point you have mastered the use of the AutoPADS utilities. You should now be able to productively design PCBs with AutoCAD on a professional basis in your daily work.

Appendix A

Gerber Format

Overview

All photoplotters create images on film using a beam of light. The original mechanical photoplotters pioneered by Gerber Scientific during the early 1960s used an optical exposure head. This was similar to a slide projector that moved over the surface of the film. The optical exposure head had 24 apertures mounted on a wheel. Film images were created by drawing traces (lines) and flashing patterns (component pads or registration targets). Each aperture defined a particular beam width or beam pattern.

Modern photoplotters utilize laser scanning technology similar to that used in laser printers. Laser photoplotters create a raster image composed of individual pixels. Virtual aperture patterns are defined in software. Most laser photoplotters can accommodate up to 245 aperture patterns.

Gerber Photoplotter Format

Gerber photoplotter format is a command language originated by Gerber Scientific for controlling their photoplotters. Gerber format has become an industry standard that is universally supported by all vendors of PCB design systems and photoplotters. It is based on the RS-274 data standard used for controlling NC machine tools. Gerber format consists of individual instructions comprised of ASCII characters. You can examine and modify a Gerber file with a text editor.

Gerber format consists of data blocks (not to be confused with AutoCAD blocks) that contains X and Y axis coordinates and/or various commands. The standard block format is:

Nnumber Gcode Xxxxxxx Yyyyyyy Dcode Mcode *

where:

Nnumber	Optional sequence number that is ignored
Gcode	Optional preparatory code that is ignored

G54	Alerts plotter to a new aperture selection
Xxxxxxx	X axis coordinate
Yyyyyyy	Y axis coordinate
Dcode	Draft code
D01	Light beam on (like pen down)
D02	Light beam off (like pen up)
D03	Flash aperture (creates a pad)
D10-255	Aperture selection (like pen change)
Mcode	Miscellaneous code
M00-02	Program stop (end of plot data)
*	End of data block character (others may be used)

Coordinates and commands can be in any order within the data block. Extraneous ASCII control characters and spaces are ignored. All coordinate information, G codes, and D codes are modal. This means that the last value is retained for all subsequent operations until it is changed.

Other aspects of Gerber format include

1. **Number format**. X and Y coordinate values may contain up to nine total digits. A decimal point is implied as part of the format specification. The number of digits precision refers to the digits behind the decimal point. The most common Gerber decimal formats are 2.3 (five digits total, three digits precision) and 2.4 (six digits total and four digits precision). For example, 125000 in 2.4 decimal format represents the number 12.5000.

2. **Absolute or incremental data**. Coordinate values can represent either absolute positions referenced to the plotter origin or incremental distances from the last position.

3. **Units**. Coordinate values can be in either inch (English) or centimeter (metric) units.

4. **Zero suppression**. Three zero suppression options include: leading zero suppression, no zero suppression, or trailing zero suppression.

Some examples of Gerber format data are as follows:

> G54D20*
>
> X000000Y000000D01*
>
> X010000Y010000D02*

The above data is in absolute 2.4 format with no zero suppression. Aperture 20 is selected and a line is drawn from X=0, Y=0 to X=1, Y=1. The G54 command is optional.

> G54D20*
>
> X000Y000D01*
>
> X1000Y1000D02*

The above data represents the same instructions in absolute 2.3 format with leading zero suppression. Aperture 20 is selected and a line is drawn from X=0, Y=0 to X=1, Y=1.

> D25*
>
> X015Y015D03*

The above data is in absolute 2.4 format with trailing zero suppression. Aperture 25 is selected and flashed at X=1.5, Y=1.5.

Aperture Assignments

Information about aperture assignments is an important part of the Gerber format specification. Each aperture referenced by a D code in the Gerber data must have a defined size and pattern. Most photoplotters support aperture sizes ranging from .001 to .250 inch. Traces are usually drawn with a round aperture pattern. Most laser photoplotters currently in use will accept D codes from D10 to D255.

Note that the aperture size and shape information is not contained in the Gerber data file. The user must provide this information as a separate document.

Image Quality Issues with AutoPADS and HPGL2GBR

Gerber data generated by the AutoPADS or HPGL2GBR utilities contains only draws; flashes are not used. Solid areas such as ground planes and pads are filled by means of stroking multiple draws. The plot driver routine embedded within the CAD software generates the stroking pattern used to fill solid areas.

Remember that you are converting data intended for a pen plotter. The spacing of draws in the stroking pattern used to fill solid areas may not be appropriate for photoplotting. Insufficient overlap may cause faint clear streaks on the photoplotted film image. Some additional overlap is generally recommended. You can create additional overlap by means of photoplotting with a slightly oversized aperture relative to the pen width defined within the CAD system.

Laser photoplotter resolution can vary from 1000 to 4000 DPI. Most newer systems are capable of 2000 DPI. For optimum image quality, the photoplotter resolution must equal or exceed the resolution of the Gerber data. If AutoPADS is configured to convert data at 2000 DPI and the photoplotter has a maximum resolution of only 1000 DPI, images will appear to have rough edges with noticeable stair stepping patterns.

Some Helpful Photoplotting Hints

Listed below is some helpful information about photoplotting Gerber data:

1. Your service bureau (or in-house department) must know both the Gerber format and the aperture assignments used for a particular file. You must provide them with a list giving the size and shape of each aperture used. This information is not part of the Gerber file.

2. Service bureaus with laser photoplotters can be found in most major metropolitan areas. Check the Yellow Pages or ask a local PCB manufacturer. Service bureaus will accept a DOS format floppy disk with Gerber files. Most have BBS systems to allow on-line file transfer by means of modem.

Determining the Gerber Format of an Unknown File

When you are going to convert Gerber data and do not know the exact format, use a text editor to examine the file and follow the suggestions listed below:

1. **Zero suppression**. As far as GBR2DXB and GBR2DXF are concerned, leading zero suppression and no zero suppression are the same. These are the most common zero suppression options. Look at some of the coordinates in the file. If you never see a trailing zero (no coordinates such as X1200), then your data probably uses trailing zero suppression.

2. **Absolute or incremental data**. Incremental data is rare. If you see any negative coordinates, you probably have incremental data. Normal absolute Gerber format should not contain negative coordinates, since the lower left hand corner of the plotter is X=0, Y=0.

3. **Total number of digits and digits precision**. Look at the data and make a reasonable guess based on all the available information. Signs (+ or –) do not count as digits. Photoplotters are limited to dimensions not exceeding 48 inches. This means that you will never see more than two digits before the decimal point when using inch units. Few PCBs have any dimensions exceeding 18 inches.

4. **Units**. Unless you are on the other side of the pond, assume inch (English) units. You can always measure the distance between some common parts, such as the spacing of IC leads, after you have loaded your converted file into CAD and verify that your choice of units is correct.

5. **End of block character**. The * character is most common. Other printable ASCII characters can be used. Non-printing ASCII control characters (such as CR or LF), cannot be used as an end of block.

Corrupt Gerber Files

Gerber format is an industry standard, but there are many variants. If you have a file that you cannot convert, use a text editor to examine the file. Does it look like Gerber data? Can you send the file to a photoplotter and get a correct plot? In general, extra spaces and ASCII control characters are ignored. GBR2DXB and GBR2DXF ignore almost any garbage that is not recognized as a part of a Gerber data block.

Appendix B

Excellon Format

Overview

Excellon NC drill data format is an industry standard originated by Excellon Automation, a manufacturer of NC drilling machines for the PCB industry. All PCB manufacturers accept Excellon data. Most can accept Excellon data on floppy disk. Providing the PCB manufacturer with NC drill data ensures accurate drilling of your PCBs and reduces tooling charges and turnaround time.

Excellon NC Drill Data Format

Excellon format is based on the RS-274 data standard used for controlling NC machine tools. It consists of individual instructions comprised of ASCII characters. You can examine and modify an Excellon file with a text editor.

Excellon format consists of data blocks (not to be confused with AutoCAD blocks) containing X and Y axis coordinates or tool select commands. The standard block format is

   Tcode Xxxxxx Yyyyyy Mcode

where:

Tcode	Tool select code (selects a given drill size)
Xxxxxx	X axis coordinate
Yyyyyy	Y axis coordinate
Mcode	Miscellaneous code
M30	End of data

Each block of data is terminated with a carriage return and linefeed. Tool commands are generally on a separate line. All tool commands are modal. This means that once a tool is selected, it is used for all subsequent drilling operations until it is changed. Each line of coordinate data causes a hole to be drilled at the specified X,Y coordinate.

Other aspects of Excellon format include

1. **Number format**. X and Y coordinate values may contain up to five total digits. A decimal point is implied. The number of digits precision (digits behind the decimal point) is three.

2. **Absolute data.** Coordinate values always represent absolute positions referenced to an origin on the PCB.

3. **Inch units**. Coordinate values are always in inch (English) units.

4. **Zero suppression**. Trailing zero suppression is used.

For example

> T1
>
> X00625Y005

The above data selects tool number one (whatever size it may be) and drills a hole at X=.625 and Y=.5 inches.

Tool Assignments

Information about tool assignments is very important. Unfortunately, Excellon format has no provision for identification of the tool size. You must give the board manufacturer a listing that gives the drill size for each tool number. By convention, tools are consecutively numbered starting with T1 for the smallest hole size.

Some companies include a text header with tool information at the beginning of the Excellon file.

Appendix C

HPGL Format

Overview

HPGL format is a command language originated by Hewlett-Packard for controlling pen plotters. HPGL format consists of individual instructions comprised of ASCII characters. You can examine and even modify an HPGL file with a text editor.

All HPGL commands share a common syntax, a two character instruction mnemonic followed by a parameter field and a terminator. The two character instruction mnemonic can be either lowercase or uppercase. The parameter field is omitted with some instructions. If more than one parameter is used, the parameters are separated with a comma or space. The terminator is generally a semicolon. In some cases the terminator can be omitted. Extraneous characters and spaces are generally ignored. For example

> PA2000,3000;

The above instruction moves the pen to the absolute position X=2000 and Y=3000.

HPGL Command Summary

A brief summary of the more common HPGL commands follows. Note that not all of these commands are supported by the conversion programs HPGL2DXB, HPGL2DXF, and HPGL2GBR. Unsupported commands are ignored. Parenthesis indicate optional parameters.

AA   **Arc Absolute**

> AA X-center, Y-center, arc angle (, chord tolerance);

> Draws arc starting from present pen position with center at X-center, Y-center, using current pen status (up or down). Positive angle causes arc to be drawn counterclockwise. Chord tolerance is optional.

AR   Arc Relative

AR X-center increment, Y-center increment, arc angle (, chord tolerance);

Draws arc starting from present pen position, using current pen status (up or down). Center of arc is calculated by adding X-center and Y-center increments to pen starting position. Positive angle causes arc to be drawn counterclockwise. Chord tolerance is optional.

CI   Circle

CI radius (, chord tolerance);

Draws a circle with the specified radius centered at the current pen position. Chord tolerance is optional

CA   Designate Alternate Character Set

CA character set number;

Designates the alternate character set (0 to 99). Used in conjunction with the SA command.

CS   Designate Standard Character Set

CS character set number;

Designates the standard character set (0 to 99). Used in conjunction with the SS command.

DI   Absolute Direction

DI run, rise;

Sets the text rotation angle.

DR   Relative Direction

DR run, rise;

Sets the text rotation angle. Run and rise coordinates are relative to plotter scaling points P1 and P2.

DT   Define Terminator

DT terminator character.

Defines an ASCII character used as terminator for text strings following a LB (label) instruction.

ES   Extra Space

ES spaces (, lines);

Sets the amount of extra space to be added between characters and lines.

The lines parameter is optional and ignored.

IP   Input (Scaling) Points

IP Xp1, Yp1 (, Xp2, Yp2);

Used to input scaling points. Refer to your Plotter Interfacing and Technical Manual for more details.

LB   Label

LB character string + terminator character;

Draws an ASCII character string.

LT   Linetype

LT pattern number (, pattern length);

Sets the linetype used for drawing entities. Valid pattern numbers range from –6 to +6. Negative pattern numbers result in the same linetype as positive numbers but with scaling based so that an entire pattern is drawn. Pattern length is optional. Omitting parameters forces a continuous linetype.

PA   Plot Absolute

PA X1, Y1 (, X2, Y2 . . . , Xn, Yn);

Moves the pen to each X, Y coordinate in sequence using the current pen status (up or down).

PD   Pen Down

PD;

Sets pen down onto medium.

PR   Plot Relative

PR X1, Y1 (, X2, Y2 . . . , Xn, Yn);

Same as PA except X, Y values are increments relative to the last pen position.

PU   **Pen Up**

PU;

Raises pen up from medium.

SA   **Select Alternate Character Set**

SA;

Selects the alternate character set previously designated with the CA instruction. Subsequent LB commands will be drawn with the alternate character set.

SC   **Scale**

SC Xmin, Xmax, Ymin, Ymax;

Used to input scale factors that affect the plotting operation. Refer to your Plotter Interfacing and Technical Manual for more details.

SI   **Character Size**

SI width, height;

Sets character width and height in centimeters.

SL   **Character Slant**

SL tangent angle;

Sets the character slant angle, in terms of the tangent of the slant angle.

SP   **Select Pen**

SP pen number;

Selects a pen from the carousel. Valid number are 0 to 8. Omitting the pen number or using pen number 0 stores the pen and is often used to signify the end of a plot.

SR   **Relative Character Size**

SR width, height;

Sets character width and height as a percentage of the distance between scaling points P1 and P2.

SS   Select Standard Character Set

SS;

Selects the standard character set previously designated with the CS instruction. Subsequent LB commands will be drawn with the standard character set. .

Commands Supported by HPGL2DXB and HPGL2DXF

A list of HPGL commands supported by HPGL2DXB and HPGL2DXF follows. Some commands establish setup of the conversion process, such as defining the scale factors for coordinates. Most commands are for plotting entities, such as lines, arcs, circles, and text. Two special commands, linetype and select pen, are used to determine the type of line with which entities will be drawn.

Plot Setup

The IP (input scaling points) and SC (scale) commands are supported for the purpose of establishing scale factors for subsequent X and Y coordinates. HPGL X and Y coordinates are normally scaled at 1016 plotter units per inch. In some cases, CAD systems change the normal scale factor to better fit a drawing image into a given plotting area. Not all HPGL files will contain IP and SC commands, which usually occur together. If these commands are not found, the default scaling of 1016 plot units per inch is used. If the IP and SC commands are found, a message will appear on the conversion screen and display the new X and Y axis scale factors.

The subject of scaling and units is very important in any conversion process involving CAD data. In most cases, mechanical and PCB design systems will use inch (English) units for the internal database and for plotting. In this case, the data will be correctly converted and coordinate units will remain in inches once the DXB or DXF file is loaded into AutoCAD.

Graphics Entities

Lines are converted with the PA (plot absolute), PR (plot relative), PU (pen up), and PD (pen down) commands. Arcs are converted with the AA (arc absolute) and AR (arc relative) commands. Circles are converted with the CI (circle) command.

Text Entities

Since AutoCAD DXB format does not provide support for text, HPGL2DXB ignores all HPGL text entities during the conversion process. However, the HPGL2DXB program recognizes and reports the LB (label) and DT (define label terminator) commands.

HPGL2DXF supports conversion of HPGL text entities. Supported commands include LB (label), DT (define label terminator), CA (designate alternate character set), CS (designate standard character set), DI (absolute direction), DR (relative direction), ES (extra space), SA (select alternate character set), SI (absolute character size), SL (character slant), SR (relative character size), and SS (select standard character set). The term *character set* is synonymous with *font*.

During the text conversion process, the DI (or DR) command determines the AutoCAD text rotation. The SI (or SR) command determines the AutoCAD text height. The SL command determines the AutoCAD text slant. The AutoCAD text width factor is determined by means of an algorithm that considers the original width factor entered on the text conversion setup screen and parameters obtained from the SI (or SR), and ES commands.

Text Fonts

HPGL supports three classes of text fonts: fixed-space vector, variable-space arc, and fixed-space arc. Fixed-space fonts have a constant spacing between characters and the variable-space font has proportional spacing between characters. The vector font is drawn with straight lines, resulting in faster plotting but giving a rough appearance. The arc fonts have a smoother appearance but require a longer plotting time. Default conversion options are as follows: the HPGL variable-space arc font is converted into the AutoCAD SIMPLEX font and the HPGL fixed-space vector and arc fonts are converted into MONOSI (a public domain, mono-spaced simplex font that can be used with AutoCAD).

Select Pen Command

CAD drawings typically use different line widths and linetypes. Special consideration must be given for this important information to be successfully converted into AutoCAD. The strategy used to convert line widths and linetypes is compatible with most users' AutoCAD design standards. Most AutoCAD users assign each line width a unique color and layer. AutoCAD supports different linetypes within a given layer.

Most CAD systems plot different line widths by selecting individual pens by means of the SP (select pen) command. HPGL supports pen numbers 0-9 (pen number 0 is generally not used for actual plotting). Linetypes (solid or various dash patterns) are generally plotted by means of stroking individual lines within the CAD program, not by use of the plotter's internal linetype commands. If you are sure that this is the case with the data you are converting, you can disable the linetype conversion option. Entities drawn in each respective line width will be placed on individual AutoCAD layers. All the entities drawn with pen number 1 will go onto AutoCAD layer 1. You can later edit the layers so that the layer assignments match your standards.

Some CAD systems plot different line widths by stroking with a given pen size. Generally this is not done because it is very time consuming, but you may encounter this situation. The data will still be converted correctly, but your AutoCAD drawing database will have multiple overlapping lines that make editing somewhat troublesome.

Linetype Command

Another situation that can arise is that the CAD system outputs plot files with HPGL linetype commands instead of stroking. HPGL supports LT (linetypes) commands with optional parameter ranging from –6 to +6. An LT command without parameter causes solid lines to be drawn. Positive parameters select dashed line patterns with fixed scaling. Negative parameters select dashed lines with scaling adjusted on the basis of plotter scaling. If the linetype conversion option is enabled and a linetype command is encountered, the AutoCAD layer used for entities drawn with that linetype is determined as follows:

AutoCAD layer = (pen number × 10) + absolute value of the linetype

If the pen number is 1 and the linetype is –6 (or 6), the data will be placed on AutoCAD layer 16. When each linetype is placed on a different layer, the linetype information is preserved. You can then edit all the entities on this layer to restore the correct linetype within AutoCAD.

Commands Supported by HPGL2GBR

A list of HPGL commands supported by HPGL2GBR follows. Some commands establish setup of the conversion process, such as defining the scale factors for coordinates. Most commands are for plotting entities, such as lines, arcs, circles, and text. Two special commands, linetype and select pen, are used to determine the type of line with which entities with be drawn.

Plot Setup

The IP (input scaling points) and SC (scale) commands are supported for the purpose of establishing scale factors for subsequent X and Y coordinates. HPGL X and Y coordinates are normally scaled at 1016 plotter units per inch. In some cases, CAD systems change the normal scale factor to better fit a drawing image into a given plotting area. Not all HPGL files will contain IP and SC commands, which usually occur together. If these commands are not found, the default scaling of 1016 plot units per inch is used. If the IP and SC commands are found, a message will appear on the conversion screen and display the new X and Y axis scale factors.

Graphics Entities

Only the line draw commands PA (plot absolute), PR (plot relative), PU (pen up), and PD (pen down) commands are converted by HPGL2GBR. Arcs and circles are ignored.

Text Entities

The LB (label) and DT (define label terminator) commands and related text commands are ignored. This rarely is an issue as few CAD systems use the HPGL text commands. Most CAD systems, including AutoCAD, use internal text fonts and send line commands to the plotter to draw the actual text.

Problems with Multiple Frames in a Plot File

Hewlett-Packard offers several plotters with a roll feed capability (such as the HP 7586). Some CAD systems will output a single plot file with multiple frames (drawings), using HPGL commands within the file to advance the paper. If you try to convert such a file, you will have multiple overlapping drawings.

If this situation occurs, you can either reconfigure the CAD system for a single sheet plotter (i.e. a HP 7580 or HP 7585) or you can use a text editor to split the file. Simply search the file for the following HPGL commands and then divide the file at the point at which you find the command.

      AF   Advance Full Page

      AH   Advance Half Page

      EC   Enable Cut Line

FR   Frame Advance

PG   Advance Full Page

Corrupt HPGL Files

HPGL is a very flexible and widely used format, but the actual data format is not rigorously defined. The HPGL2DXB, HPGL2DXF, and HPGL2GBR utilities have been designed to accommodate most HPGL variants. In general, if the HPGL file can be plotted on a Hewlett-Packard plotter, it can be converted.

If you have a file that you cannot convert, the file may be corrupted. Use a text editor to examine the file. Does it look like HPGL data? Can you send the file to a plotter and get a correct plot? In general, extra spaces, extra commas, and ASCII control characters are ignored. The semicolon terminator is optional. The conversion utilities ignore almost any garbage that is not recognized as a supported HPGL command.

In some cases the plot data directed to a file may not match the plot data actually sent to an on-line plotter. You may need to eavesdrop on the plotter as explained in Chapter 7.

Appendix D

Information About the Disk Supplied with this Book

Disk Contents

This book includes a disk that contains the AutoPADS conversion utilities, a shareware version of the LIST utility, schematic symbol, and PCB part libraries and sample files for the tutorial exercises. The files on the disk are listed in Table D-1.

Table D-1   Disk Files

Filename	Description
AUTOPADS <DIR>	AutoPADS conversion utilities
LIST91M.EXE	Shareware list utility self extract
MONOSI.SHX	Mono spaced font for AutoCAD
TUTOR1 <DIR>	Sample files for Tutorial 1 (Chapter 2)
TUTOR2 <DIR>	Sample files for Tutorial 2 (Chapter 3)
TUTOR3 <DIR>	Sample files for Tutorial 3 (Chapter 4)
TUTOR4 <DIR>	Sample files for Tutorial 4 (Chapter 5)
TUTOR5 <DIR>	Sample files for Tutorial 5 (Chapter 6)
TUTOR6 <DIR>	Sample files for Tutorial 6 (Chapter 7)
TUTOR7 <DIR>	Sample files for Tutorial 7 (Chapter 8)
TUTOR8 <DIR>	Sample files for Tutorial 8 (Chapter 9)
TUTOR9 <DIR>	Sample files for Tutorial 9 (Chapter 10)
README.TXT	Text file with any updated information not available when the book was printed

The sample files for the tutorial exercises files are intended to help complete the exercises and to serve as examples of finished designs.

Requirements and Compatibility

The files are supplied on a MS-DOS formatted 1.4MB 3.5 inch floppy disk. The AutoPADS conversion utilities and the two shareware utility programs should run on any MS-DOS/PC-DOS compatible computer capable of running AutoCAD. At least 5MB of free hard disk space is recommended to allow for the files created during the tutorial exercises.

Please note that the AutoPADS conversion utilities do not support long filenames when running from a DOS window in Windows 95.

Shareware List Utility

The self-extracting archive file LIST91M.EXE contains the LIST.COM shareware file list utility and associated documentation. The copyright for this material belongs to Vernon Buerg. Any use, including use as part of the tutorial exercises in this book, requires payment of a registration fee and is subject to the software license in the program documentation.

You can install LIST.COM and the associated documentation files on your root directory or any subdirectory on your PC's path. For example, to install the files from floppy disk on your A: drive to the root directory on your hard drive, type:

>   **A:<ENTER>**
>
>   **COPY LIST91M.EXE C:\<ENTER>**
>
>   **C:<ENTER>**
>
>   **LIST91M<ENTER>**

The list utility can then be run by typing **LIST<ENTER>** at the C: prompt. This will bring up a file directory and you can highlight the file to list by using the cursor keys and then pressing the Enter key. You can also directly list a specific file by including the filename with the command, that is by typing **LIST filename.ext<ENTER>**. Refer to the documentation supplied with the program for more details.

Schematic Symbol Library

The file SCH1_LIB.DWG in the TUTOR1 subdirectory contains the library of schematic symbols listed in Table D-2. All schematic symbols are defined as AutoCAD blocks. Refer to Figures 2-1 through 2-13 for details.

Table D-2   **Schematic Symbols in SCH1_LIB.DWG**

AutoCAD Block Name	Description
ANT	Antenna
BT	Battery
C	Capacitor, non-polarized
C_FED	Capacitor, feed through
C_POL	Capacitor, polarized (electrolytic)
C_VAR	Capacitor, variable
D	Diode
D_CAP	Diode, variable capacitance (varactor)
D_LED	Diode, LED
D_PHT	Diode, photo
D_SCH	Diode, Schottky
D_ZEN	Diode, Zener
F	Fuse
F_THER	Circuit breaker, thermal
GND	Ground
GND_EARTH	Ground, earth
GND_PWR	Ground, power
J_BNC	Jack, BNC
J_MLX-12	Jack, Molex 12 pin
J_PHONE	Jack, phone
JP	Jumper
JUNC	Junction
K	Relay, SPDT
L	Inductor
L_IRON	Inductor, iron core
LS	Speaker
M_MOT	Motor, DC
M_MTR_MA	Meter, DC milliamp
MK	Microphone
P_AC	Plug, AC line
P_DB9_FEM	Plug, DB9 female
P_DB9_MALE	Plug, DB9 male
PWR	Power
Q_IGBT	Transistor, IGBT N channel
Q_MOS_N	N channel MOSFET
Q_MOS_P	P channel MOSFET
Q_NPN	Transistor, NPN
Q_NPN_DARL	Transistor, NPN Darlington
Q_NPN_PHT	Transistor, NPN photo

Table D-2 (Cont.)   Schematic Symbols in SCH1_LIB.DWG

AutoCAD Block Name	Description
Q_PNP	Transistor, PNP
Q_SCR	SCR
Q_TRI	Triac
R	Resistor (industrial symbol)
R_ALT	Resistor (common symbol)
R_VAR	Resistor, variable (industrial symbol)
R_VAR_ALT	Resistor, variable (common symbol)
RN_DIP16_ISO	Resistor network, 16 pin DIP isolated
RN_SIP10	Resistor network, 10 pin SIP, pin 1 common
S_DIP8	Switch, 8 pin DIP 4PST
S_MOM_NC	Switch, momentary, normally closed
S_MOM_NO	Switch, momentary, normally open
S_SPDT	Switch, SPDT
S_SPST	Switch, SPST
SIG_IN	Intersheet connection symbol, input
SIG_IO	Intersheet connection symbol, input/output
SIG_OUT	Intersheet connection symbol, output
SIG_UNSPEC	Intersheet connection symbol, unspecified
T	Transformer, iron core
T_AIR	Transformer, air core
U_AND	Logic symbol, AND gate
U_BUF	Logic symbol, buffer
U_CMOS_4013	CMOS 4013 flip-flop, gate A
U_CMOS_4013_ALT	CMOS 4013 flip flop, gate B
U_CMOS_4516	CMOS 4516 binary counter
U_INV	Logic symbol, inverter
U_NAND	Logic symbol, NAND gate
U_NOR	Logic symbol, NOR gate
U_OPA	Logic symbol, OP amp/comparator
U_OPA_ALT	Logic symbol, OP amp/comparator (alternate)
U_OPTO	Opto isolator
U_OR	Logic symbol, OR gate
U_REG	Voltage regulator, LM7805
U_TGT	Logic symbol, CMOS transmission gate
U_TTL_373	TTL 373 octal latch
U_XNOR	Logic symbol, XNOR gate
Y	Crystal
Y_RES	Resonator, ceramic

PCB Parts Libraries

The file PCB1_LIB.DWG in the TUTOR2 subdirectory contains the library of through hole PCB parts listed in Table D-3. The PCB1_LIB is intended for use with single and double sided boards that do not require SMT parts. The file PCB2_LIB.DWG in the TUTOR4 subdirectory contains the library of through hole and SMT parts listed in Table D-4. The PCB2_LIB library has the additional layers required for SMT designs. SMT parts are identified by the SMD (surface mount device) suffix. All library parts are defined as AutoCAD blocks. Note that LS refers to lead spacing in inches.

Table D-3   PCB Parts in PCB1_LIB.DWG

AutoCAD Block Name	Description
CAP_10LS	Capacitor, .10 LS
CAP_20LS	Capacitor, .20 LS
CAP_40LS	Capacitor, .40 LS
D_30LS	Diode, .30 LS
D_40LS	Diode, .40 LS .037 hole size
D_40LSA	Diode, .40 LS .045 hole size
D_50LS15	Diode, .50 LS
DIP_18	DIP IC, 18 pin .30 row spacing
DIP_8	DIP IC, 8 pin, .30 row spacing
ECAP_10LS20A	Electrolytic capacitor, .10 LS, .20 diameter
ECAP_10LS25A	Electrolytic capacitor, .10 LS, .25 diameter
F_20LS15	Fuse, .20 LS (used for Raychem polyfuse)
JP_10LS	Jumper block, .10 LS
LED_10LS15	LED, .10 LS, .15 diameter
LED_10LS25	LED, .10 LS, .25 diameter
OPB_32LS	Optek slotted sensor, .32 LS
PAD_100R62	Pad, .100 diameter, .062 hole size
PAD_250R145	Pad, .250 diameter, .145 hole size
PAD_60R37	Pad, .060 diameter, .037 hole size
PAD_60S37	Pad, .060 square, .037 hole size
PAD_80R45	Pad, .080 diameter, .045 hole size
PAD_80S45	Pad, .080 square, .046 hole size
R_15LS	Resistor, .15 LS (1/2W stand up mounting)
R_20LS	Resistor, .20 LS (1W stand up mounting)
R_40LS	Resistor, .40 LS (1/4W)
R_60LS	Resistor, .60 LS (1/2W)
SIP_3P	SIP package, 3 pin
SIP_4P	SIP package, 4 pin

Table D-3 (Cont.)   PCB Parts in PCB1_LIB.DWG

AutoCAD Block Name	Description
SW_BCD_A7C	Switch, BCD Omron A7C series
SW_END_A7C	Switch end cap, Omron A7C series
TO220_DNA	Transistor, TO-220 (flat mounting)
TO220_UPA	Transistor, TO-220 (stand up mounting)
VIA	Via, .055 diameter, .031 hole size
VRES_50D	Potentiometer, panel mount, .50 diameter
XTAL_HC18UP	Crystal, HC18 package (stand up mounting)

Table D-4   PCB Parts in PCB2_LIB.DWG

AutoCAD Block Name	Description
CAP_10LS	Capacitor, .10 LS
CAP_1206_SMD	Capacitor, 1206 SMD
CAP_20LS	Capacitor, .20 LS
CAP_40LS	Capacitor, .40 LS
CAP_805_SMD	Capacitor, 805 SMD
CAP_805_SMD_SOLDER	Capacitor. 805 SMD, solder side
D_30LS	Diode, .30 LS
D_40LS	Diode, .40 LS .037 hole size
D_40LSA	Diode, .40 LS .045 hole size
D_50LS15	Diode, .50 LS
D_LL41_SMD	Diode, LL-41 SMD
DIP_16SO	SOIC, 16 pin SMD
DIP_18	DIP IC, 18 pin .30 row spacing
DIP_8	DIP IC, 8 pin, .30 row spacing
DIP_8SO	SOIC, 8 pin SMD
ECAP_10LS20A	Electrolytic capacitor, .10 LS, .20 diameter
ECAP_10LS25A	Electrolytic capacitor, .10 LS, .25 diameter
ECAP_30SQ_SMD	Electrolytic capacitor, .30 square SMD
ECAP_3216_SMD	Tantalum capacitor, 3216 SMD
F_20LS15	Fuse, .20 LS (used for Raychem polyfuse)
JP_10LS	Jumper block, .10 LS
LED_10LS15	LED, .10 LS, .15 diameter
LED_10LS25	LED, .10 LS, .25 diameter
MICROVIA	Micro via, .031 dia, .018 hole size (for SMD)
OPB_32LS	Optek slotted sensor, .32 LS
PAD_100R62	Pad, .100 diameter, .062 hole size
PAD_250R145	Pad, .250 diameter, .145 hole size
PAD_60R37	Pad, .060 diameter, .037 hole size

Table D-4 (Cont.)   PCB Parts in PCB2_LIB.DWG

AutoCAD Block Name	Description
PAD_60S37	Pad, .060 square, .037 hole size
PAD_80R45	Pad, .080 diameter, .045 hole size
PAD_80S45	Pad, .080 square, .046 hole size
R_15LS	Resistor, .15 LS (1/2W stand up mounting)
R_20LS	Resistor, .20 LS (1W stand up mounting)
R_40LS	Resistor, .40 LS (1/4W)
R_60LS	Resistor, .60LS (1/2W)
R_805_SMD	Resistor, 805 SMD
R_805_SMD_SOLDER	Resistor, 805 SMD, solder side
RV_3224_SMD	Varistor (surge absorber), 3224 SMD
SIP_3P	SIP package, 3 pin
SIP_4P	SIP package, 4 pin
SW_BCD_A7C	Switch, BCD Omron A7C series
SW_END_A7C	Switch end cap, Omron A7C series
TO220_DNA	Transistor, TO-220 (flat mounting)
TO220_UPA	Transistor, TO-220 (stand up mounting)
VIA	Via, .055 diameter, .031 hole size
VRES_50D	Potentiometer, panel mount, .50 diameter
XTAL_HC18UP	Crystal, HC18 package (stand up mounting)

Index